RDF

IDS-Southall

XML, WEB SERVICES, AND THE DATA REVOLUTION

Frank P. Coyle

Addison-Wesley

Boston • San Francisco • New York • Toronto
Montreal • London • Munich • Paris • Madrid
Capetown • Sydney • Tokyo • Singapore • Mexico City

Many of the designations used by manufacturers and sellers to distinguish their products are claimed as trademarks. Where those designations appear in this book and Addison-Wesley was aware of a trademark claim, the designations have been printed in initial capital letters or in all capitals.

The author and publisher have taken care in the preparation of this book, but make no expressed or implied warranty of any kind and assume no responsibility for errors or omissions. No liability is assumed for incidental or consequential damages in connection with or arising out of the use of the information or programs contained herein.

The publisher offers discounts on this book when ordered in quantity for special sales. For more information, please contact:

Pearson Education Corporate Sales Division
201 W. 103rd Street
Indianapolis, IN 46290
(800) 428-5331
corpsales@pearsoned.com

Visit Addison-Wesley on the Web: www.aw.com/cseng/

Library of Congress Cataloging in Publication Data

Coyle, Frank P., 1945–
      XML, Web services, and the data revolution / Frank P. Coyle.
            p. cm.—(The Addison-Wesley information technology series)
      Includes bibliographical references and index.
      ISBN 0-201-77641-3
      1. XML (Document markup language) I. Title. II. Series.
QA76.76.H94 C69 2002
005.7'2—dc21   2002018355

ISBN 0-201-77641-3
Text printed on recycled paper
12345678910—CRW—0605040302
First Printing, March, 2002

Contents

1

XML: Extending the Enterprise

2

The XML Technology Family

3

XML in Practice

4

SOAP

5

Web Services

6

.NET, J2EE, and Beyond

7

XML Security

Contents

8

Back to the Future

Foreword

XML and XML-based Web services have been the "next big thing" for the last couple of years, and will increasingly touch the lives and careers of most of us in the software and Internet industries in the future. There is a tendency among many observers to treat the World Wide Web as part of the "high technology" industry and describe its development as driven by some vaguely understood technological imperative. Web Services are (as of this writing) a particularly clear example of the "if we build it, they will come" assumption that tends to go along with the view of the Web as just a corner of the High-Tech sector. Executives of large software companies tend to make speeches extolling the coming era of Web services without explaining how or why this will come about. There's much talk about the new "paradigm," but little explanation of how anyone besides software vendors desiring a guaranteed revenue stream will benefit if it is technically possible to sell software as a service rather than on a CD.

We are starting to see more sophisticated analyses of the Web phenomenon and the role that XML may play in its evolution. To understand where the Web is going, we not only need to understand the technologies that define it, but also to understand how they have interacted with one another and with the social and economic system to produce something very much greater than the sum of the technological parts. In this view, the Web was not *designed*; it *is evolving* in ways not foreseen by the inventors of the technologies out of which it emerged. No visionary drew a picture of what we have today and proselytized until it became a reality, and no committee laid out requirements for the Web and reviewed designs to achieve it. Instead, its features are the *emergent properties* that appeared when TCP/IP and HTTP produced a reasonably reliable universal network and the simple but powerful HTML (and later XML) markup languages became almost universally supported in browsers and authoring tools.

This is not to downplay the role of good engineering in the success of the many great products that define its individual components, such as IP routers, HTTP servers, and HTML/XML browsers and editors. The principles of sound engineering are the same as those that contribute to evolutionary survival—simplicity, modularity, ease of use, low cost of ownership, etc. Conversely, if it's hard to understand, it will be hard to build; if it's hard to build, it will break; if it breaks, it won't survive. Nevertheless, to understand how the "Web" as we know it emerged from the separate components, and to predict how it will evolve in the future, a higher-level, less technology-driven perspective is necessary.

Frank Coyle's *XML, Web Services, and the Data Revolution* does a great job of explaining the Web/XML phenomenon by clearly describing where it came from, why it has proved so useful, and where it is likely to take us. It provides a solid technical overview to the various XML-related specifications and standardization organizations, especially those relevant to Web services. More importantly, he explains how they all fit together, and what a real business might be able to do with them today and in the near future. By combining these bottom-up and top-down approaches, Coyle's book can be fruitfully read by technologists needing an introduction to the fast–moving and confusing world of XML and Web services specifications, by managers trying to come to grips with the business implications of it all, and by architects who need to integrate both perspectives.

The book's greatest strength is to show how XML accepts and extends the architectural principles that have fostered the World Wide Web:

- *Simplicity.* When in doubt, choose the simplest (to implement) solution.

- *Modularity.* Don't try to build software that "does it all." Components should do one thing well so that they can be re-used in unanticipated ways.

- *Loose coupling.* Components should know as little as possible about one another, allowing components to be interchanged and upgraded as needed. With loosely coupled systems such as the Web, designers don't attend to every detail; they maximize the possibility of interaction and watch systems grow.

- *Emergent behavior.* Surprising possibilities are opened up when simple, modular, loosely coupled components are connected and re-used in new ways.

In other words, powerful systems emerge when built on an infrastructure made of simple, loosely coupled components; The future of the XML-powered Web is not being designed in the labs or meeting rooms of the largest companies, but it will evolve in unanticipated ways as XML liberates data from the applications that create it. SOAP, the most fundamental standard for Web services, is a good example of this phenomenon. Large companies struggled for years to get various proprietary "remote procedure call" tools to work well and become widely used by developers, and an industry group worked hard to perfect a platform-neutral, vendor-neutral standard to do the same thing. Java RMI™, Microsoft's COM/DCOM, and OMG's CORBA are all solid, widely deployed technologies, but none generated much in the way of "buzz." SOAP, however, has created a phenomenal amount of excitement even though it has fewer features and is less mature than its predecessors, basically because it solves many previously difficult problems simply by leveraging the installed base of interoperable HTTP servers and the platform neutrality of XML. Coyle's readers will quickly recognize SOAP's "emergent properties" that arise when complementary technologies are combined to produce a new compound that is something more than the sum of its parts.

This liberation of data from applications is the "Data Revolution" noted in the title. Unlike EDI systems (which specify both data formats and protocols) or Java RMI (which is tied to the Java Virtual Machine operating environment), XML is "pure" data, free to be used in any environment and to be exchanged by any feasible means. By declaring the independence of data from programming and transport issues, XML processing components can be even more modular and assembled into even more loosely coupled systems than is possible in any object-centric approach, even those such as Java or CORBA that have tried very hard to be platform-neutral. Furthermore, once data is in XML form, it doesn't matter whether the information encoded in XML is "really" a document, a message, an RPC invocation, or whatever; there are an ever-growing array of specifications and tools to query, manipulate, validate, transform, and display the XML data. Those operations that cannot be performed in an XML technology per se can be defined with any modern software development language or tool.

As an example of how the message of *XML, Web Services, and the Data Revolution* may apply in real life, consider a couple of exercises in informed speculation. First, many computer industry pundits believe that XML will not come into its own until industry-standard schemas are in place to define the format of messages between businesses in a supply chain; they believe that the adoption of XML is hindered by the "Tower of Babel" or the "balkanization" of XML efforts. There is undoubtedly much truth in this analysis, but think about it from a loosely coupled "Web" perspective rather than the conventional tightly coupled perspective. With loosely coupled systems that only know the bare minimum about each other (e.g., WSDL descriptions of the calling conventions of a Web service), designers can effectively maximize the possibility of interaction rather than forcing every component to conform to the master plan. Loosely coupled Web services may open up possibilities as components are connected and reused in new ways in some of the same ways that HTML and HTTP liberated the text world from tight coupling between applications and proprietary formats and protocols.

Likewise, while Coyle does not discuss the point explicitly, it seems to follow from his analysis that since the success of the Web and XML depends on simplicity, modularity, and loose coupling, it may be necessary to resist the inevitable tendency for standards groups to add "power" to these specifications and for vendors to combine implementations into more "efficient" packages. So long as new features are layered on top of existing modules (optimizations do not change the external behavior of Web components) or new simple, modular, loosely coupled technologies are added to the "menu," such progress is desirable. Ease of use and performance that compromise the fundamental principles of the Web, however, may not be sufficient reasons to jeopardize the evolution of the system that has brought us so many unanticipated benefits.

However history judges (or ignores) these arguments, they illustrate some ways in which a thoughtful reading of *XML, Web Services, and the Data Revolution* may change the way one thinks about XML and Web technology. Frank Coyle offers both a fresh perspective and solid detail on the role of XML in the various software, Internet, and data revolutions that we are living through. Reading this book will help one to understand XML technology as well as how and where to employ it.

—Michael Champion
Advisory Research and Development Specialist
Software AG, Darmstadt, Germany

Preface

The aim of this book is to try to tell the story that we're now all a part of—
a story not just about emerging technologies such as XML and Web services,
but also about how these technologies are coming together and combining
in new ways, creating new applications for which the requirements have
yet to be written.

Structure of the Book

Except for the first and last chapters, the book is essentially a
bottom-up view of the XML-driven, open systems world in which
we now find ourselves. Chapter 1 describes the big picture: how
XML and the Web have changed our perspective about data so that
instead of regarding data as something to be stored in a database and
shuttled across networks by object systems locked in a tight transport protocol embrace, data is now free (thanks to XML and its family of standards) to move about the Web and create new synergies
based on asynchronous loose coupling. After the next six chapters
have described the current state of the technology, Chapter 8 then
takes a top-down look at where we have arrived and explores some
of the new kinds of interactions to expect in environments made up
of traditional client-server networks, even more traditional mainframe applications, and the Web.

Chapter Overviews

Chapter 1 is an attempt to draw the big picture: how the Web
and a data description technology known as XML have initiated

fundamental changes in computing through a shift in focus from tightly coupled computing environments to loosely coupled networks centered around the Web and XML. The effect of this shift has been to spawn three revolutions. The first revolution, the data revolution, is the story of XML and its impact on how data businesses represent data. Although initially viewed as a data description language, XML in combination with HTTP, the Web transport protocol, quickly took on emergent properties, giving rise to SOAP. Today SOAP is the basis for communicating across loosely coupled Web space and is the key driver behind Web services. The second revolution is about software architectures and the move to loosely coupled distributed systems that are both an alternative and a complement to the more tightly coupled systems such as Common Object Request Broker Architecture (CORBA), Distributed Component Object Model (DCOM), or Remote Method Invocation (RMI). The third revolution, the software revolution, involves a changing model of software construction influenced by the World Wide Web Consortium (W3C) in its effort to build a universal Web. Instead of trying to construct software that "does it all," this new era of software assembly is based on the principles of simplicity and modularity, encouraging combination with other software entities.

Chapter 2 covers the core XML technologies, XML 1.0 and namespaces, and explores the family of technologies surrounding this core that provides the support system for delivering structured content across the Web. We examine the applicability of the various support technologies from the perspective of a fictitious company, ZwiftBooks, that has decided to adopt XML in an effort to build its business around Web standards and protocols. The chapter focuses on two important categories of XML support: presentation and transformation. For data presentation we look at cascading style sheets, Extensible Stylesheet Language (XSL), Extensible Hypertext Markup Language, and VoiceXML, each offering options for delivering XML to a variety of devices in different formats. For XML manipulation we look at XSL Transformations, XPath, and XQuery, three technologies used to transform, process, and query XML data. Finally, to round out our tour, we look at Resource Description Framework and the XML Information Set, which permit different XML technologies to integrate more effectively, helping foster what the W3C refers to as the seamless Web.

Chapter 3 looks at XML in practice: how XML has been put to use in a variety of ways, from simple industry-driven data description languages, to vocabularies for configuration and action, to the use of XML as a protocol language that has changed the fundamental assumptions about distributed object computing.

Chapter 4 takes a detailed look at the forces and technologies behind SOAP. SOAP is an example of what can happen when you put two technologies such as the Web and XML together. True to the Web's spirit of emergent behavior, SOAP has created a framework for building loosely coupled confederations of servers that communicate by exchanging XML data over XML protocols. The surprise here is a new set of options that provide alternatives to the tightly coupled network islands of CORBA, DCOM, and RMI. SOAP and its associated protocol, XML Remote Procedure Call, have the balance of power in the computer industry, creating new paradigms based on message-oriented middleware and dynamic discovery and interaction that are the basis for Web services.

Chapter 5 examines the playing field of Web services. Building on a framework of loosely coupled networks, Web services takes object technology's goal of reusability to the next level, by defining XML protocols for discovery and connection. These protocols include Universal Description, Discovery, and Integration (UDDI) and Web Services Description Language (WSDL). UDDI is a protocol for the discovery and deployment of Web services. WSDL describes how to connect to Web services. We examine details of both UDDI and WSDL to get a sense of how these technologies combine to create a new, developing framework for Web services.

Chapter 6 looks at how the software industry is reacting and adapting to the changes brought about by XML-driven loosely coupled networks and the emergence of Web services. Throughout the 1990s, the major network players—Microsoft, Sun, and the Object Management Group (OMG)—have been competing with their respective object-technology-based alternatives for distributed computing. Microsoft's DCOM, the OMG's CORBA and Sun's Java 2 Enterprise Edition (J2EE) represent competing options for building tightly coupled distributed networks. The advantage of these distributed networks is that they provide efficient communication and handle the complex interactions required for transactions and security. The downside is that each comes with its own object model and transport technology, so that connection outside their own universes is possible only with gateway software. Thus, what we're seeing—in Microsoft's .NET initiative, and in various J2EE implementations from Sun, IBM, HP, BEA, and others—are attempts to bridge the gap between tightly coupled, transaction-aware space (DCOM and J2EE) and the loosely coupled, XML-driven, message-centric space of the Web.

Chapter 7 is about securing the XML traffic as it travels across the loose fabric of the Web. XML's ability to structure data provides both opportunities and challenges for applying encryption, authentication, and digital signatures to XML-encoded data. For example, in a workflow environment where XML documents move between participants, and where a digital signature implies some commitment or assertion, participants may wish to sign only parts of a document to minimize liability. Existing secure Web standards, such as the HyperText Transfer Protocol over Secure Socket Layer, that support secure Web transmissions are not able to address XML-specific issues relating to partial document signing or to deal with the fact that XML documents may be processed in stages along loosely coupled network paths. To deal with this reality, three new XML-related security initiatives are explored: XML Encryption, for encoding individual parts of an XML document; XML Signature, for managing the integrity of XML as it moves across the Web; and the XML Key Management Specification for dealing with public key verification and validation.

Chapter 8 takes a high-level look at some of the forces driving the new hybrid world in which we now find ourselves, an amalgam of three architectures: (1) loosely coupled Web space driven by SOAP messaging, (2) tightly coupled transaction-capable; object systems with their own transport protocols; and (3) legacy applications, mostly mainframe based, that have long been difficult to integrate into client-server systems. The irony here is that the central repository model made possible by the mainframe, and made obsolete by client-server network computing, is now undergoing a renewed interest due to the need to manage collaborative peer-to-peer efforts over the loosely coupled Web.

Acknowledgments

Thanks are in order for the many individuals who knowingly and unknowingly contributed to this book.

Special thanks go to Michael Brint who helped give shape to the book during numerous conversational walks and discussions.

Thanks to Simon Johnston, Capers Jones, Cameron Laird, Eve Maler, and Anne Manes whose time and comments were invaluable.

A special thanks go to Mary O'Brien for her encouragement and to the staff at Addison-Wesley who worked hard to make this book a reality.

At home, my family—Judy, Alex, and Nick—were invaluable assets, for both research and humor.

And thanks to Mom and Dad for keeping the coffee table available.

About the Author

Frank P. Coyle is director of the Software Engineering Program at Southern Methodist University in Dallas, Texas. A well-known XML authority, he has extensive experience teaching XML-related technologies in both university and industry settings. A frequent speaker at XML and Java conferences, Frank has also written widely on XML and is the author of *Wireless Web* (Addison-Wesley, 2001).

Introduction

This book is about understanding and navigating the change brought about by Extensible Markup Language (XML) and the World Wide Web. To understand the momentum behind XML, it's important to realize that XML and the Web are not separate phenomena but very much interrelated. Both are part of a paradigm shift in computing based on software assembly and emergence rather than software creation. This phenomenon is changing how we think about software and is the driving force behind the market strategies of the major players in the software industry: Microsoft, Sun, IBM, and others. The layering of XML on top of the existing Web infrastructure is disrupting the status quo, giving rise to new initiatives such as the Simple Object Access Protocol (SOAP), and Web services.

Like other disruptive technologies before them, the Web and XML bring with them a new wave of possibilities and challenges. In terms of software architecture, the Web and XML open up a new way of assembling systems based on loosely coupled confederations of servers exchanging XML data. Unlike servers with tight dependencies upon each other, this new loose confederation is capable of establishing dynamic connections through message-oriented middleware and asynchronous interaction. As with any technology that makes it possible to solve old problems in new, more efficient ways, the net effect is an upset in the balance of power in the computer industry.

To appreciate the speed with which these changes have occurred, it's instructive to look at the Web and XML in the context of another recent technology innovation, the personal computer. The PC revolution started with the invention of the microprocessor in the 1970s, moved to the hobbyist realm in the mid-1970s, received

IBM's blessing in 1981, and by the mid-1980s was making inroads into the mainframe and minicomputer world. Fueling the PC's rise was the emergence of networks, both local and wide area, that moved the focus of computing from centralized mainframes to the desktop where sharing was handled by local servers, ushering in the era of client-server computing. But whereas this process took years to unfold, the the Web arrived almost overnight.

How do we explain this? How is the Web different from other large-scale software efforts such as the U.S. Air Traffic Control System, the Sabre airline reservation system, or an enterprise-wide software framework such as SAP, each taking years to specify, more years to implement, and even more years to get right? The difference is that the Web wasn't programmed; it was assembled from simple con-stituent parts. It seemed to appear so quickly because the Web *emerged* from its constituent building blocks and in the process took everyone by surprise.

No team defined use cases for the Web, formulated detailed require-ments, considered design alternatives, moved to an implementation phase, or published delivery schedules. If we had tried to build the Web this way, it simply would not exist.

The Web as we know it today has emerged from four building blocks, limited in scope yet open to combination: an Internet driven by TCP/IP that provides reliable global communication; HTTP, a simple protocol for delivering files; HTML, a tag-based language for specifying how data should be displayed; and the browser, a graphical user interface for displaying HTML data. Each in its own right does something interesting, but taken together, the whole turned out to be greater than the sum of its parts, a principle long known to systems engineers and, before them, to the Gestalt psychologists.

Emergence

There is emergent behavior all around us. In chemistry the product of a chemical reaction is most often very different from any of its constituent ingredients. Consider sodium (Na) and chlorine (Cl), two volatile and dangerous chemicals that react violently when placed in proximity. Put sodium and chlorine together and, after the smoke clears, a totally new substance emerges: table salt (NaCl), not at all dangerous, in fact essential to human life.

That the Web arrived with the force of a chemical reaction is not an accident. Software designers and architects faced with the inability of over-designed systems to adapt to change have long sought alternatives to conventional systems building, which is based on the attempt to anticipate, up front, all possible system functionality and to building a system that satisfies a complete specification.

In an article entitled "Architectural Principles of the Internet," Brian Carpenter of the Internet Architecture Board's Network Working Group provides an informative description of the architectural philosophy underlying the Web:

> In searching for Internet architectural principles we must remember that technical change is continuous. In this environment, some architectural principles inevitably change. Principles that seemed inviolable a few years ago are deprecated today. Principles that seem sacred today will be deprecated tomorrow. The principle of constant change is perhaps the only principle of the Internet that should survive indefinitely.[1]

---

[1] Brian Carpenter, "Architectural Principles of the Internet," Request for Comments 1958, Internet Architecture Board, June 1996, http://www.isi.edu/in-notes/rfc1958.txt.

On simplicity and modularity, he has this to say: "Keep it simple. When in doubt during design, choose the simplest solution." He adds, "Modularity is good. If you can keep things separate, do so."

As you work your way through the various chapters of this book, it's important to keep in mind that simplicity, modularity, and emergent behavior are the driving forces behind the technology revolution that surrounds the Web, XML, and Web services.

For the big players in the software industry, the difficulty is predicting the effects of a software chemical reaction. Consider for a moment the Napster phenomenon. Napster, the Web-based, peer-to-peer music distribution system, exploded on the scene almost overnight, not planned or designed in the traditional software sense, but emerging from the assembly of a loosely coupled network infrastructure plus some simple parts. Despite legal attacks on the Napster, the genie is out of the bottle. The music industry will never be the same. Nor will the software industry.

The major industry players, now well aware of the power of emergent software, are driven both by both desire and fear: the desire to leverage the Web to enhance their bottom lines, but also the fear that if they aren't experimenting with new combinations and possibilities, new technologies will emerge from the primordial software soup and make what they are doing obsolete.

1

XML: Extending the Enterprise

Extensible Markup Language (XML) is a simple data description language with profound implications. It affects how we build software and how we think about distributed systems. Surrounding XML is a family of standards and technologies that have opened up new possibilities for exchanging information across the World Wide Web and building communication infrastructures.

XML derives much of its strength in combination with the Web. The Web provides a collection of protocols for moving data; XML represents a way to define that data. The most immediate effect has been a new way to look at the enterprise. Instead of a tightly knit network of servers, the enterprise is now seen as encompassing not just our traditional networks but also the Web itself, with its global reach and scope.

In this chapter we look at XML's role in the expanding view of the enterprise. From its beginnings as a language for describing vertical industry data, XML has blossomed to include not only horizontal applications but also protocols that challenge the conventional wisdom about how to do distributed computing and that open the door to new ways of discovery and connection. Web services represents the most recent visible effect of this change.

In this chapter we also try to establish the context for the changes brought about by XML and the Web. To place events in perspective we explore three technology revolutions: data, architecture, and software. Together the changes in these areas are fostering new ways of thinking about the enterprise and about application development in general. The new paradigm that emerges is the result of global Web-based communication infrastructure, the ability to describe data with XML, and the emergence of XML-based protocols such as Simple Object Access Protocol (SOAP) that contribute to a fabric of loosely coupled distributed systems. As we'll see, these forces are driving initiatives such as Microsoft's .NET and Sun's Java 2 Enterprise Edition (J2EE) that are looking at XML as the bridge between the more traditional space of tightly coupled object systems and the more freewheeling loosely coupled space of the Web.

Extending the Enterprise

The Web has opened up new possibilities for engagement.

The story behind XML is very much the story of the Web. In just a few short years the Web has affected almost every aspect of our lives, from work, to play, to social interaction. However, until recently, the Web's impact has been primarily on individuals, providing a quick and efficient way to check email, search for information, and buy things online. The global scope of the Web and its possibilities have not gone unnoticed by companies looking to gain competitive advantage. This global connectivity, coupled with accepted Internet standards for communication, has spawned new ideas about how to leverage this new capability.

The extended enterprise includes B2C, B2B, and B2E interaction.

As Figure 1.1 illustrates, there are three major aspects to extending the enterprise from a relatively constrained network to the broad reach of the Web. The most commonly considered aspect is the business-to-consumer (B2C) connection, exploiting opportunities that abound in online commerce. Another area is the business-to-employee (B2E) connection, adding efficiencies in operations and customer contact by using the Web instead of proprietary networks. A third area, and one of particular interest to businesses trying to survive in competitive environments, is the business-to-business (B2B) connection made possible by the Web. Together, these opportunities are driving what is seen as the extended enterprise, a mix of traditional networks and the loose space of the Web.

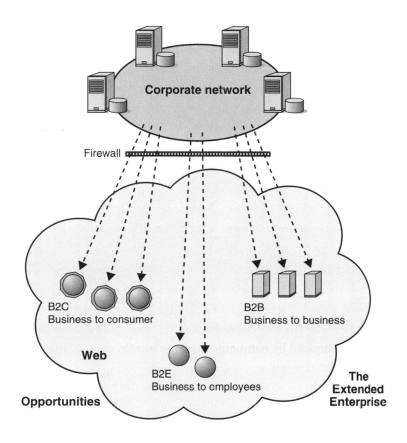

Figure 1.1 **The extended enterprise combines traditional networks with the power of the Web, opening up new opportunities in B2B, B2C, and B2E commerce.**

But to turn these possibilities and visions of global connectedness into a reality requires data, not only for the consumer, but for employees who need data and information to do their jobs wherever they are, and for the B2B transactions that are the essential ingredient for partners and suppliers. That's where XML comes in.

Data is the key to the extended enterprise.

The Role of XML

XML is a metalanguage (literally a language about languages) defined by the World Wide Web Consortium (W3C), one of the main organizations driving the push to open Web standards. In its simplest sense, XML is a set of rules and guidelines for describing

XML is a specification for defining new markup languages.

structured data in plain text rather than proprietary binary repre-sentations. However, as a phenomenon, XML goes beyond its tech-nical specification. Since its standardization by the W3C in 1998, XML has been the driving force behind numerous other standards and vocabularies that are forging a fundamental change in the soft-ware world.

XML has enabled industry vocabularies and protocols.

In its short history, XML has given rise to numerous vertical indus-try vocabularies in support of B2B e-commerce, horizontal vocab-ularies that provide services to a wide range of industries, and XML protocols that have used XML's simple power of combination to open up new possibilities for doing distributed computing. As Fig-ure 1.2 shows, XML's influence has been felt in three waves, from industry-specific vocabularies, to horizontal industry applications, to protocols that describe how businesses can exchange data across the Web. One of the key developments has been SOAP, the protocol

Figure 1.2 XML has been widely used as a language for a variety of applications ranging from vertical industry vocabularies, to horizontal industry applications, to protocols.

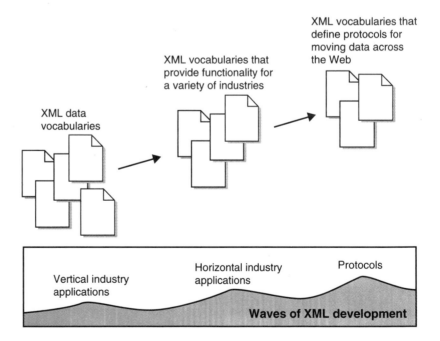

XML vocabularies that define protocols for moving data across the Web

XML vocabularies that provide functionality for a variety of industries

XML data vocabularies

Vertical industry applications

Horizontal industry applications

Protocols

Waves of XML development

that has opened the Web to program-to-program communication and, as we'll see in Chapter 5, is the basis for Web services.

XML: Just Tags?

XML is simple. Technically, it's a language for creating other languages based on the insertion of tags to help describe data. However, XML is actually more than just tags. To see what we mean by this, let's begin with a simple XML data description.

XML supports user-defined languages that add meaning to data.

XML is a combination of tags and content in which the tags add meaning to the content. The following is a simple XML markup of customer information. Start tags such as <Name> begin an element that contains the actual data. End tags such as </Name> mark the end of an element definition.

```
<Customer>
    <Name>John von Neumann</Name>
    <PhoneNum>914.631.7722</PhoneNum>
    <FaxNum>914.631.7723</FaxNum>
    <E-Mail>Johnny@cd.com</E-Mail>
</Customer>
```

However, elements are only one way to describe data. It's also possible to represent the data using attributes within a single element:

```
<Customer name="John von Neumann" phone="914.631.7722"
fax="914.631.7723" email="Johnny@cd.com"/>
```

In both these examples, the data is the same, but the form is different. There are several important basic points to observe about these definitions.

❏ XML allows data to be stored in either elements or attributes.
❏ Elements and attributes can be named to give the data meaning.

❑ Start tags and end tags define elements that are the basis for XML tree-structured representations of documents.

❑ Elements can contain text data and/or other elements.

While XML is more than just a few simple rules, its essential aspects can be grasped and understood quite easily. What's important about XML is what it brings to enterprise computing and how it is affecting many aspects of software development and e-commerce.

The XML Advantage

Several aspects of XML have contributed to its success.

XML has had an impact across a broad range of areas. The following is a list of some of the factors that have influenced XML's adoption by a variety of organizations and individuals.

❑ XML files are human-readable. XML was designed as text so that, in the worst case, someone can always read it to figure out the content. Such is not the case with binary data formats.

❑ Widespread industry support exists for XML. Numerous tools and utilities are being provided with Web browsers, databases, and operating systems, making it easier and less expensive for small and medium-sized organizations to import and export data in XML format.

❑ Major relational databases now have the native capability to read and generate XML data.

❑ A large family of XML support technologies is available for the interpretation and transformation of XML data for Web page display and report generation.

XML: Design by Omission

Much of XML's success stems from what it does not address.

In addition to XML's explicit advantages, it's important to realize that much of XML's widespread success and use derives more from what it does *not* address. There are three key design elements that by omission contribute to XML's success:

1. No display is assumed. Unlike HTML, XML makes no assumptions about how tags will be rendered in a browser or other display device. Auxiliary technologies such as style sheets add this capability.
2. There is no built-in data typing. DTDs and XML Schema provide support for defining the structure and data types associated with an XML document.
3. No transport is assumed. The XML specification makes no assumption about how XML is to be transported across the Internet. This has opened the door to creative ideas about delivering XML by means of HTTP, FTP, or Simple Mail Transfer Protocol (SMTP).

These design-by-omission principles can be reformulated by saying that XML explicitly limits the scope of ambitions to maximize interaction with other technologies.

XML and the Web

XML's capability to work with other technologies has greatly expanded the possibilities for navigating the space of the new extended enterprise. Figure 1.3 shows how XML may be used to communicate directly with partners and suppliers. Instead of exchanging data about purchases and orders either manually or over proprietary networks, data vocabularies can be defined using XML and delivered from server to server using standard protocols such as HTTP or FTP.

XML integrates with standard Web protocols such as HTTP and FTP.

Associated with this ability to move data freely across the Web is the rise in the use of messaging servers and software that sit between conversational participants. These servers, supporting what is known as Message Oriented Middleware, are playing an increasingly important role in the new extended enterprise by providing guarantees of delivery and the ability to broadcast communications to multiple recipients.

Messaging middleware supports the asynchronous delivery of XML.

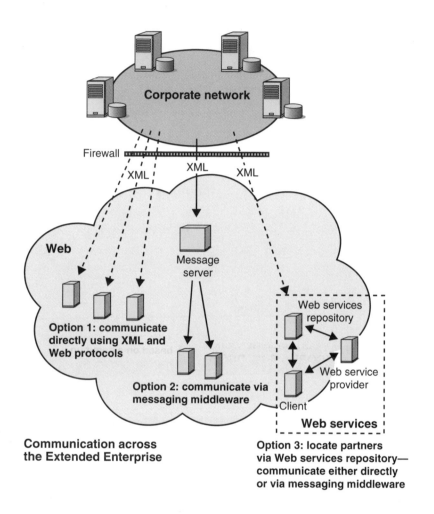

Figure 1.3 **XML fits into the fabric of a new architecture built around Internet protocols and loosely coupled systems.**

Web services makes B2B direct connections feasible over the Web.

A third aspect of the new extended enterprise is the emergence of Web services. For some, Web services represents the next evolutionary step for the Web, extending it from a network that provides services to humans to one that provides services to software looking to connect with other software. Web services is an ambitious initiative that is moving the Web to new levels of B2B (that is, software-to-software) interaction while trying to fulfill object technology's promise of reusable components from a service interface perspective. In Chapter 5 we take a closer look at Web services, but for now it's important to see the growing momentum behind Web services as an effort (but by no means the only effort) to structure B2B activity over the Web.

SOAP

SOAP is the XML glue that lets clients and providers talk to each other and exchange XML data. As Figure 1.4 shows, SOAP builds on XML and common Web protocols (HTTP, FTP, and SMTP) to enable communication across the Web. As we discuss in more detail in Chapter 4, SOAP brings to the table a set of rules for moving data,

SOAP is an XML based protocol.

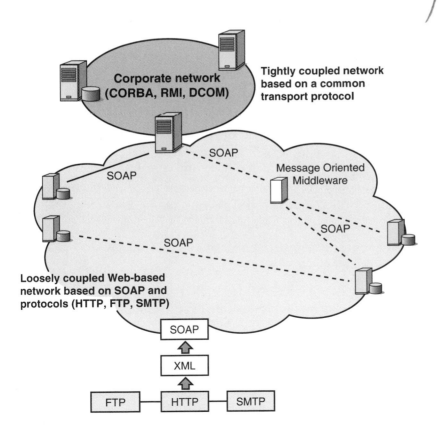

Figure 1.4 **SOAP, an XML-based protocol, gains its global scope through the power of combination with Internet protocols such as HTTP, FTP, and SMTP.**

either directly in a point-to-point fashion or by sending the data through a message queue intermediary.

SOAP opens up new options for distributed computing.

One of the main implications of SOAP is a change in how we think about distributed computing. Prior to SOAP, there were three basic options for doing distributed computing: Microsoft's Distributed Component Object Model (DCOM), Java's Remote Method Invocation (RMI), or the Object Management Group's Common Object Request Broker Architecture (CORBA). These technologies are still in widespread use today. Their drawback is that they limit the potential reach of the enterprise to servers that share the same object infrastructure. With SOAP, however, the potential space of interconnection is the entire Web itself, which is why there is such intense interest in technologies that can leverage the power of SOAP. One of these technology efforts is Web services.

Web Services

Web services builds on a SOAP foundation.

Web services is both a process and set of protocols for finding and connecting to software exposed as services over the Web. By assuming a SOAP foundation, Web services can concentrate on what data to exchange instead of worrying about how to get it from point A to point B, which is the job of SOAP. To make things even easier, SOAP also defines an XML envelope to carry XML and a convention for doing remote procedure calls so that a service can advertise "call me here" and a program will be able to do so without concern for language or platform. Although SOAP may be used with a variety of protocols, the only bindings specified in the proposed SOAP specification are for HTTP.

Web services facilitates software interaction.

A Web service can be anything from a movie review service, to a real-time weather advisory, to an entire hotel- and airline-booking package. The Web services technical infrastructure ensures that services even from different vendors will interoperate to create a complete business process. Web services takes the object-oriented vision of assembling software from component building blocks to the next level. With Web services, however, the emphasis is on the assembly of services that may or may not be built on object technology.

As Figure 1.5 illustrates, the interconnections opened up by the Web make possible a new way of interacting through the registration, discovery, and connection of software packaged as Web services. As we'll see in Chapter 5, there are three major aspects to Web Services:

Web services = repository + client | provider.

❏ A *service provider* provides an interface for software that can carry out a specified set of tasks.

❏ A *service requester* discovers and invokes a software service to provide a business solution. The requester will commonly invoke a remote procedure call on the service provider, passing parameter data to the provider and receiving a result in reply.

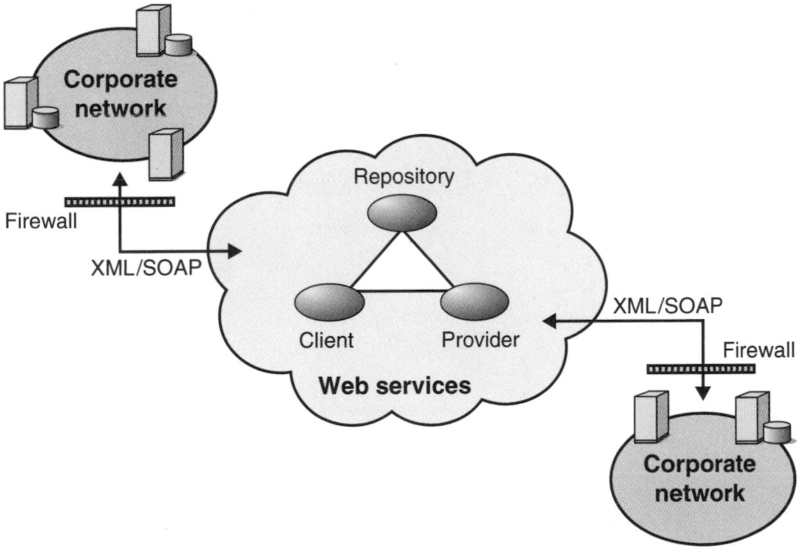

Figure 1.5 **The Web services framework provides protocols and a process for clients to discover and connect to web-based services.**

❑ A *broker* manages and publishes the service. Service providers publish their services with the broker and requests access those services by creating bindings to the service provider.

.NET and J2EE

Messaging, transactions, security, and identity are key ingredients for Web commerce.

While Web services represents one way to exploit the power and reach of the Web, there is a caveat. Web services and SOAP-based connections do not currently have the key building blocks for industrial-strength Web-based e-business. As Figure 1.6 shows, what's needed is support for the four pillars of Web-based e-business: messaging, transactions, security, and identity.

.NET and J2EE are options for building an extended enterprise.

As we'll see in Chapter 6, messaging, security, transactions, and identity are the essential ingredients in managing interactions across the extended enterprise. In the current software world, these capabilities are being provided from two directions. On one side is Microsoft's .NET, a Windows-centric framework for extending Windows-based

Figure 1.6 .NET and J2EE add capability for messaging, security, identity, and transactions to loosely coupled networks based on SOAP.

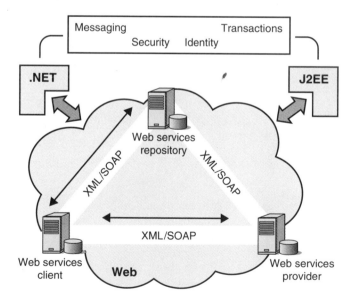

networks into the extended space of the Web. On the other side is J2EE, a Java-centric specification that is being implemented by several companies including Sun, IBM, BEA, HP, Oracle, and others. While we'll defer until Chapter 6 taking a look at how these competitive forces are playing out, it's important to keep the big picture in mind as we explore each of these concepts in subsequent chapters.

Now that we've seen where we'll be going, let's step back and take a broader look at some of the forces at play in the rapidly changing world of the Web. As we do so, we'll fill in some details that will help in subsequent chapters and explore how XML is playing an integral part in three revolutions.

XML: The Three Revolutions

At the beginning of this chapter we outlined several areas in which XML's impact has been felt. To understand the changes that are occurring in today's software world, it's helpful to look at XML in the context of three revolutions in which XML is playing a major role.

The three revolutions: data, architecture, and software.

As Figure 1.7 illustrates, the three areas of impact are data, which XML frees from the confines of fixed, program-dependent formats; architecture, with a change in emphasis from tightly coupled distributed systems to a more loosely coupled confederation based on the Web; and software, with the realization that software evolution is a better path to managing complexity than building monolithic applications. In the following sections we'll explore each in more detail.

The Data Revolution

Prior to XML, data was very much proprietary, closely associated with applications that understood how data was formatted and how to process it. Now, XML-based industry-specific data vocabularies provide alternatives to specialized Electronic Data Interchange (EDI)

Data is now free to travel the Web.

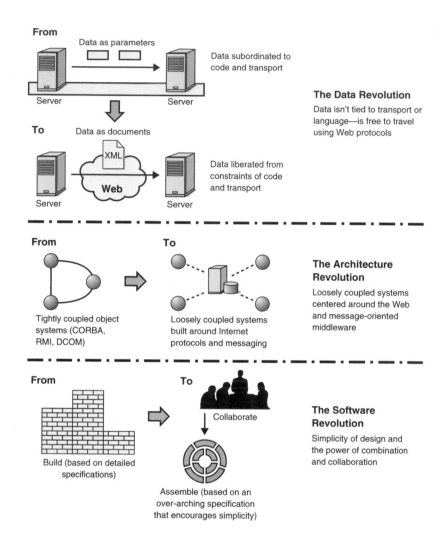

Figure 1.7 **The three XML revolutions: data, architecture, and software.**

solutions by facilitating B2B data exchange and playing a key role as a messaging infrastructure for distributed computing.

XML enables the creation of program-independent data formats.

XML's strength is its data independence. XML is pure data description, not tied to any programming language, operating system, or transport protocol. In the grand scheme of distributed computing this is a radical idea. The implication is that we don't require lock-in to programmatic infrastructures to make data available to Web-connected platforms. In effect, data is free to move about globally without the constraints imposed by tightly coupled transport-dependent architectures. XML's sole focus on data means that a variety of transport technologies may be used to move XML across the Web. As a result, protocols such as HTTP have had a tremendous impact on XML's viability and have opened the door to alternatives to CORBA, RMI, and DCOM, which don't work over TCP/IP. XML does this by focusing on data and leaving other issues to supporting technologies.

XML: Origin and Cultures

Although XML is a relatively new technology, its lineage extends back over several decades. Approved by the W3C in 1998, XML is an effort to simplify the Standard Generalized Markup Language (SGML), which, until XML, was the ISO standard for defining data vocabularies. Technically, XML is a subset of SGML designed to facilitate the exchange of structured documents over the Internet. Although SGML, which became an ISO standard in 1986, has been widely used by organizations seeking to structure their documents and documentation (for example, the General Motors parts catalog), its pre-Web complexity has been the main stumbling block to its widespread use and acceptance by the Web community. Figure 1.8 illustrates the relationship between SGML and XML and shows some of the languages derived from each.

XML's origins are in SGML.

The designers of XML took the best parts of SGML and, based on their experience, produced a technology comparable to SGML but much simpler to use. In fact, simplicity and ease of programming were requirements imposed by the W3C on the Working Group responsible for the final XML specification.

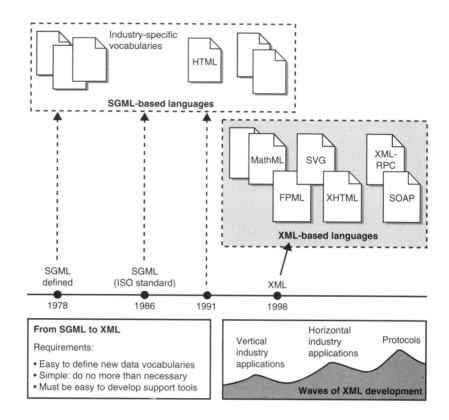

Figure 1.8 XML is the successor to SGML. Both are metalanguages that are used to define new data-oriented vocabularies.

The Code, Data, and Document Cultures

XML has emerged from a document culture.

To understand XML's impact on the computing world, it's useful to place XML in perspective. As Figure 1.9 shows, XML comes out of a document culture that is distinct from the code and data cultures that are the hallmarks of the mainstream computer industry. The code culture is characterized by a focus on programming languages, beginning with FORTRAN and evolving through Algol to C, C++, and Java. The data culture is characterized by COBOL, data processing, and databases. Both the data and code cultures carry with them a built-in propensity to view the world through either a code or a data lens. From a code perspective, data is something to be transported by

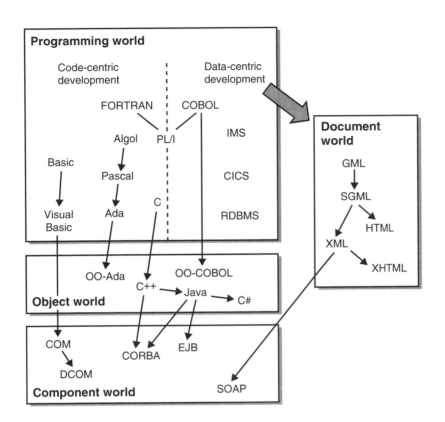

Figure 1.9 **Evolution: from programming languages to objects to components.**

procedure calls. From a data perspective, data is something to be stored in databases and manipulated.

The late 1980s and early 1990s saw code and data combine in the form of object-oriented languages such as C++, Smalltalk, Java, and Object COBOL. And yet, object technology was only a partial answer. As practitioners in the data world had long realized, transactions—the ability to update multiple databases in an all-or-none manner—are essential to serious industrial-strength enterprise applications. Because component frameworks provide transactions as a service to applications regardless of language origins, the playing field quickly shifted from objects to components. Thus infrastructures

Code and data have defined systems thinking.

such as CORBA, DCOM, and Enterprise JavaBeans (EJB) provide interconnection, security, and transaction-based services for extending the enterprise. In the mid 1990s, components were the only way to extend legacy. However, XML changed the rules of the game.

XML opens up options for treating code as data.

XML's emergence from the data-oriented document culture has forced a rethinking about application development, particularly for those accustomed to thinking of building applications from a code-based perspective. What XML brings to the computing world is a technology that allows data to be freed from the constraints created by code-centric infrastructures. Instead of requiring data to be subordinated to parameters in a procedure call, XML now permits data to stand on its own. More radically, it allows code to be treated as data, which has been the driving force behind using XML for remote procedure calls. As Figure 1.10 illustrates, XML offers an alternative

Figure 1.10 XML in combination with Web protocols allows data to be independent of network, programming language, or platform.

The Data Revolution

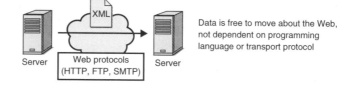

Data is free to move about the Web, not dependent on programming language or transport protocol

Server   Web protocols (HTTP, FTP, SMTP)   Server

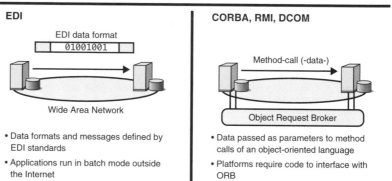

EDI

EDI data format

`01001001`

Wide Area Network

- Data formats and messages defined by EDI standards
- Applications run in batch mode outside the Internet
- Proprietary wide area network required to deliver EDI messages

CORBA, RMI, DCOM

Method-call (-data-)

Object Request Broker

- Data passed as parameters to method calls of an object-oriented language
- Platforms require code to interface with ORB

to both EDI and technologies such as CORBA, RMI, and DCOM that lock data transfer into underlying networks and object infrastructures. It is this change in perspective that is driving the widespread use of XML across the entire computing industry and opening up new patterns of interaction, including Web services.

The Architectural Revolution

Together these XML-based technology initiatives open up new possibilities for distributed computing that leverage the existing infrastructure of the Web and create a transition from object-based distributed systems to architectures based on Web services that can be discovered, accessed, and assembled using open Web technologies. The focal point of this change in architectural thinking has been a move from tightly coupled systems based on established infrastructures such as CORBA, RMI, and DCOM, each with their own transport protocol, to loosely coupled systems riding atop standard Web protocols such as TCP/IP. Although the transport protocols underlying CORBA, RMI, and DCOM provide for efficient communication between nodes, their drawback is their inability to communicate with other tightly coupled systems or directly with the Web.

Simplicity and the ability to combine different standards are driving forces behind W3C deliberations.

Loosely coupled Web-based systems, on the other hand, provide what has long been considered the Holy Grail of computing: universal connectivity. Using TCP/IP as the transport, systems can establish connections with each other using common open-Web protocols. Although it is possible to build software bridges linking tightly coupled systems with each other and the Web, such efforts are not trivial and add another layer of complexity on top of an already complex infrastructure. As Figure 1.11 shows, the loose coupling of the Web makes possible new system architectures built around message-based middleware or less structured peer-to-peer interaction.

XML and the Web have enabled the loose coupling of software components.

Figure 1.11 **XML in combination with Web protocols has opened up new possibilities for distributed computing based on message passing as well as peer-to-peer interaction.**

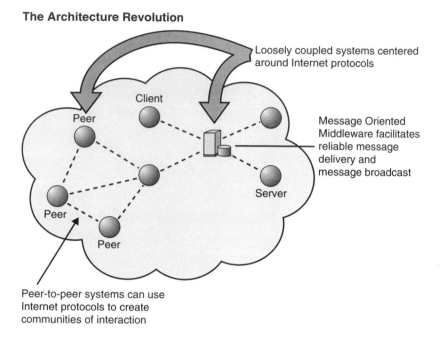

The Architecture Revolution

Loosely coupled systems centered around Internet protocols

Client

Peer

Message Oriented Middleware facilitates reliable message delivery and message broadcast

Server

Peer

Peer

Peer-to-peer systems can use Internet protocols to create communities of interaction

The Software Revolution

XML is part of a software revolution centered around combination and surprise.

XML is also part of a revolution in how we build software. During the 1970s and 1980s, software was constructed as monolithic applications built to solve specific problems. The problem with large software projects is that, by trying to tackle multiple problems at once, the software is often ill-suited to adding new functionality and adapting to technological change. In the 1990s a different model for software emerged based on the concept of simplicity. As Figure 1.12 illustrates, instead of trying to define all requirements up front, this new philosophy was built around the concept of creating building blocks capable of combination with other building blocks that either already existed or were yet to be created.

The Web is an example of the power of combination.

A case in point is the Web. After decades of attempts to build complex infrastructures for exchanging information across distributed networks, the Web emerged from an assemblage of foundational

The Software Revolution

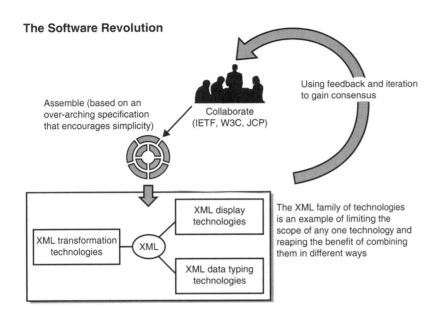

Assemble (based on an over-arching specification that encourages simplicity)

Collaborate (IETF, W3C, JCP)

Using feedback and iteration to gain consensus

XML transformation technologies

XML

XML display technologies

XML data typing technologies

The XML family of technologies is an example of limiting the scope of any one technology and reaping the benefit of combining them in different ways

Figure 1.12 **The software revolution: simplicity and collaboration.**

technologies such as HTTP, HTML, browsers, and a longstanding networking technology known as TCP/IP that had been put in place in the 1970s.

Figure 1.13 illustrates how the Web as we know it was not something thought out in strict detail. Each of the contributing technologies focused on doing one thing well without inhibiting interconnection with other technologies. The essential idea was to maximize the possibility of interaction and watch systems grow. The result is the Web, a product of the confluence of forces that include the Internet, HTML, and HTTP. Let's now look at how these same forces of combination and collaboration are driving the revolution in software.

Software and Surprise

One byproduct of this new way of thinking about software combination is the element of surprise. Conventional software built around an ongoing series of requirements poses few surprises (except if it comes in under budget and on time). The Web, however, was different. It

Combination often leads to surprise.

Figure 1.13 **The Web itself is an example of combinatoric simplicity in action. HTTP, a simple protocol, combines with browser technology to give us the Web as we know it today.**

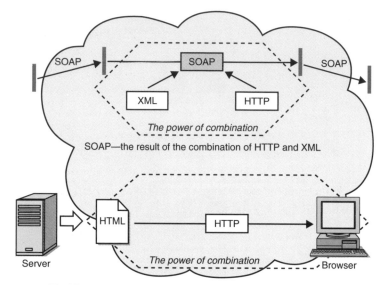

The power of combination

SOAP—the result of the combination of HTTP and XML

The power of combination

Server

Browser

The Web—the result of the combination of HTML, Browsers, and HTTP

Design Principles

While Tim Berners-Lee gets the credit for assembling the pieces that ultimately composed the Web, a look at what Berners-Lee has to say in a 1998 article entitled "Principles of Design"[1] sheds some light on the thinking behind the software revolution. In this article, Berners-Lee focuses on several fundamental principles that are driving a new way of creating software.

❏ *Simplicity:* Often confused with ease of understanding, simplicity refers to the ease with which a concept or construct achieves its goal.

❏ *Modular design:* When you want to change a system (and change is inevitable), modular design lets you

[1] Tim Berners-Lee, "Principles of Design," 1998, http://www.w3.org/DesignIssues/Principles.html.

introduce change with minimal impact on the workings of other system components.

❑ *Decentralization:* Systems should be constructed so that no one element serves as a single point of failure for the entire system.

❑ *Test of independent invention:* This involves a thought test. If someone else had invented your system, would theirs work with yours? This property means that in design, you should try to do one thing well and avoid having to be the center of the universe.

❑ *Principle of least power:* Computer science from the 1960s to the 1980s put great effort into constructing systems as powerful as possible, systems that tried to do it all. The principle of least power asserts that less powerful solutions ultimately are better suited for analysis and manipulation by applications yet to be invented. One hundred years in the future, software will probably have an easier time figuring out the content of an XML document than of a C++ program.

took just about everyone by surprise. Like a chemical reaction, the elements reacted in combination, giving rise to totally new structures.

Another example of the power of combination and surprise is Napster, a radical way of distributing music over the Internet. Napster relied on peer-to-peer connectivity rather than centralized distribution. Napster wasn't the result of a team of dedicated software professionals, but was created by a twenty-something upstart drawing on the power of assembly. The music industry will never be the same.

Napster was a surprising Web-based application.

Combination and Collaboration

Collaboration is
being applied
to requirements
and design.

The power of combination is finding its way not only into software construction but up the development chain to software specification and design. Rather than hoping to meet the needs of users, design is now more collaborative, bringing in stakeholders early to ensure maximum feedback and the benefits of collaborative thinking. Figure 1.14 illustrates how this collaborative model is used by the W3C, the Internet Engineering Task Force, and Sun in its Java Community Process.

Figure 1.14 Part of the software revolution includes collaboration on specification and design. Examples include the Internet Engineering Task Force, the W3C, and Sun's Java Community Process.

Collaboration in Software Specification and Design

Internet Engineering Task Force

- Formed in 1992
- Charter: build an international community of network designers, operators, vendors, and researchers concerned with the evolution of the Internet's architecture and operation
- Standards include those for Internet infrastructure including security, routing, and user services

World Wide Web Consortium

- Formed in 1994
- Charter: lead the World Wide Web to its full potential by developing common protocols that promote its evolution and ensure its interoperability
- Standards (published as W3C Recommendations) include XML, XSLT, CSS, HTML, XHTML, DOM, and XML namespaces

Java Community Process

- Formed in 1995
- Charter: develop and revise Java technology specifications, reference implementations, and technology compatibility kits
- Standards are based on Java Specification Requests which describe both proposed and final specifications for the Java platform. There are currently over 100 JSRs including standards for Java 2 Enterprise Edition and Java Server Pages

The W3C

Regarding standards from the W3C, it's important to realize that the word "Recommendation," in W3C parlance, means final specification or standard. Understanding the W3C's process in moving from idea to Recommendation is important in tracking where the Web is going. Having the status of an approved Recommendation means that software vendors and developers can be confident that the technology described in the Recommendation has general industry-wide consensus.

There are several steps along the W3C path from submitting a proposal to ultimate approval as an official Recommendation, as Figure 1.15 illustrates.

❑ *Submission:* Any W3C member may submit a document to the W3C for possible review. A Submission indicates only that the document has been placed in a W3C in-box. It says

The W3C is the driving force behind open Web standards.

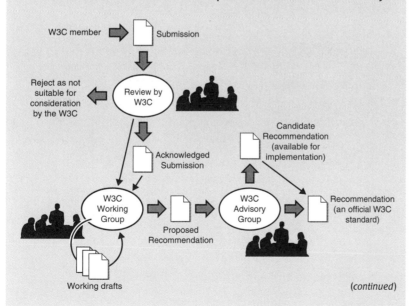

Figure 1.15 The W3C approval process from Submission to Recommendation.

(*continued*)

The W3C (continued)

nothing about what the W3C thinks about it. The next step is for the W3C to determine whether it warrants further consideration as an Acknowledged Submission or should be dropped. This decision is based on whether the Submission is within the scope of the W3C charter.

❑ *Note:* A Note is a W3C document that has followed a formal submission process and gets an official date stamp. It carries no commitment on the part of the W3C to pursue the work any further.

❑ *Acknowledged Submission:* A Submission or Note that has been reviewed by the W3C becomes an Acknowledged Submission, which results in the formation of a Working Group, typically composed of the member group that authored the original Submission plus any other interested parties. The Working Group is tasked with producing Working Drafts that go up for public review.

❑ *Working Draft:* Working Groups produce Working Drafts. A Working Draft is a document in progress. When consensus is reached within the Working Group, a Proposed Recommendation is released. Often a Working Draft will be implemented by vendors who provide feedback to the Working Group about the viability of the proposed idea.

❑ *Proposed Recommendation:* The Working Group's consensus is formulated in a Proposed Recommendation that is sent to the W3C Advisory Committee for review.

❑ *Candidate Recommendation:* For complex proposals, the W3C Advisory Committee may release the document as a Candidate Recommendation, which indicates that there is consensus within the Working Group but that the W3C would like additional public review and feedback,

> particularly from implementers of a specification. These developers also get a head start in bringing the technology to market before it acquires Recommendation status.
>
> ❑ *Recommendation:* A Recommendation represents consensus within the W3C that the idea is ready for prime time. Developers can be confident that a Recommendation will remain stable and that software can be built around it.

Summary

The simplicity of XML in combination with the Web has opened up new possibilities for moving data and for building new application architectures centered around common Internet protocols. Some of the changes brought about by XML include:

❑ Reduced dependence on proprietary data formats for applications

❑ A new way to do B2B data exchange using XML instead of the formats defined by traditional EDI systems

❑ A shift from relying on tightly coupled systems such as CORBA, RMI, and DCOM to a more loosely coupled Internet-based framework centered around XML and SOAP

❑ A change in focus from object-oriented to service-oriented software

❑ The emergence of Web services as technology for discovering and connecting to Internet-based services

❑ A move away from monolithic applications that attempt to do it all to a more organic software model that derives new capabilities from the combination of well-defined, limited software modules

❑ The consolidation of the software industry around two competing architectures, Microsoft's .NET and Sun's J2EE, specifications implemented by many of the major middleware vendors including IBM, Sun, BEA, Oracle, HP, and others

Placed in context, these changes reflect a major shift in the software industry from monolithic applications to applications built up from constituent pieces in an environment that fosters open, collaborative development.

Resources

Article

Jon Bosak and Tim Bray, "XML and the Second-Generation Web," *Scientific American*, May 1999.

Two Web pioneers discuss how hypertext and a global Internet started a revolution and how XML is poised to finish the job. A convenient online version of their article with hyperlinks is available at http://www.scientificamerican.com/1999/0599issue/0599bosak.html.

Web

http://www.simonstl.com/articles/civilw3c.htm

"An Outsider's Guide to the W3C," authored by Simon St. Laurent, offers a list of frequently asked questions about the W3C, providing insights into its workings and philosophy.

http://www.w3.org/DesignIssues/

Hosts a broad-ranging collection of personal notes and articles written by Tim Berners-Lee over the past decade describing the architectural design philosophy behind the Web.

http://www.oasis-open.org/cover/xml.html

"The Cover Pages," an encyclopedic Web site of news and articles about every aspect of XML maintained and updated daily by Robin Cover.

http://www.webservices.org/

A vendor-neutral site with hundreds of links to news and articles about all aspects of Web services.

2

The XML Technology Family

XML's strength is its simplicity. Its primary focus is data. All the rest—formatting, display, type checking, manipulation, search, and query—are associated with one of the family of technologies that surround an XML core. In this chapter we examine the XML core and its surrounding technologies. At the heart are XML and namespaces, which together provide a foundation for unambiguously delivering structured documents across the Web. Moving beyond the core we find a collection of technologies for presentation, data typing, and manipulation.

In regard to presentation, we look at cascading style sheets (CSS), Extensible Hypertext Markup Language (XHTML), Extensible Stylesheet Language (XSL) formatting, and VoiceXML, which provide options for delivering XML to a variety of devices in a number of different formats. For data typing we look at document type definitions (DTDs) and XML Schema. For client- and server-side manipulation and transformation, we examine XSL Transformations (XSLT), XPath, XLink, and XQuery, technologies for transforming, navigating, and extracting XML. Finally, to round out our discussion, we examine the XML Information Set (InfoSet) and its metadata capabilities that provide a basis for XML technologies to work together with a common semantic meaning, and then look at the Resource Description Framework (RDF) as the basis for what is referred to as the Semantic Web.

XML Technologies

XML is not just a technology for defining data vocabularies. Surrounding XML is a wide variety of XML standards and initiatives that act in combination with XML to address many of the issues associated with bringing XML into mainstream computing, namely presentation, structure, and transformation. As Figure 2.1 shows,

XML derives its strength from a variety of supporting technologies.

the XML core includes XML itself, based on the XML 1.0 specification, and namespaces, the specification that allows XML documents from different sources to be combined and yet be able to disambiguate elements with the same name from different sources. Following is a list of other categories in the XML technology:

❑ *Structure and data types:* When using XML to exchange data among clients, partners, and suppliers, it's important to be able to define how XML documents should be structured. DTDs and XML Schema provide this capability. DTDs come out of the world of Standard Generalized Markup Language (SGML), focusing primarily on structure by specifying what elements and attributes are considered valid for a particular XML instance document. DTDs have limited capability to specify data types, a circumstance that can be explained historically by considering their origins in the document culture (see Figure 1.9 in Chapter 1). XML Schema is a more recent initiative of the World Wide Web Consortium (W3C) that puts a more

Figure 2.1 **The XML technology family.**

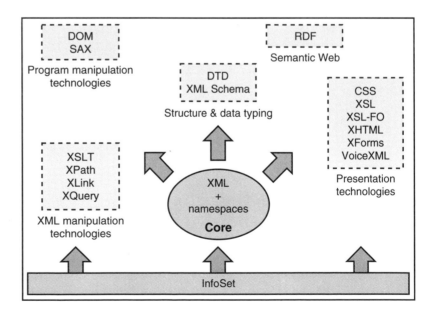

conventional data processing spin on describing XML data with more precision than with DTDs.

❑ *XML presentation technologies:* In keeping with an important design pattern for robust systems, XML intentionally separates data content from presentation through the introduction of supporting technologies that focus on delivering content to users via a variety of devices and presentation media. Among the technologies for presentation are XHTML, a modular XML-conformant replacement for HTML; CSS for controlling the display properties of HTML or XML in Web browsers; XSL and XSL Formatting Objects (XSL-FO) for formatting XML for various output media; XForms for collecting data from Web forms and returning XML; VoiceXML, for delivering content to voice-enabled devices; and Wireless Markup Language (WML), for delivery to wireless devices enabled for Wireless Application Protocol (WAP).

❑ *XML manipulation technologies:* Manipulation technologies provide the capability to extract and transform XML in different ways. These technologies play an important role in server-based XML processing for business-to-business (B2B) data manipulation and exchange. XSLT is widely used to transform XML from one format to another; XPath is a technology used by other XML technologies to navigate through an XML tree structure and zero in on particular elements or subtrees; XLink is a technology for creating and describing links between resources and for enabling links that go beyond the simple unidirectional links of the current Web; and XQuery is an evolving technology for extracting and querying XML repositories.

❑ *Other related technologies:* The XML family of technologies also includes initiatives for working with metainformation, which is literally information about the information contained in an XML document. Technologies in this space include RDF and InfoSet.

Leveraging the XML Technology Family

*Zwiftbooks—
an enterprise
looking to use XML
technologies in
its operations.*

In the following section we explore aspects of the different XML technologies from the perspective of a fictitious company called ZwiftBooks. ZwiftBooks is a company that has decided to build its business around XML, not unlike many companies today that are trying to leverage XML and its various supporting technologies.

ZwiftBooks' business is rapid book delivery. Its customers are people who just have to get their hands on a particular book, often within a matter of hours. ZwiftBooks fills this need by offering a local number that customers can call and get a guaranteed price and maximum waiting time for a book based on the customer's zip code. ZwiftBooks maintains a warehouse of in-demand books and does business in a city heavily populated with pager-carrying cyclists and skateboarders who are happy to earn extra money by zooming around town delivering books. When an order for a book comes in, the operator at the telephone desk sends out a paging message for all available riders to call in and report their locations. The operator uses rider location to determine estimated pickup and delivery times and gives the job to the closest rider. Within minutes the customer is given a price and a guaranteed delivery time. If the customer agrees, the closest delivery person is given the go-ahead and another ZwiftBooks customer is soon handed the vital book.

As we follow Zwiftbooks in its effort to XML-ize its operations, sometimes we'll find immediate applications for a new technology; at other times we won't, especially if the technology has not ripened into a W3C Recommendation, an indication of stability in the world of open standards. But even if a supporting technology is still under development, it can be useful to consider whether the expected capabilities of the technology fit in any way with corporate strategic objectives and vision. If a technology is promising, ZwiftBooks should at least begin to think about how it might utilize it once it is formalized or ZwiftBooks is ready to adopt it. What's important for ZwiftBooks to keep in mind is that, as it steps into the XML world, the XML family's ability to combine technologies results in being able to get to market more quickly with applications that simply plug into new technology capabilities. This is not to say that development is without cost, only that using capabilities and features of supporting technologies designed to plug into an XML foundation can reduce both cost and risk.

In the following sections we'll look at several XML technologies to determine if any can contribute to ZwiftBooks' objective to take its business global. It's not the intent here to provide a tutorial on XML syntax and structure, but rather to give a broad overview of the technology in the context of a business application. Those looking for more detail about XML can consult Appendix A or one of the references listed at the end of this chapter.

XML 1.0

For a company like ZwiftBooks, deciding on an XML representation for their data is a first step. In trying to come up with an XML data vocabulary that may be useful in automating operations, it's helpful to examine use cases that describe what occurs during a business interaction. Figure 2.2 illustrates the essence of a ZwiftBooks customer request and response.

Let's look at three different simple XML definitions: one for a customer request, one for the ZwiftBooks response to that request, and a third that illustrates an XML vocabulary for structuring the book data maintained by ZwiftBooks.

XML provides a variety of options for describing data.

It should be noted that these examples of XML are created more with an eye toward explaining how ZwiftBooks might use XML technologies rather than as a final take on ZwiftBooks' commercial

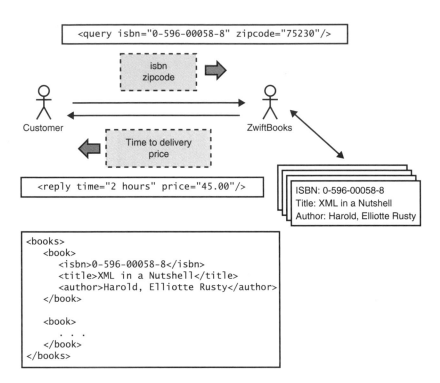

Figure 2.2   A ZwiftBooks business scenario and some XML representations.

```
<query isbn="0-596-00058-8" zipcode="75230"/>
```

isbn
zipcode

Customer

ZwiftBooks

Time to delivery
price

```
<reply time="2 hours" price="45.00"/>
```

ISBN: 0-596-00058-8
Title: XML in a Nutshell
Author: Harold, Elliotte Rusty

```
<books>
   <book>
      <isbn>0-596-00058-8</isbn>
      <title>XML in a Nutshell</title>
      <author>Harold, Elliotte Rusty</author>
   </book>

   <book>
      . . .
   </book>
</books>
```

distribution system, which of course would involve additional data elements and definitions.

Let's begin with the customer query.

```
<query isbn="0-596-00058-8" zipcode="75230"/>
```

Technically this represents an XML element called query with the data represented as the value of the two attributes isbn and zipcode. Because we are packing all the information into this one element, we've elected to write this element using an "empty" element tag ending with a slash. Empty element tags stand alone and are generally used when only attributes are specified and there is no element or subelement content.

The `reply` element is similarly defined, using attributes to hold the data.

```
<reply time="2 hours" price="45.00"/>
```

To maintain information about ZwiftBooks' inventory, we create a hierarchy of elements.

```
<books>
  <book>
   <isbn>0-596-00058-8</isbn>
   <title>XML in a Nutshell</title>
   <author>Harold, Elliotte Rusty</author>
  </book>
  <book>

</book>

   ...
  </book>
</books>
```

This XML structure differs from the `query` and `reply` elements in that the data is stored as the content of individual `isbn`, `title`, and `author` elements. Another difference is that the `books` and `book` elements do not have content but instead are used to contain other elements. It is this hierarchy or tree structure, implicit in all XML documents, that is processed and understood by the many XML-based tools available today.

Using these XML definitions as a starting point, let's move on and explore how other XML technologies can fit into ZwiftBooks' effort to bring its manual operation into the Internet age.

Elements versus Attributes

The ZwiftBooks example illustrates a classic issue in XML design: whether to use elements or attributes to represent data. Technically, it doesn't matter which you do. However, there are several factors to consider:

- ❏ Attributes cannot be further subdivided into subelements, but elements can always be subdivided. If there is any possibility of a need to break down data into more detail, then one should chose elements over attributes.

- ❏ Programs that process XML data often have to call special modules to handle attributes. While not a major issue, it does result in slightly more complex logic, which may take programmers longer to get right.

- ❏ Attributes are more compact and therefore more readable by humans. This is the main reason we're using attributes in this example.

Some organizations specifically require that only elements should be used to define application data. Others don't care and freely mix attributes with elements. A maxim that makes sense is to use elements for application data and attributes to describe metainformation about the application data. For example, attributes might be used to add security or transaction information pertaining to domain-specific data.

XML Namespaces

Namespaces eliminates the ambiguity of the same name from different providers.

Having at least begun to define some ZwiftBooks XML data, we learn from a bit of research on the Internet that several other companies also use the tag name query, but they use it to describe requests for types of information other than data about books. The potential problem this creates is confusion when ZwiftBooks' XML is merged with XML from other sources. An XML processor will not be able to distinguish between a ZwiftBooks `query` and another company's `query`. Similar problems can arise with the ZwiftBooks definitions for `reply` and `book`. The solution to this potential confusion in working with XML from different sources is what XML namespaces is all about.

XML namespaces is a simple technology solution that allows ZwiftBooks' element and attribute names to be distinguished from the similarly named elements and attributes of other XML users. Figure 2.3 illustrates how a namespace may be used to disambiguate duplicate element names. XML namespaces solves the problem of clashing names by providing for a unique prefix to be attached to the beginning of element and attribute names. In practice, a company's Web address is often used as the unique prefix, but technically the namespaces specification allows any Uniform Resource Identifier (URI) to be used. URIs are more general than the common Uniform Resource Locator (URL) and include just about any unique name one wants to use. The usual result, though, is that when namespaces are used in an XML document, the official element name is actually a two-part name: the name of the XML namespace plus the name of the element or attribute.

Namespaces use URIs to distinguish names.

Namespaces are needed to distinguish between identical
element names from different data sources

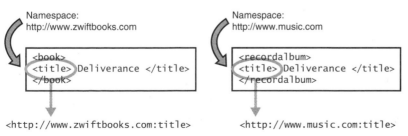

Unambiguous element names with namespace prefixes

Figure 2.3 The XML namespaces Recommendation allows identical element names from different sources to be distinguished.

A URL such as http://www. zwiftbooks.com does not imply the existence of such a site.

For ZwiftBooks, the namespace selection was easy: We use the address of the planned company Web site, www.zwiftbooks.com, as the namespace prefix to uniquely distinguish ZwiftBooks' XML from that of other companies. An important point to realize about this decision to use a future Web site as the namespace identifier is that XML namespaces makes no assumptions about the existence of a Web site for any URI used as the unique namespace prefix. This is something that often causes confusion when people first look at namespaces. The use of a URL such as http://www.zwiftbooks.com says nothing about the existence or nonexistence of the Web site. As it turns out, many URLs used as namespace identifiers do exist on the Web and often have links to DTDs or other information that pertains to their company's XML initiatives, but there is nothing in the namespace specification that requires an actual site to exist.

Namespace Declarations

There are several ways to add a namespace to an XML document so that, when software is processing XML data from ZwiftBooks, it will see ZwiftBooks elements as `http://www.zwiftbooks.com:title` instead of just `title`. The simplest approach is to declare a namespace in a top-level element and let all the elements and attributes under the top element come under the scope of the namespace. For example, the following XML document adds a ZwiftBooks namespace to an XML book description document.

```
<book xmlns="http://www.zwiftbooks.com">
    <isbn>0-596-00058-8</isbn>
    <title>XML in a Nutshell</title>
    <author>Harold, Elliotte Rusty</author>
</book>
```

In this example, the namespace declaration is applied to the `book` element by adding the predefined attribute `xmlns` and giving as its value the unique URL of ZwiftBooks, `http://www.zwiftbooks.com`. Because the `xmlns` attribute appears in the `book` element, all subelements (`isbn`, `title`, and `author`) are included in the namespace.

But what happens if the namespace declaration appears at some element other than the root element of the document? As you might expect, the namespace applies only to the element where it is declared and all its child elements. This ability to specify namespaces based on element hierarchies allows multiple namespaces to be used in the same document, which is why namespace is around after all: to help XML processors distinguish elements that have the same name but come from different sources.

Namespaces may span a range of elements or target just one element.

Figure 2.4 illustrates the use of multiple namespaces within the same document and how namespaces are useful in distinguishing which elements are which. In this example, the top-level element, `supercatalog`, is in its own namespace. Its two `book` subelements, technically within the scope of the `supercatalog` namespace declaration, define their own namespaces, so that we end up with three namespaces within the XML.

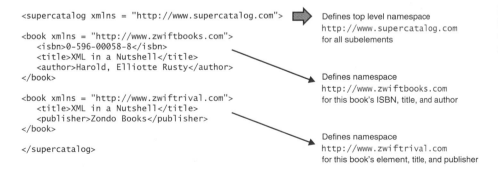

```
<supercatalog xmlns = "http://www.supercatalog.com">

<book xmlns = "http://www.zwiftbooks.com">
    <isbn>0-596-00058-8</isbn>
    <title>XML in a Nutshell</title>
    <author>Harold, Elliotte Rusty</author>
</book>

<book xmlns = "http://www.zwiftrival.com">
    <title>XML in a Nutshell</title>
    <publisher>Zondo Books</publisher>
</book>

</supercatalog>
```

Defines top level namespace
http://www.supercatalog.com
for all subelements

Defines namespace
http://www.zwiftbooks.com
for this book's ISBN, title, and author

Defines namespace
http://www.zwiftrival.com
for this book's element, title, and publisher

Figure 2.4 An XML document with multiple namespaces.

Figure 2.5 An XML document using a namespace abbreviation.

The shortcut term zbooks now refers to the namespace http://www.zwiftbooks.com

```
<zbooks:book xmlns:zbooks="http://www.zwiftbooks.com">
    <zbooks:isbn>0-596-00058-8</isbn>
    <zbooks:title>XML in a Nutshell</title>
    <zbooks:author>Harold, Elliotte Rusty</author>
</zbooks:book>
```

All elements that begin with zbooks: belong to the http://www.zwiftbooks.com namespace

Namespace Abbreviations

Namespace abbreviations may be used to simplify writing and reading the XML.

The namespaces specification also makes it possible to use abbreviations for namespaces in order to make XML documents more readable. Figure 2.5 shows how we can define a shortcut name, zbooks, so that anywhere that zbooks appears in a document, a software program processing the document will replace it with the actual namespace, http://www.zwiftbooks.com.

The ZwiftBooks data shown in Figure 2.4 is identical in meaning to the XML in Figure 2.5. There are several issues to be aware of when using the shortcut abbreviation. One is that you may use whatever shortcut name you like within an XML document, and an XML processor reading the document will replace whatever shortcut you use with the URI namespace. Another point is that, if you declare you will use a shortcut by including xmlns:shortcut ="some URI", then everywhere the shortcut is not used in an element name, the assumption is that the element is *not* part of the namespace.

Structuring with Schemas

Having defined some XML and come up with a namespace for ZwiftBooks, it's now time to think how we might use our new data representation to begin to accept queries as XML over the Internet.

When using XML to exchange data among clients, partners, and suppliers, it's important to be able to define how XML documents should be structured. What's needed is a schema.

"Schema" is a general term that describes the form of data. Originally the term was used to define the structure of databases. A schema is a formal specification of the grammar for a specific XML vocabulary. Schemas are useful in validating XML document content, determining whether the XML document conforms to the grammar expressed by the XML Schema, and describing XML structure to others, which enables the exchange of structured information between collaborating applications or business partners in a platform- and middleware-neutral manner.

A schema defines a data representation.

In the XML world, there are two schemas: DTDs and XML Schemas. Figure 2.6 illustrates how either may be used to define a family of XML document instances. DTDs focus primarily on structure, allowing an XML vocabulary designer to specify the elements and attributes

XML may be specified with DTDs or XML Schema.

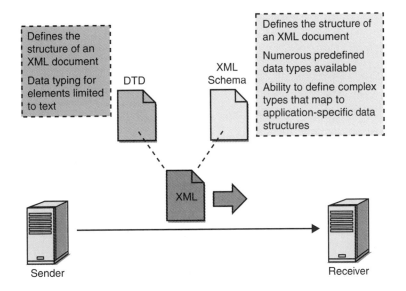

Figure 2.6 Both DTDs and XML Schemas may be used to define the structure of an XML document.

that are appropriate for a set of XML instance documents. However, DTDs have limited capability to describe data types within an XML document.

XML Schema is a newer technology, adopted by W3C as an official Recommendation in May 2001, intended to provide the kind of detailed structure often associated with programming languages' data types and useful in enabling solutions for the exchange of XML-based information where it is helpful to check data format accuracy before processing begins.

Let's look at how ZwiftBooks could use schemas to help it move its business to an Internet base.

DTD

A DTD may be used by both a sender and a receiver of XML.

Figure 2.7 shows how a DTD can be used by both the sender and receiver of a ZwiftBooks document. When ZwiftBooks publishes its DTD for a query, senders can use the DTD to create XML documents that the ZwiftBooks server will understand. On the receiving end, the server can compare an incoming XML document against the DTD and determine if the incoming XML data is valid with respect to the DTD. If not, it can return a message indicating an error in the incoming data format.

DTD structure and syntax are covered in more detail in Appendix A. There are several points to keep in mind:

❑ DTDs are written using a different syntax from XML. This is because DTDs were first developed in the SGML world before XML existed.

❑ DTDs define the elements and attributes that can validly appear in our ZwiftBooks XML documents.

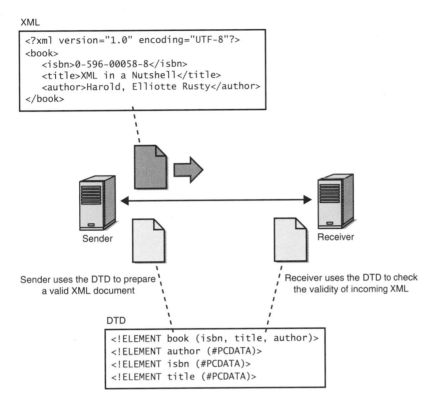

XML

```
<?xml version="1.0" encoding="UTF-8"?>
<book>
    <isbn>0-596-00058-8</isbn>
    <title>XML in a Nutshell</title>
    <author>Harold, Elliotte Rusty</author>
</book>
```

Sender

Receiver

Sender uses the DTD to prepare
a valid XML document

Receiver uses the DTD to check
the validity of incoming XML

DTD

```
<!ELEMENT book (isbn, title, author)>
<!ELEMENT author (#PCDATA)>
<!ELEMENT isbn (#PCDATA)>
<!ELEMENT title (#PCDATA)>
```

Figure 2.7 A ZwiftBooks DTD can be used by both the sender and receiver of an XML document.

❑ DTDs are not able to define distinctions about data types. For example, a DTD cannot declare that an element must contain a valid date or numeric field or even an ISBN number. A DTD is limited to declaring that an element must contain text; it cannot control what kind of text, as, for example, by distinguishing between numeric and alphabetic characters.

XML Schema

The alternative to using DTDs to specify what constitutes a valid ZwiftBooks XML document is to use XML Schemas. The XML Schema Recommendation goes beyond the basic text-based descriptors provided by DTDs. It provides more detail about the kind of data that

An XML Schema is itself an XML document.

43

can appear as part of an XML document. Unlike the non-XML syntax of a DTD, XML Schema is itself an XML vocabulary that defines rules governing the structure and content of elements and attributes in an XML document. Because XML Schemas are XML, they can be processed and managed like any XML instance.

XML Schemas can reduce the burden of processing XML.

XML Schemas take a giant step in moving XML from the document world into the data processing world. Schemas support a broad range of data types, and include useful features like range constraints that let XML authors describe bounds for data that can be enforced by schema processors. The advantage of using XML Schemas over DTDs is that XML Schemas eliminate the need for hand-coded data checking of XML data fields. Off-the-shelf software can validate XML data against a broad range of built-in data types.

As Figure 2.8 illustrates, XML Schema data types form a hierarchy. All data types derive, directly or indirectly, from the root `anyType`, which can be used to indicate any value at all. Below `anyType`, the hierarchy branches into two groups consisting of simple types and complex types.

XML Schema supports different ways to define data types.

As we move down the tree, types derive from their parents by modifying in some way the properties of parent types. There are four kinds of derivation rules: restriction, enumeration, list, and union. Restriction works by constraining a parent base type. For example, `positiveInteger` inherits from `nonNegativeInteger` by restricting the scope of values to positive values. Enumeration constrains by restricting legal values to a set based on an underlying type. For example, it's possible to declare a `holiday` data type that allows only values from a list of company holidays (such as "12-25", "01-01", and "02-14"). List constraint is similar to enumeration except that multiple values are permitted. For example, the list data type option could be used to define a data item such as `personalHoliday` that reflects an employee's

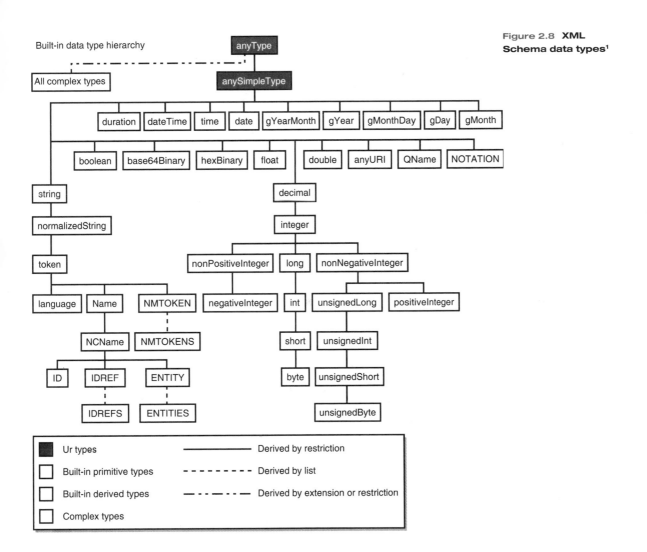

[1] http://www.w3.org/TR/2001/REC-xmlschema-2-20010502/.
Copyright © 2001 World Wide Web Consortium (Massachusetts Institute of Technology, Institut National de Recherche en Informatique et en Automatique, Keio University). All Rights Reserved. http://www.w3.org/Consortium/Legal/. Recommendation date May 2001.

Figure 2.8 **XML Schema data types[1]**

ability to pick three out of ten listed days as personal holidays. Union allows the mixing of data types, such as positiveInteger and String. For example, a company that used 9 as the internal code for the rank of vice president could use either the integer 9 or the string "Vice President" within a companyRank element in its XML.

Complex Types

Complex types can be used to model application-specific data.

Complex types are an important aspect of XML Schema that allow application developers to define application-specific data types that can be checked by programs that check XML documents for validity. As Figure 2.8 shows, XML Schema divides complex types into two categories: those with simple content and those with complex content. Both varieties allow attributes, but simple content types can contain only characters, whereas complex content types can contain child elements.

ZwiftBooks and XML Schema

Let's follow ZwiftBooks on the path to XML Schema. It should consider moving from DTD to XML Schema mainly to be able to specify more accurately the structure of documents sent over the Web and to allow both sender and receiver to validate the XML against the schema using off-the-shelf tools. For example, DTDs can specify only text in the zipcode data item, while with XML Schema the text can be refined to numeric data for the zip code.

Figure 2.9 illustrates ZwiftBooks' use of XML Schema to describe a complex data type called book. Because a schema definition is an XML document, we must be careful to distinguish between elements associated with the XML Schema namespace and ZwiftBooks' elements. Thus the declaration

```
<xsd:schema xmlns:xs="http://www.w3.org/2001/XMLSchema">
```

allows us to use the short-cut term xs in place of the official namespace, http://www.w3.org/2001/XMLSchema. We then use

XML

```
<?xml version = "1.0" encoding = "UTF-8"?>
<book>
    <isbn>0-596-00058-8</isbn>
    <title>XML in a Nutshell</title>
    <author>Harold, Elliotte Rusty</author>
</book>
```

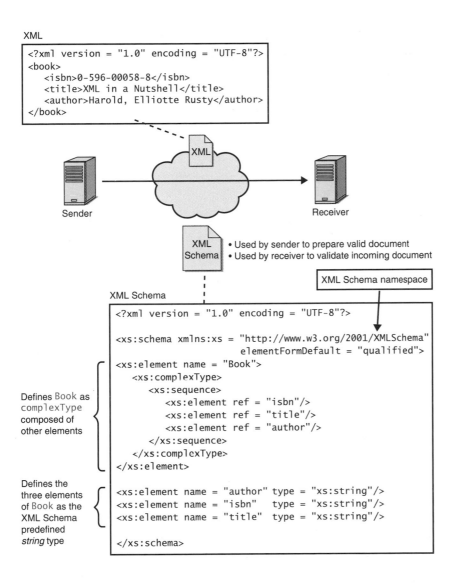

Sender   Receiver

XML
Schema • Used by sender to prepare valid document
        • Used by receiver to validate incoming document

XML Schema namespace

XML Schema

```
<?xml version = "1.0" encoding = "UTF-8"?>

<xs:schema xmlns:xs = "http://www.w3.org/2001/XMLSchema"
                      elementFormDefault = "qualified">
<xs:element name = "Book">
    <xs:complexType>
        <xs:sequence>
            <xs:element ref = "isbn"/>
            <xs:element ref = "title"/>
            <xs:element ref = "author"/>
        </xs:sequence>
    </xs:complexType>
</xs:element>

<xs:element name = "author" type = "xs:string"/>
<xs:element name = "isbn"   type = "xs:string"/>
<xs:element name = "title"  type = "xs:string"/>

</xs:schema>
```

Defines Book as
complexType
composed of
other elements

Defines the
three elements
of Book as the
XML Schema
predefined
string type

Figure 2.9 A ZwiftBooks schema to describe the data associated with a book.

`<xs:element name="Book">` to define our new complex data type that consists of three subelements, `isbn`, `title`, and `author`.

Schemas in Practice

XML Schema provides a rich catalog of element descriptions.

Schemas provide a flexible and rich language to specify, package, publish, and exchange both structured and unstructured information across application or business boundaries. Schemas may be used in several ways with XML documents. Through use of the `xsi:type` attribute, an element can explicitly assert its type within a specific XML document instance. Such assertions can be used to validate an element against a predefined XSL type. To handle versioning and time-related processing, the XML Schema type `timeInstant` may be used to specify a particular instant of time. Values for `timeInstant` are compliant with the ISO 8601 time and date standard. The XML Schema `uriReference` data type can handle links to URIs, which may be specified using an absolute or relative syntax.

XML Processing

When XML arrives at a server, it is typically validated against a DTD or XML Schema and then stored, transformed, or processed in some way depending on the application. Both validation and processing can be performed by XML parsers. In the XML parsing and processing world there are two major alternatives: the Document Object Model (DOM) and the Simple API for XML (SAX).

DOM

DOM is a W3C Recommendation.

DOM is a W3C-supported standard application programming interface (API) that provides a platform- and language-neutral interface to allow developers to programmatically access and modify the content and structure of tree-structured documents such as HTML or XML. Because DOM is language neutral, programmers can use scripting languages or programming languages such as Java to process XML.

DOM is constantly evolving to keep up with changes in the XML world. It includes the following levels, each of which provides more capability to the DOM API:

- ❑ *DOM Level 0* informally refers to the functionality available to scripting languages in Netscape Navigator 3.0 and Microsoft Internet Explorer 3.0. There is no W3C specification for Level 0.

- ❑ *DOM Level 1* is a W3C Recommendation completed in October 1998. Level 1 provides support for XML 1.0 and HTML processing.

- ❑ *DOM Level 2* is a W3C Recommendation completed in November 2000. Level 2 extends Level 1 with support for XML 1.0 with namespaces and CSS. It also provides support for user interface and tree manipulation events and adds additional DOM tree manipulation capabilities.

- ❑ *DOM Level 3* is still under development as of this writing. Level 3 is intended to extend Level 2 by adding user interface keyboard events. It will also support DTDs, XML Schema, and XPath.

DOM falls under the category of tree-based APIs which are useful for a wide range of applications but can strain system resources when documents are large. Also, because DOM is language neutral, processing in a strongly typed language such as Java can introduce unwanted complexities when going from DOM interfaces to language-specific data structures. To overcome these drawbacks, developers began to look at event-based processing models that reduced system memory requirements and let developers create their own data structures. The result was SAX.

DOM requires significant system resources for large documents.

SAX

SAX is an example of a grass-roots development effort to provide a simple, Java-based API for processing XML. It began with design discussions taking place publicly on the XML-DEV mailing list. One

SAX is simple.

month after discussions began, the first draft interface was released in January 1998. After further mailing list discussion, SAX 1.0 was released.

SAX is event-driven.

SAX differs from DOM in that SAX is event-driven. Programmers define event handlers that are notified when elements are found in an XML document. The handler code uses the information delivered by SAX to perform application-specific processing tasks.

SAX supports processing pipelines.

SAX2 was released in May 2000 and provides support for other languages besides Java. SAX2 also supports filter chains that may be used to construct event processing pipelines. Filter chains are useful in building complex XML applications that can be partitioned into tasks modeled as simple SAX components. In a SAX filter chain, each SAX component does some processing and passes data on to the next SAX component in the chain. (See Chapter 4 for additional discussion of filter architectures.)

SAX requires programmers to maintain state.

While SAX is simple, there is a downside. Programmers working with SAX must build their own data structures to help keep track of where they are in a document. In effect, they have to maintain state as they process XML using SAX. This can make programs complex and more difficult to maintain. Thus it's important that developers understand both SAX and DOM and choose their API based on the requirements of the application.

Presentation Technologies

Representing data with XML opens up new possibilities for transport and distribution. XML presentation technologies provide a modular way to deliver and display content to a variety of devices. Here we examine some technologies for display, including CSS, XSL, Xforms, and VoiceXML.

CSS

Cascading style sheets is an XML-supporting technology for adding style display properties such as fonts, colors, or spacing to Web documents. CSS origins may be traced to the SGML world, which used a style sheet technology called DSSSL to control the display of SGML documents. Style sheet technology is important because it lets developers separate presentation from content, which greatly enhances software's longevity.

As Figure 2.10 shows, a style sheet tells a browser or other display engine how to display content. Each rule is made up of a selector—typically an element name such as an HTML heading (H1) or paragraph (P), or a user-defined XML element (Book)—and the style to be applied to the selector. The CSS specification defines numerous properties (color, font style, point size, and so on) that may be defined for an element. Each property takes a value which describes how the selector should be presented.

Style rules have the following syntax.

```
selector { property: value }
```

Multiple style declarations for a single selector are separated by a semicolon. The following code segment shows how a CSS element

CSS is used to control document display.

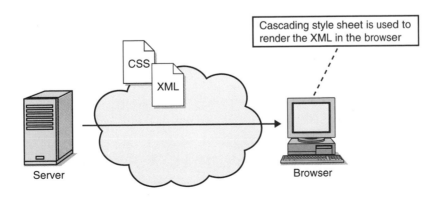

Cascading style sheet is used to render the XML in the browser

CSS

XML

Server

Browser

Figure 2.10 HTML or XML may be delivered to a browser with CSS, which controls how data is presented on the screen.

can be added to an HTML or XML document to define the color and font size properties for TITLE and AUTHOR elements:

```
<STYLE TYPE="text/css">
TITLE  { font-size: x-large; color: red }
AUTHOR { font-size: large; color: blue }
</STYLE>
```

This style sheet tells the browser to show the content of TITLE elements in an extra-large red font, and to show the content of AUTHOR elements in a large blue font. Although CSS technology was designed to allow finer control of how HTML is displayed, CSS makes no assumptions about the tags' names, which is why cascading style sheets can be used just as easily with XML as with HTML.

CSS is a W3C Recommendation.

Because style sheet technology is important for the Web design industry, the CSS specification has undergone significant evolution. The CSS1 specification, which defines all properties and values that can be applied to a Web document, received its W3C Recommendation status in December 1996. It describes the CSS language as well as a simple visual formatting model. CSS2, which itself became a W3C Recommendation in May 1998, builds on CSS1 and adds support for style sheets for specific media such as printers and audio devices, as well as downloadable fonts, element positioning, and tables.

CSS has limitations for complex displays.

However, there are two drawbacks with CSS that should be noted. The first is that CSS describes only those tags that are to be treated in a special way; the browser decides how to display elements that the style sheet says nothing about. While this typically works fine for HTML, with XML, where it may be desirable not to display certain data, CSS does not help. The second drawback is that with CSS technology it is up to the browser to implement CSS correctly, and some implementations may not always be consistent.

XSL

XSL 1.0 is a W3C Recommendation that provides users with the ability to describe how XML data and documents are to be formatted. XSL does this by defining "formatting objects," such as footnotes, headers, or columns.

The XSL initiative began as an effort to develop a styling technology more suited to the needs of XML than CSS. However, in pulling together a Working Group to define XSL, something interesting happened. The Working Group realized that the kind of styling performed by technologies such as CSS was only one instance of a more general "transformation" process of taking an XML document and turning it into another kind of document. After much deliberation the XSL Working Group split into two subgroups, one focused on trying to build a better display-oriented style sheet technology and a second group trying to define a transformation language that could be used to transform XML into a variety of target languages including HTML, other dialects of XML, or any text document, including a program. The result of this effort was XSLT, which achieved W3C Recommendation status in November 1999 and which we discuss in the next section of this chapter.

XSL began as an effort to provide a better CSS.

An XSL style sheet is basically a series of pattern-action rules and looks like an XML document with a mixture of two kinds of elements: those defined by XSL and those defined by the object language. The patterns are similar to CSS's selectors, but the action part may create an arbitrary number of "objects." The action part of the rule is called the "template" in XSL, and a template and a pattern together are referred to as a "template rule."

XSL is based on applying rules or templates to an XML document.

The result of applying all matching patterns to a document recursively is a tree of objects, which is then interpreted top-down according to the definition of each object. For example, if they are

HTML objects, an HTML document will be generated; if they are XML objects, XML will be the result.

CSS Compared to XSL

The fact that the W3C has started developing XSL in addition to CSS has caused some confusion. Why develop a second style sheet language when implementers haven't even finished the first one? The W3C has answered this question with the information in Table 2.1.

In practice, both CSS and XSL may be used in conjunction with each other. Figure 2.11 illustrates some of the different options for using CSS and XSL to create displays based on HTML or XML. The general principle is that if the document is to be simply rendered and not transformed in any way through the addition or deletion of items, then CSS is the more straightforward approach.

XForms

Forms are widely used in all aspects of e-commerce.

Soon after HTML began to be used to deliver content from Web sites to browsers, it became apparent that it was also necessary to push data from browsers to servers. The result was HTML forms. Since

Table 2.1 Comparison of CSS and XSL

	CSS	XSL
Can be used with HTML?	yes	no
Can be used with XML?	yes	yes
Transformation language?	no	yes
Syntax	CSS	XML

SOURCE: http://www.w3.org/Style/. Copyright © 2001 World Wide Web Consortium (Massachusetts Institute of Technology, Institut National de Recherche en Informatique et en Automatique, Keio University). All Rights Reserved. http://www.w3.org/Consortium/Legal/. Last updated November 2001.

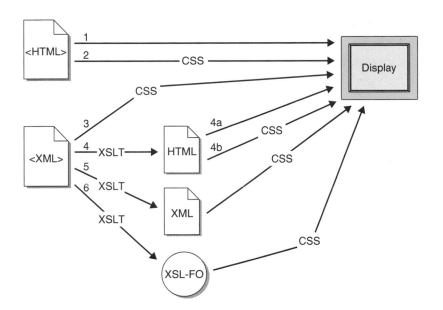

Figure 2.11 **Options for using CSS and XSLT with XML and HTML.**[2]

their introduction in 1993, forms have become a critical aspect of Web-based e-commerce. However, existing mechanisms for form data capture are limited, especially when complex data spanning multipart forms must be collected and complex logic is required.

XForms is an XML approach that overcomes the limitations of HTML forms. XForms is a GUI toolkit for creating user interfaces and delivering the results in XML. Because XForms separates what the form does from how it looks, XForms can work with a variety of standard or proprietary user interfaces, providing a standard set of visual controls that replaces the primitive forms controls in HTML and XHTML. Included in XForms are a variety of buttons, scrollbars, and menus integrated into a single execution model that generates XML form data as output.

XForms delivers XML.

---

[2] http://www.w3.org/Style/CSS-vs-XSL. Copyright © 2001 World Wide Web Consortium (Massachusetts Institute of Technology, Institut National de Recherche en Informatique et en Automatique, Keio University). All Rights Reserved. http://www.w3.org/Consortium/Legal/. Updated July 1999.

Figure 2.12 illustrates how a single device-independent XML form definition, called the XForms Model, has the capability to work with a variety of standard or proprietary user interfaces. For example, the Voice Browser Working Group is looking at developing voice-based user interface components for XForms.

There are currently several XForms implementations:

❑ *X-Smiles* is a Java-based XML browser from Helsinki University of Technology. It implements a large part of XForms and uses XForms together with XSL-FO on the user interface side. It also supports XSLT, Synchronized Multimedia Integration Language 1.0, and Scalable Vector Graphics.

❑ *Mozquito XForms Preview* is an XML-based Web development software that implements XForms and gives current Web browsers the ability to send, receive, and process XML data

Figure 2.12 XForms provides a standard way to collect form data through a variety of device interfaces.

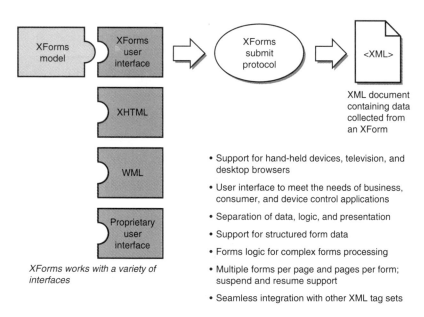

XForms works with a variety of interfaces

XML document containing data collected from an XForm

• Support for hand-held devices, television, and desktop browsers

• User interface to meet the needs of business, consumer, and device control applications

• Separation of data, logic, and presentation

• Support for structured form data

• Forms logic for complex forms processing

• Multiple forms per page and pages per form; suspend and resume support

• Seamless integration with other XML tag sets

easily and effectively. It reads and writes XML instances without the need for XSL.

XHTML

XHTML is an effort by the W3C to replace HTML with a more flexible approach to displaying Web content. XHTML differs from HTML in that it is based on XML, not SGML. Thus, XHTML conforms to the XML 1.0 Recommendation. The long-term goal of the XHTML spec is that XHTML will continue to be useful in environments where there are no preconceived notions about how elements should be rendered in a browser. The approach is one in which developers will be able to extend in unanticipated ways as new technologies and display media emerge. Its modular design reflects the realization that a one-size-fits-all approach to the Web no longer works, especially when browsers differ significantly and cell phones have limited memory and screen size for display.

XHTML brings HTML into conformance with XML.

XHTML Modularization

The capability of XHTML to be more flexible than HTML is attributable to the use of XHTML modules for creating XHTML-conforming markup languages. New XHTML-compliant languages must use the basic XHTML framework as well as other XHTML modules. As illustrated in Figure 2.13, modules plug together within the XHTML framework to define a markup language that is task or client specific. Documents developed based on the new markup language will be usable on any XHTML-conforming clients.

XHTML modules build a base for the future.

In some instances, people will create complete, proprietary markup languages using XHTML. People may also create new, reusable modules that will find use within their own or other organizations. The architecture and technology behind XHTML are already finding use within the W3C by organizations such as the Organization for the

XHTML allows specialized markup languages to be developed.

Figure 2.13 The structure of XHTML.

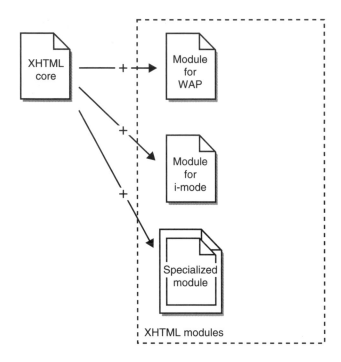

Advancement of Structured Information Standards (OASIS) and Project Gutenberg, which are using XHTML modularization to create new markup languages for industry-specific applications. XHTML is also finding applicability within the wireless industry that sees it as the next-generation language of choice for NTT DoCoMo's i-mode cell phones and as the WAP Forum's replacement technology for WML.

VoiceXML

VoiceXML uses XML text to drive voice dialogs.

VoiceXML is an emerging standard for speech-enabled applications. Its XML syntax defines elements to control a sequence of interaction dialogs between a user and an implementation platform. The elements defined as part of VoiceXML control dialogs and rules for presenting information to and extracting information from an end-user using speech. For ZwiftBooks, VoiceXML opens up options for extending its service to voice through cellular networks.

As Figure 2.14 illustrates, VoiceXML documents are stored on Web servers. Translation from text to voice is carried out either on a specialized server that delivers voice directly to a phone or by the device itself using speech processing technology.

Just as a Web browser interprets HTML and displays it on the screen, a VoiceXML browser understands VoiceXML markup and interprets it for presentation over the telephone or directly to an audio channel. As mobile devices such as cell phones acquire additional processing power, it will be possible to deliver VoiceXML documents directly to cell phones for VoiceXML processing.

The VoiceXML document specifies each interaction dialog. User input affects dialog interpretation and is collected into requests that

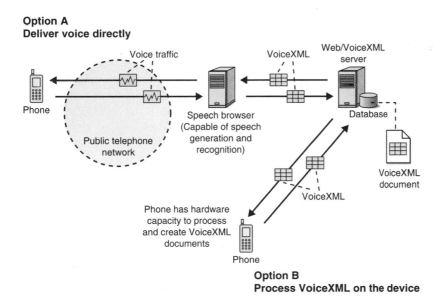

Option A
Deliver voice directly

Voice traffic

VoiceXML

Web/VoiceXML server

Phone

Public telephone network

Speech browser
(Capable of speech generation and recognition)

Database

VoiceXML document

VoiceXML

Phone has hardware capacity to process and create VoiceXML documents

Phone

Option B
Process VoiceXML on the device

Figure 2.14
VoiceXML documents are used to drive voice interactions over conventional or wireless phones.

go back to the VoiceXML server. The server may reply with another VoiceXML document to continue the user's session with other dialogs.

A VoiceXML document includes tags defining both audio prompts and logic. For example, the content of a `prompt` tag is converted by a VoiceXML browser to speech. Other VoiceXML tags include `form` for building a voice-driven form to collect user information and `menu`, which leads an end-user through a series of menu selections.

Forms and Menus

VoiceXML supports both forms and menus.

There are two kinds of dialogs: forms and menus. Forms define an interaction that collects values for a group of fields. Each field may specify a grammar that controls the allowable inputs for that field. Menus present the user with a choice of options and then transition to another dialog based on that choice.

Forms also contain subdialogs that provide a mechanism for triggering a new interaction and returning to the original form. Subdialogs can be used to create a confirmation sequence that may require a database query, a set of components for sharing among documents in a single application, or a reusable library of dialogs shared across many applications.

Transformation

XML is supported by several technologies that allow XML to be manipulated and modified in various ways. These technologies include XSLT, XLink, XPath,and XQuery.

XSLT

XSLT is an XML-based language used to transform XML documents into other formats such as HTML for Web display, WML for display on WAP devices, alternate XML dialects for B2B data transfer, or just plain text.

To perform an XSL transformation, a program referred to as an XSLT processor reads both an XML document and an XSLT document that defines how to transform the XML (see Figure 2.15). An XSLT processor has the capability to read the XML source document, and rearrange and reassemble it in a variety of ways, even adding new text and tags.

XSLT is used to transform an XML document.

The XSLT Model

Writing XSLT is different from writing a program that specifies in a step-by-step manner what a processor is expected to do. XSLT transformations occur through a series of tests that compare parts of an XML document against templates defined in an XSLT document. Templates act like rules that are matched against the contents of a document; when a match occurs, whatever the template specifies

XSLT uses templates as rules.

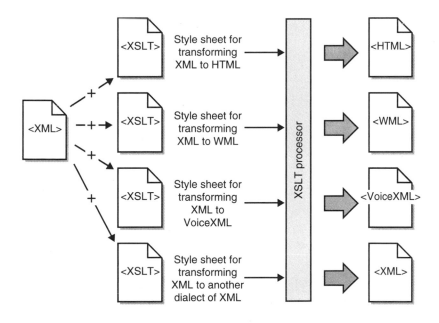

Figure 2.15 **The transformation language XSLT may be used to transform XML into a variety of formats.**

is output. For example, assume an XML document contains the fragment

```
<title> A History of PI </title>
```

Given a template that matches for a title element

```
<xsl:template match="title">
  <H2>
   <xsl:value-of/>
  </H2>
</xsl:template>
```

the output will be

```
<H2> A History of PI </H2>
```

where the `<xsl:value-of/>` tag is replaced by the actual value of the title element. Using this capability, one can go from XML to HTML or other forms of XML.

The following is a complete style sheet that generates a Web page of all books in an XML document:

```
<?xml version="1.0"?>
<xsl:stylesheet version="1.0"
   xmlns:xsl="http://www.w3.org/1999/XSL/Transform">

<xsl:template match="/">
   <xsl:apply-templates/>
</xsl:template>

<xsl:template match="books">
   <html>
   <head>
       <title>ZwiftBooks - At Your Doorstep</title>
   </head>
   <body>
```

```
    <h2>Weekly Specials</h2>

    <xsl:apply-templates/>

    </body>
    </html>
</xsl:template>

<xsl:template match="book">
    <p></p><b>Title:</b>  <xsl:value-of select="title/><br/>
            <em>Author:</em>  <xsl:value-of select="author"/>
            <em>ISBN:</em>  <xsl:value-of select="isbn"/>

    <xsl:apply-templates/>
</xsl:template>

</xsl:stylesheet>
```

Let's look at a portion of this page in a bit more detail.

```
<xsl:template match="/">
    <xsl:apply-templates/>
</xsl:template>
```

The slash in the first line tells the processor that this node applies to the root level of the XML document. Think of the root level as an imaginary pair of tags surrounding the entircty of an XML document which must be addressed before you can get to the actual tags. The apply-templates tag tells the processor to look at everything that occurs beneath the current level; in this case it means, "examine everything." This command can be found in most XSLT documents.

In our example note that there are two templates: one that matches for books and another that matches for a book. When a books element is found, the outer structure of an HTML page is printed. Within the books template there is another apply-templates element which says to keep trying to find more matches in the XML document. When the XSLT matches a book element, the book template is activated and details of the book are printed as HTML.

This short example only touches the surface of the power of XSLT. The syntax for XSLT is quite involved and there is a significant learning curve associated with becoming competent at using it to transform documents. In keeping with the W3C spirit of simplicity and combination, XSLT uses XPath as the language for zeroing in on elements within an XML tree. XSLT also provides "if-then" and "choose" functions for embedding program logic into an XSLT style sheet. Such features allow a wide range of manipulation for XML content.

XSLT and CSS

XSLT and CSS may complement each other.

Both XSLT and CSS may be used to generate data for display, either alone or in combination. As we saw in Figure 2.11, there are a variety of options for using the two technologies. For example, when beginning with HTML, one can generate a display by going directly to a browser (Option 1) or by using CSS to control how the HTML is displayed (Option 2). When beginning with XML, one may use CSS to generate display (Option 3) or use XSLT to generate HTML (Option 4). It's also possible to go from XML to another form of XML and then use CSS to control the display (Option 5). Another option is to use XSLT to generate an XML Formatting Object (Option 6) and then use CSS to generate display.

XSL-FO is the formatting part of XSL, an XML-based markup language that allows fine control of display, including pagination, layout, and style. Because XSL-FO markup is fairly complex and verbose, it is recommended that XSLT be used to actually generate an XSL-FO source document. As a result of the current paucity of tools that support XSL-FO, it is not nearly as widely used as XSLT, or XSLT with CSS.

XLink

The notion of resources is universal to the World Wide Web. According to the Internet Engineering Task Force, a "resource" is any addressable unit of information or service. Examples include files, images, documents, programs, and query results. These resources are addressed using a URI reference. What XLink brings to the table is the ability to address a portion of a resource. For example, if the entire resource is an XML document, a useful portion of that resource might be a single element within the document. Following an XLink might result, for example, in highlighting that element or taking the user directly to that point in the document.

XLink will enable bidirectional Web linking.

XPath

XPath gets its name from its use of a path notation to navigate through the hierarchical tree structure of an XML document. Because all XML documents can be represented as a tree of nodes, XPath allows for the selection of a node or group of nodes through the use of a compact, non-XML syntax. It is an important XML technology due to its role in providing a common syntax and semantics for functionality in both XSLT and XPointer.

XPath is used to navigate XML tree structures.

Figure 2.16 shows that XPath operates on the hierarchical tree structure of an XML document rather than its tag-based syntax. It is capable of distinguishing between different types of nodes, including element nodes, attribute nodes, and text node.

XQuery

XQuery is a W3C initiative to define a standard set of constructs for querying and searching XML documents. The XML Query Working Group draws its membership from both the document and the database communities, trying to hammer out an agreement on XML-based query syntax that meets the needs of both cultures.

XQuery brings database query processing to XML.

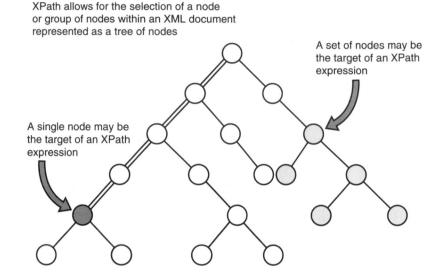

Figure 2.16 XPath is used to specify nodes using their location in an XML tree.

XPath allows for the selection of a node or group of nodes within an XML document represented as a tree of nodes

A set of nodes may be the target of an XPath expression

A single node may be the target of an XPath expression

Although the final form of the XQuery language is still open to definition as of this writing, the Working Group has published a set of queries in the form of use cases, which the final draft of the XQuery specification is expected to address. Although it's too early to implement for XQuery, ZwiftBooks can strategically look ahead to see if it can leverage any of the immediate functionality provided by emerging XQuery examples.

For example, selection and extraction are fundamental database operations. A typical select-and-extract operation is to select all titles of books in the ZwiftBooks catalog published by Addison-Wesley after 1993. The result, in XML, might look like this:

```
<books>
    <book year="1994">
    <title>Object Oriented Programming</title>
    </book>
```

```
        <book year="1994">
        <title>Design Patterns for Object-Oriented Software
                Development</title>
        </book>
</books>
```

The following is how extraction of this data might look in XQuery:

```
<books>
{
FOR $b IN document("http://www.zwiftbooks.com")/bib/book
WHERE $b/publisher = "Addison-Wesley" AND $b/@year > 1993
RETURN
<book year={ $b/@year }>
{ $b/title }
</book>
}
</books>
```

In this example, note how XML tags are interspersed with XQuery code embedded between open and close curly brackets. In the following sections we examine other examples of some of the functionality that ZwiftBooks may expect from XQuery.

Flattening

This function creates a new flattened list of all the title-author pairs, with each pair enclosed in a new result element. The expected result is

```
<results>
 <result>
   <title>Object Oriented Programming</title>
   <author>
    <last>Cox</last>
```

```
        <first>Brad</first>
      </author>
    </result>
    <result>
      <title>Object-Oriented Design Heuristics</title>
       <author>
        <last>Riel</last>
        <first>Arthur</first>
      </author>
    </result>
    <result>
      <title>A History of PI</title>
      <author>
       <last>Beckman</last>
       <first>Petr</first>
      </author>
     </result>
  </results>
```

Changing Structure by Nesting

Often the result of a query will need to have a structure different from the original XML document. XQuery supports restructuring an XML document. Thus it is possible to create a new XML document that groups each author with that author's titles. This requires the equivalent of a relational database join that creates a new element out of existing elements.

Changing Structure by Explicit Grouping

Combining information from different parts of a document is useful when merging information from multiple sources. For example, a second data source from a site such as www.bookreviews.com/reviews.xml may contain book reviews and prices organized in a completely different way from the ZwiftBooks site. XQuery will allow creating a query that searches both documents and lists all books with their prices from both sources.

Sorting

In our earlier example, all titles of books published by Addison-Wesley after 1993 were generated in no specific order. XQuery will support the sorting of query results using any combination of elements so that, for example, titles may be listed alphabetically.

Tag Variables

XML documents do not always come with a DTD. Therefore provision must be made to query documents without knowledge of structure or tag names. To handle this situation, XQuery supports queries that match element tags based on a regular expression or on phrases. For example, it is possible to match against an element that contains the text "author" or "editor" and whose value is "Jones" by building such a query directly into the XQuery.

XML Infrastructure Technologies

InfoSet

The InfoSet specification results from the fact that we're in a software world where it is important to be able to combine Web technologies for previously unanticipated purposes. This means specifications don't stand in isolation. W3C specs generally do one of two things: they describe what they do in natural language, most commonly English, or they provide a syntax or a grammar. Both approaches can prove difficult when trying to determine the exact meaning of XML specifications.

InfoSet is the basis for a variety of XML technologies.

For example, consider the concept of empty elements in XML. The XML 1.0 specification says that one may either provide a start and end tag with no content, such as

```
<foo></foo>
```

or use an empty element tag, such as

```
<foo/>
```

In most XML vocabularies the distinction is irrelevant. However, there are certain situations where the distinction matters. For example, some applications might want to treat `<foo></foo>` as signifying "data with the value NULL" and `<foo/>` as signifying "no data." The problem is, one cannot predict how XML will be used and what environment will be processing the XML.

InfoSet supports distinctions that are important when different XML specifications must interoperate.

While in one sense the two forms are equivalent, they are still different constructs. Is one interchangeable with the other? Most would say yes, they are interchangeable. However, it's possible to give one a semantic interpretation that makes them quite different. For example, it could be argued that the single-tag empty element emphasizes a lack of content, since it is impossible to provide content with just a single tag. The contentless start and end tags, on the other hand, are at least open to the possibility of content.

Secure communication requires unambiguous assumptions.

While it may seem that we're splitting hairs here, the problem is real. Consider, for example, a situation with possible legal implications. If I generate a digital signature to sign an XML document, do I want to invalidate that signature by changing `<foo></foo>` to `<foo/>` or vice versa? To answer such questions we need some way to talk about the structure of an XML document that goes beyond the grammatical rules of the language. We need to talk about the language in some universally communicable way. We need a metadiscourse. We need an InfoSet: a consistent set of definitions for use in other specifications that need to refer to the information in a well-formed XML document. (See the resources section at the end of this chapter for links to more detail on InfoSet.)

RDF

RDF is an effort to bring order to the Web. It is part of the W3C's Semantic Web initative, an effort not to create a separate Web but to extend the current one in a way that gives information well-defined meaning, better enabling computers and people to work in cooperation. Because there are billions of pieces of data on the Web, the problem is getting to the information you really need. Most search engines fail miserably, returning thousands of unhelpful links because Web pages don't provide information about their content. However, some search engines do better than others because they use metadata.

RDF is part of the Semantic Web.

Technically metadata is data about data. The search engines Yahoo and Google use metadata to build useful search links. When you search Yahoo, you're searching through human-generated subject categories and site labels. Google, on the other hand uses a method that ranks relevant Web sites based on the structure of the Internet itself. For example, Google interprets a link from page A to page B as a vote for page B by page A. More votes or links that connect to a page mean a higher rank for that page. Also, votes cast by "important" Web pages count more than links from "unimportant" pages. Either way, smart search requires metadata.

Yahoo and Google use metadata to improve search results.

Metadata

Metadata includes the indexing and organization required to retrieve library material such as books by author, title, or subject. It is the software infrastructure behind a large video store catalog that lets a customer find a movie directed by Quentin Tarantino or all movies where the director also appears in the film (*Reservoir Dogs, Apocalypse Now*). Then when the customer gets the movie home, the metadata of the yellow pages lets one find the phone number for pizza delivery so there will be something to eat while watching the movie.

Metadata: information about information.

The common thread here is information about information. In each case, there is a need for information about what you're looking for—the book's location, the video's name, the pizza shop's phone number—to zero in on your goal.

Metadata isn't
needed but it
certainly helps.

Is metadata required? In theory, no. The brute–force approach—looking through a library one book at a time, or wandering past video store shelves until you find a movie, or calling all the possible numbers in your area code until you hit on pizza delivery—is always a possibility. But that would be far too time consuming. Without metadata there wouldn't be time for much else beside brute-force searching.

MetaData: Beyond Search

Although metadata is most commonly used to find things, metadata is also used to support the business side of an enterprise. The video store uses metadata to determine how often videos are being rented, when it's time to move rentals to the for-sale bin, and who its best customers are. Running a viable video store operation would be impossible without metadata.

The Components of RDF

RDF helps
organizations
exchange metadata.

RDF is used to identify the commonality behind different ways of categorizing data and to represent that commonality in such a way that Web architects can use it to build new and more complex technologies. The Resource Description Framework, as its name implies, is a framework for describing and interchanging metadata. It is built on the following three definitions.

Resources

All things described by RDF expressions are called resources. A resource may be an entire Web page, such as the HTML document http://www.w3.org/Overview.html. A resource may also be a part of a Web page, such as a specific HTML or XML element within the document. A resource is anything that can have a URI; this includes all the Web's pages, as well as individual elements of an XML document.

Properties

Properties are specific aspects, characteristics, attributes, or relations used to describe resources. A particular property is a resource that has a name and can be used as a property, for example Author or Title. In many cases, all we really care about is the name; but a property needs to be a resource so that it can have its own properties.

Statements

A statement consists of a resource, a property, and a value. These parts are known as the subject, predicate, and object of a statement. A typical statement is, "The Author of http://davenet.userland.com/2001/09/10/openSourceIn2001 is Dave Winer." The value can be just a string, for example "Dave Winer," or it can be another resource, as in the example, "The Home-Page of http://davenet.userland.com/2001/09/10/openSourceIn2001 is http://davenet.userland.com."

A specific resource together with a named property plus the value of that property for that resource is an RDF statement. The object of a statement (that is, the property value) can be another resource or it can be a literal, such as a resource (specified by a URI) or a simple string or other primitive data type defined by XML. In RDF terms, a literal may have content that is XML markup but is not further evaluated by the RDF processor.

Consider as a simple example the sentence, "Dave Winer is the creator of the resource http://davenet.userland.com/2001/09/10/openSourceIn2001." This sentence has the following parts:

Subject (resource):   http://davenet.userland.com/2001/09/10/
openSourceIn2001

Predicate (property): Creator

Object (literal):   "Dave Winer"

RDF Vocabularies

RDF may be used to define specialized vocabularies.

Properties standing alone, however, are not very useful. The expectation is that properties will be packaged, for example, as a set of basic bibliographic properties such as Author, Title, and Date. Over time, property collections or vocabularies will emerge in competition with each other, such as vocabularies for online learning or wine connoisseurship. This means that opinions, pointers, indexes, or anything that helps discovery will have high value. Diversity of ideas inevitably leads to a diversity of vocabularies, since anyone can come up with a vocabulary, advertise it, and charge a fee. The market will help the good ones survive.

RDF is designed to have the following characteristics:

❑ *Independence:* Properties that tell us something about a resource can be invented by anyone. There is no one list of accepted ways to categorize things. Although different categorization schemes already exist (for example, those of the Library of Congress), RDF is flexible enough to admit other schemes that have not yet been invented.

❑ *Interchangeability:* RDF statements are convertible into XML, which means they can be exchanged across the Web.

❑ *Scalability:* RDF statements are simple, three-part records (resource, property, value), so they are easy to handle and retrieve data from, even when they exist in large numbers.

❑ *Properties functioning as resources:* Properties themselves can have properties that can be discovered and manipulated like any other resource. This recursive aspect of RDF is important because, for example, I might want to know if anyone out there has defined a property that describes the genre of a movie, with values like Comedy, Horror, Romance, or Thriller. I'll need metadata to help with that.

❑ *Values functioning as resources:* Most Web pages have a property named Home-Page which points to the Web site from which the page came. This value is itself a resource. Therefore it's important that values of properties must be able to include resources.

❑ *Statements functioning as resources:* Statements themselves can have properties. Because there is so much varied information on the Web, we'll need to do lookups based on other people's categorizations (as is done with Yahoo). This means that any statement, such as "The Subject of this page is Java Technology," needs to have properties that tell us "Who said so? And when?" Thus statements need properties.

For Tim Berners-Lee, the real power of the Semantic Web will come about when program agents collect Web content from a variety of sources and exchange their results with other programs and agents. The effectiveness of these agents will increase as more Web content and services become available. The dream is that a Semantic Web will allow agents not explicitly designed to work together to transfer data by using RDF semantics that describe what the data really is all about.

The Semantic Web is seen as an evolving data repository.

Summary

XML is not just one technology or specification but a family of technologies that work together to enable an infrastructure for describing, presenting, and manipulating XML-based data. At the core is XML and the XML namespaces Recommendations, which form the basis for defining data unambiguously. For description, there are DTDs and

XML Schema, which provide a way to describe the structure and content of XML documents. These schema can be used by both clients and servers to determine document validity, thereby reducing the need for specialized programmatic document checking. For display, there are a variety of technologies including XForms, VoiceXML, and XHTML that offer modular options for working with many different kinds of user interfaces. For XML manipulation and transformation, XSLT is a key technology supported by XLink, XPath, and XQuery. Finally, InfoSet provides a mechanism that allows different XML technologies to work together, and RDF opens up the possibility of an expanding, evolving Semantic Web. While these topics do not by any means cover all the technologies in the XML family, they provide a good starting point to begin to understand the scope and power of XML and how it can be applied to a variety of problems.

Resources

Books

St. Laurent, Simon, *XML : A Primer,* 3rd ed. (Foster City, CA: IDG Books, 2001)
The third edition of this classic includes new discussions of XLink, XPointer, XPath, and XSLT.

Harold, Elliotte Rusty, *XML Bible* (Foster City, CA: IDG Books, 2001)
A comprehensive discussion of XML and its supporting technologies.

Web
General XML
http://www.xml.com/axml/testaxml.htm
The annotated XML 1.0 specification by Tim Bray. One window displays the actual specification and an adjacent window provides commentary. Just click on commentary links.

http://www.w3.org
The Web site of the W3C. Contains specifications and links to all things XML.

http://www.xml.org
Hosted by OASIS, this Web site advertises itself as the XML Industry Portal. It maintains regularly updated links to XML industry news.

http://xml.coverpages.org/
A Web site with literally thousands of links relating to XML and its numerous associated technologies. Maintained by Robin Cover, the site is a cornucopia of XML information.

http://www.w3.org/TR/REC-xml-names/
The W3C XML Namespaces Recommendation.

http://www.xml.com/pub/a/1999/01/namespaces.html
Article by Tim Bray on using namespaces.

http://www.xml.com/
A site maintained by the O'Reilly publishing group. Contains numerous links to XML articles and books.

http://ibm.com/developerworks/xml/
IBM's Web site dedicated to XML technology.

http://www.xmlhack.com
A news and resource site for XML developers.

http://www.zvon.org/
Billed as a guide to the XML galaxy, the site maintains numerous links, tutorials, and downloads.

http://www.w3schools.com/

A Web site (not part of the W3C) with numerous tutorials on XML and related technologies.

XML Schema

http://www.xml101.com/dtd/

Tutorials on how to build and use DTDs.

http://www.w3.org/XML/Schema

The W3C XML Schema home page.

http://www.oasis-open.org/cover/schemas.html

Robin Cover's collection of schema information covering DTDs, XML Schema, and more.

XML Presentation

http://www.xhtml.org/

A central site for articles and tutorials on XHTML.

http://www.w3.org/TR/xforms/

W3C site for XForms.

http://www.renderx.com/tutorial.html

Tutorial for XSL-FO.

http://www.w3.org/TR/voicexml/

The W3C's VoiceXML Web site.

http://www.voicexml.org

Web site of the VoiceXML Forum.

XML Manipulation

http://www.w3.org/Style/XSL/

W3C specifications for XSL, XSLT, XPath, and more.

http://www.xslt.com/

XSLT related tools, tutorials, and resources.

http://www.w3.org/1999/09/ql/docs/xquery.html

"XML Query Languages: Experiences and Exemplars".

http://www.w3.org/DOM/

The W3C DOM home page. Contains links to all the DOM versions.

http://www.saxproject.org/

The official SAX Web site.

http://www.megginson.com/SAX/

David Megginson's SAX Web site. Megginson led the initiative that created SAX.

http://www.w3.org/TR/xpath

The W3C XPath 1.0 Recommendation.

http://www.w3.org/TR/xlink/

The W3C XML Linking Language (XLink) Version 1.0 Recommendation.

XML Infrastructure

http://www.w3.org/RDF/

The W3C home page for RDF.

http://www.w3.org/TR/NOTE-xml-infoset-req

The W3C requirements for InfoSet.

http://www.w3.org/2000/10/swap/Primer.html
A primer on RDF and the Semantic Web written by Tim Berners-Lee
(with his director's hat off).

**http://www.scientificamerican.com/2001/0501issue/
0501berners-lee.html**
Scientific American article on the Semantic Web.

3

XML in Practice

This chapter looks at a broad range of XML in practice, taking us from XML dialects targeting specific industries to XML initiatives that span a wide range of industries. The common threads for all these applications are data and XML's ability to define vocabularies for that data. We'll see that XML's ability to play a role in so many different arenas comes from its simple focus on data and its capability to combine with other technologies.

For each area we'll look at concrete examples of how XML is being applied to solve real-world problems. We'll also look at how XML has evolved by going beyond simple data descriptions and assuming aspects of code-related functionality through its ability to describe configurations and action. Finally we'll look at how, with the help of HTTP, XML has moved into the area of protocols, applications, and technologies that challenge conventional models of distributed computing.

The Dimensions of XML in Practice

Although XML is a relatively new technology, in just a few short years it has been applied in a variety of areas. Because of XML's origins in the Standard Generalized Markup Language (SGML) world, the first XML applications were versions of existing SGML applications. These were primarily vocabularies for specific industries such as finance, banking, science and technology, and human resources.

XML is used as a data description language for various vertical industries.

However, as Figure 3.1 makes clear, XML is not limited to industry-specific data descriptions. XML has been successfully applied to problems that span industry segments. These applications, known as horizontal industry applications, provide functionality and services that are more general in nature and can be applied in different ways to different

XML is used to provide cross-industry functionality.

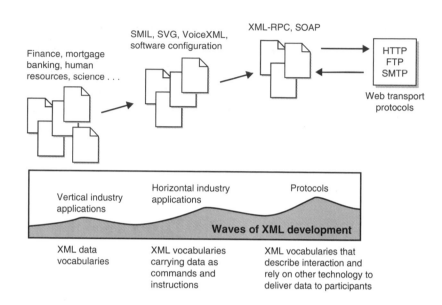

Figure 3.1 XML in practice across vertical and horizontal industry areas.

industries. Typically, these XML vocabularies go beyond simple data description and take on issues of configuration and action. Included in this category are XML vocabularies such as Scalable Vector Graphics (SVG) for describing two-dimensional graphics in XML; Synchronized Multimedia Integration Language (SMIL), which defines elements and attributes that describe the presentation of multimedia presentations; VoiceXML, for describing dialogs between a server and an end-user with access to a telephone or voice-enabled browser; and Enterprise JavaBeans (EJB) description languages that are used to configure EJB software on servers. These applications, characterized by using XML to describe both data and declarative actions, open up new ways of delivering application functionality using a simple tag-based syntax.

The XML Application Spectrum

In the following sections we explore details of XML as it is applied to vertical industry segments, horizontal cross-industry applications, and Web-based distributed computing. As an aid to understanding the various initiatives launched by XML, it's useful to view the application of XML as occurring in three waves. Figure 3-1 illustrates the characteristics of these waves as they move XML from a vertical industry vocabulary language to vocabularies that add aspects of configuration and action, while adding instructions as data to the XML mix. Finally we see XML's simple design and ability to combine with other technologies as the springboard that takes XML into the new dimensions of distributed computing and XML protocols. For each of these categories, we explore several concrete examples of XML in practice, pointing out along the way details of how designers use elements and attributes to build XML vocabularies.

Wave One: Vertical Industry Data Descriptions

As Figure 3.2 shows, the first wave of XML vocabularies centered on defining structures for specific or vertical industries: applications of XML or SGML—such as schemas, document type definitions (DTDs),

XML is used to meet the needs of specific industries.

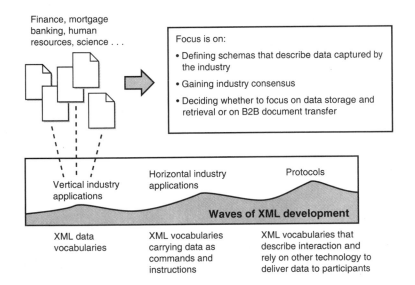

Figure 3.2 **The first wave of XML applications: vertical industry data descriptions.**

namespaces, and style sheets—were used to leverage the Web for business purposes. Many of the early applications of XML were extensions of prior development based on SGML, so that many companies working with SGML were able to get a head start in XML.

Companies seeking to position themselves in the global economy find XML attractive for several reasons:

❏ XML provides an opportunity to establish a data standard for an organization that is tied to global standards organizations.
❏ There is wide industry support for XML integration. Conversion utilities are being provided with Web browsers, databases, and operating systems, making it easier and less expensive for small- to medium-size businesses to import and export data in an XML format.
❏ Data is immediately accessible via browsers through the use of style sheet technology.

In this section we'll look at just a few of the hundreds of vertical industry initiatives centered around XML. These include the Open Financial Exchange (OFX), Mortgage Industry Standards Maintenance Organization (MISMO), and the HR-XML Consortium, an initiative to standardize data for human resources with a focus on recruitment. Each brings to the table its own challenges and solutions, many still in the formative stage, but since with XML we're not constrained by lock-in to binary data representations, data descriptions can evolve with requirements.

Industry issues: XML for data exchange versus storage.

In looking at different vertical industry approaches to defining XML vocabularies, we notice that two themes recur. One is the struggle over whether to use elements or attributes to represent data. The second theme, which is more subtle, is whether to focus on defining XML for data storage across an industry or whether to concentrate on data representations for exchanging data between partners within an industry. As we'll see in the following examples, OFX and MISMO tackle the problem of XML for data exchange, while HR-XML takes on the challenge of defining XML formats for persistent data storage.

Finance: OFX

One of the great ironies of the computer revolution is that it has pushed many clerical responsibilities up the corporate ladder so that many of us now find ourselves typing and editing our own documents and using financial software to track our personal finances. However, one of the real challenges of any data management system is to keep data synchronized. The OFX specification is an XML-based language that enables brokerage clients to download account information directly into their accounting or tax-preparation software, such as Quicken or TurboTax. OFX also supports the exchange of financial information among financial services companies, their technology outsourcers, and consumers using Web- and PC-based software.

OFX uses XML to bridge the gap between brokerage databases and personal software.

As in any effort to define an industry standard, consensus is required. OFX is an open consortium created by CheckFree, Intuit, and Microsoft in early 1997, and it now has the support of over 1,000 financial institutions, technology solution providers, and payroll companies. Major financial players in the OFX initiative include Prudential, TD Waterhouse Group, Inc., and T. Rowe Price. OFX supports a range of financial activities, including consumer and small-business banking, consumer and small-business bill payment, bill presentment, and investment download and tracking, including stocks, bonds, and mutual funds.

As Figure 3.3 shows, OFX enables the downloading of brokerage information to a user's PC. Downloads can go directly into Web and PC tax software and may include information from 401(k), 1099, and W2 tax forms. OFX also allows consumers to pay bills directly over the Web.

Figure 3.3 **OFX**
enables brokerage
clients to download
account information
directly into tax
preparation software.

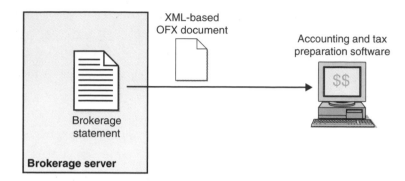

Figure 3.3 **OFX enables brokerage clients to download account information directly into tax preparation software.**

As is often the case in broad-based initiatives of this sort, the umbrella consortium allows its members (financial services companies) to enhance application capability by adding new XML content, giving them an opportunity to support value-added features and help position themselves in a competitive marketplace.

The focus of the OFX XML vocabulary has been on data exchange, not data storage. OFX makes no recommendation about how data should be represented in the permanent data stores of participants. The important objective for OFX is to define the data formats for moving data from one platform to another.

OFX has taken a strong stance in the elements versus attributes controversy, coming down strongly in favor of elements. The DTD for the financial data exchange defines over 450 elements and *no* attributes. The DTD does, however, make extensive use of entities, XML shortcut abbreviations that make the DTD and XML documents themselves more readable.

Human Resources and HR-XML

HR-XML defines a common vocabulary for storing human resources data.

The hiring and employee management done by human resources departments are data intensive. HR-XML is a nonprofit consortium dedicated to enabling an XML-based e-commerce and human resources data interchange format. The objective is to spare employers and vendors the risk and expense of having to agree upon and implement an ad hoc data exchange mechanism. By developing and publishing an XML representation for HR data, it will be easier for any company to do business with other companies without having to implement a one-of-a-kind interchange mechanism. HR-XML's current work focuses on standards for staffing and recruiting, benefits enrollment, payroll, competencies, and workforce management.

For any organization attempting to define an XML data representation, it's important to create consensus among stakeholders. HR-XML includes a group called the Cross-Process Objects (CPO) Workgroup with three related roles within the HR-XML Consortium:

❑ Developing a common HR vocabulary and model for the consortium

❑ Developing schemas for common HR objects used across the consortium's domain-specific workgroups (Recruiting and Staffing, Benefits Enrollment, Payroll, and so on)

❑ Reviewing the specifications produced by other HR-XML work groups for appropriate use of common HR objects

The CPO oversees teams that work on models and schemas for common HR objects. Driving the CPO effort is the fact that XML-HR specifically targets XML for data storage, not B2B transactional data. The usage scenario is one in which résumés will be written to a server as XML files. A program will load information from these files to a system of distributed databases where an intranet-based query program will allow precise skills matches against the databases.

What's a Person?

One of the challenges confronted by the HR-XML Consortium has been to arrive at a consensus on what it means to be a Person (at least as far as hiring managers are concerned). While Person is often used in introductory XML examples, it's not trivial to define, given

XML data definitions need to accommodate the requirements of different users.

the requirement that any definition should be capable of global use in a consistent manner. The definition of a Person schema for HR-XML includes a number of requirements:

❑ Must be able to handle various name formats without significant overhead

❑ Syntax must be self-documenting

❑ Must take cultural context into account. Cultural context drives the sort order for a name. It also determines how the various parts of the name are put together to form the whole name.

❑ Should be able to handle effective dating

❑ Must be able to handle multiple purposes or contexts of the name (Employee, Supervisor, Dependent, Beneficiary, and so forth)

HR-XML uses elements for data and attributes for metadata.

The result of the effort was the DTD shown in Listing 3.1. It's included here because it illustrates a short, readable design that mixes elements and attributes according to the well-respected schema design principle, "Use elements to represent domain data; use attributes for metadata." For example, the element `FormattedName`, which is used to describe the full name as it will appear on some document, includes an attribute called `type`, which is intended to describe the kind of presentation it indicates, for example, a legal form of the name, a form suitable for sorting, or just a default presentation that might be used to address an envelope. Similarly, the element `Affix`, intended to allow a title of some kind to be included with a name, is supported by an attribute that adds information about the affix, such as whether it represents an academic rank (Professor), an aristocratic title (Lord), or a military title (Colonel).

Listing 3.1 A DTD for the Person Element in the HR-XML Definition for Human Resources Applications[1]

```
<!ELEMENT PersonName (FormattedName* , LegalName? ,
    GivenName* , PreferredGivenName? , MiddleName? ,
    FamilyName* , Affix*)>

<!ELEMENT FormattedName (#PCDATA)>

<!ATTLIST FormattedName type (presentation | legal |
    sortOrder ) 'presentation' >
<!ELEMENT LegalName (#PCDATA)>

<!ELEMENT GivenName (#PCDATA)>

<!ELEMENT PreferredGivenName (#PCDATA)>

<!ELEMENT MiddleName (#PCDATA)>

<!ELEMENT FamilyName (#PCDATA)>

<!ATTLIST FamilyName primary (true | false | undefined )
    'undefined'
    prefix CDATA #IMPLIED >
<!ELEMENT Affix (#PCDATA)>

<!ATTLIST Affix  type  (academicGrade |
                        aristocraticPrefix |
                        aristocraticTitle |
                        familyNamePrefix |
                        familyNameSuffix |
                        formOfAddress |
                        generation |
                        qualification )  #REQUIRED >
```

---

[1] Copyright, The HR-XML Consortium. All Rights Reserved. http://www.hr-xml.org.

Examples of XML that satisfy the DTD in Listing 3-1 include an XML `PersonName` for Major John Smith:

```
<PersonName>
    <GivenName>John</GivenName>
    <FamilyName>Smith</FamilyName>
    <FormattedName>John Smith</FormattedName>
    <Affix type="formOfAddress">Major</Affix>
</PersonName>
```

and for Mrs. Jane H. Doe:

```
<PersonName>
    <GivenName>Jane</GivenName>
    <MiddleName>H.</MiddleName>
    <FamilyName>Doe</FamilyName>
    <Affix type="formOfAddress">Mrs.</Affix>
</PersonName>
```

Mortgage Banking: MISMO

MISMO's XML definitions focus on data transfer.

Just about everyone who purchases a home acquires a mortgage loan. Mortgage loans are available through lending institutions such as banks and mortgage companies that supply the cash to buy the home. In order for lending institutions to continue to have money to deliver to borrowers, the loans are sold to companies such as Fannie Mae and Freddie Mac and packaged as mortgage-backed securities. This is big business. Over $378 billion in mortgage-backed securities were issued by Fannie Mae and Freddie Mac in 2000, a statistic which indicates the importance of the transfer of data between lending institutions and Fannie and Freddie.

In 1999 a group of industry representatives formed MISMO and in 2000 began to address electronic commerce issues in the mortgage industry. Their objective was to define an XML schema in the form of DTDs that could be used as the basis for data exchange within the industry.

In formulating an XML schema, MISMO has been very explicit about what they are working to standardize. Unlike HR-XML, they are not trying to come up with formats for storing long-term data but are only attempting to standardize loan data as it moves between two organizations at some point in time. Of course, companies are free to archive data as it moves between servers, but the intent is only to describe the data that is needed to carry out the B2B transactions between lenders and Fannie Mae and Freddie Mac.

In developing a schema for B2B data interchange it's important to establish consensus, which depends on communication. Along the path to standardization, MISMO released a draft version of its dictionary of common data items for review, focusing on information associated with mortgage loan applications. MISMO uses a centralized Web-based repository to provide a single location for managing data elements and generating XML document definitions. The DTD that has evolved is extensible so that other underwriting organizations can use it and add to it with additional data they may need for their own particular transactions. As Listing 3.2 shows, the DTD is designed around a top-level definition so that parts can be reused in other loan-related transactions.

MISMO's industry acceptance is based on collaboration and consensus.

Listing 3.2 A Portion of the DTD for MISMO

```
LOAN_APPLICATION ( _DATA_INFORMATION? ,
     ADDITIONAL_CASE_DATA?,
     AFFORDABLE_LENDING?,
     ASSET*,
     DOWN_PAYMENT*,
     GOVERNMENT_LOAN?,
```

```
                         INTERVIEWER_INFORMATION?,
                         LIABILITY*,
                         LOAN_PRODUCT_DATA?,
                         LOAN_PURPOSE?,
                         LOAN_QUALIFICATION?,
                         MORTGAGE_TERMS?,
                         PROPERTY?,
                         PROPOSED_HOUSING_EXPENSE*,
                         REO_PROPERTY*,
                         TITLE_HOLDER*,
                         TRANSACTION_DETAIL?,
                         BORROWER+ )>


         DOWN_PAYMENT _Type ( BridgeLoan |
                 CashOnHand |
                 CheckingSavings |
                 DepositOnSalesContract |
                 EquityOnPendingSale |
                 EquityOnSoldProperty |
                 EquityOnSubjectProperty |
                 GiftFunds |
                 LifeInsuranceCashValue |
                 LotEquity |
                 OtherTypeOfDownPayment |
                 RentWithOptionToPurchase |
                 RetirementFunds |
                 SaleOfChattel |
                 SecuredBorrowedFunds |
                 StocksAndBonds |
                 SweatEquity |
                 TradeEquity |
                 TrustFunds |
                 UnsecuredBorrowedFunds )  #IMPLIED>
```

Tracking XML Standards

The explosion of XML vocabularies has led to a need for a central repository to track the various XML initiatives. The Organization for the Advancement of Structured Information Standards (OASIS), is a nonprofit international consortium that creates interoperable industry specifications based on public XML and SGML standards. One aspect of the OASIS mission is to develop vertical industry applications, conformance tests, and interoperability specifications that make vertical standards usable. Table 3.1 lists various areas for which there are XML initiatives.

OASIS is an organization that tracks and promotes XML standards.

OASIS does not compete with but rather builds upon and supplements the work done by standards bodies such as W3C (for XML) or ISO (for SGML). OASIS's technical work generally falls into one of the following categories:

- ❏ *Vertical industry applications:* Development of applications of XML or SGML, such as schemas, DTDs, namespaces, style sheets, and so forth that may be used in specific vertical industries

- ❏ *Horizontal and e-business framework:* Development of specifications defining how to build systems for the electronic exchange of business information

- ❏ *Interoperability:* Development of specifications and standards that define how other standards will work together, or how earlier, non-XML standards can work in an XML world

- ❏ *Conformance testing:* Development of test scenarios and cases that can determine what it means to conform to specific standards; for example, what does it really mean to "be XML"?

In keeping with the spirit of the Web and open standards, OASIS has adopted a Technical Committee Process that governs its technical work and provides a vendor-neutral home for standards, giving all interested parties, regardless of their standing in a specific industry, an equal voice in the creation of technical work.

OASIS maintains directories of industry-specific vocabularies.

Table 3.1 Some Vertical Industry XML Dialects Registered at OASIS

Accounting	Education	Professional Service
Advertising	Energy/Utilities	Publishing/Print
Aerospace	Environmental	Real Estate
Agriculture	ERP	Retail
Arts/Entertainment	Financial Services	Robotics/AI
Automotive	Food Services	Science
Banking	Healthcare	Software
Business Services	Human Resources	Supply Chain
Chemistry	Insurance	Transportation
Construction	Legal	Travel
Customer Relation	Manufacturing	Waste Management
E-Commerce	Marketing/PR	Weather
Economics	Mining	
EDI	Multimedia	

Wave Two: Configuration and Action

XML may be used to treat instructions as data.

The first wave of XML gave us (and continues to provide) industry-specific vocabularies focusing on describing data for B2B interaction or defining data for permanent storage in order to create the possibility for B2B interplay. However that's not all that can be said or done with data, particularly if we step beyond the conventional sense of the word "data" as "data processing" and look at it more generally as a description of instructions to be carried out by some processing engine. This is data the way John von Neumann, one of the great pioneers in computing, formulated it in his 1940s design for computers that is still relevant after half a century. His idea, which spawned the computer industry as we know it today, was to treat programs as data, store them in memory, and feed them to the CPU for execution. This simple yet powerful concept turned out to be the turning point for an industry that for over 50 years (from the 1890 census through the rise of IBM in the 1920s) had been locked into designing business machines with hardwired instruction sets.

It is this use of data as instructions or code that has sparked what we call the second wave of XML applications that use XML to go beyond simple vocabularies for vertical industries and step into the world of XML as instruction. Figure 3.4 illustrates the second wave of XML, and in the following section we explore a few of these XML initiatives to illustrate XML's use as a configuration and action language.

EJB and XML

EJB is component architecture for building distributed object-oriented business applications in Java. The basic idea behind EJB is to allow developers to build distributed applications by assembling components rather than to build monolithic applications from scratch. Component frameworks such as EJB free developers from having to write complex, low-level software to handle transactions, state

EJB uses XML for software configuration.

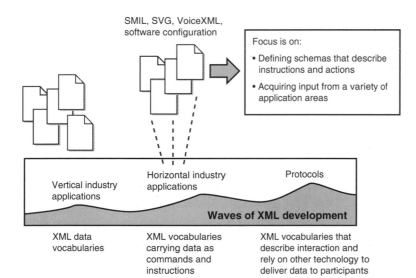

Figure 3.4 **The second wave of XML applications: using XML for declarative action and instruction.**

management, multi-threading, and connection pooling that are notoriously difficult to get right. The philosophy behind EJB is that modular software units can be developed and deployed in different ways on different platforms depending on an XML descriptor file that specifies the details.

Figure 3.5 illustrates the assembly of EJB components being controlled by an XML document known as an EJB deployment descriptor. The XML-based deployment descriptor contains two kinds of information:

Figure 3.5 The EJB architecture showing an XML-based EJB deployment descriptor. The XML is used to indicate that the program code should be executed as part of a transaction.

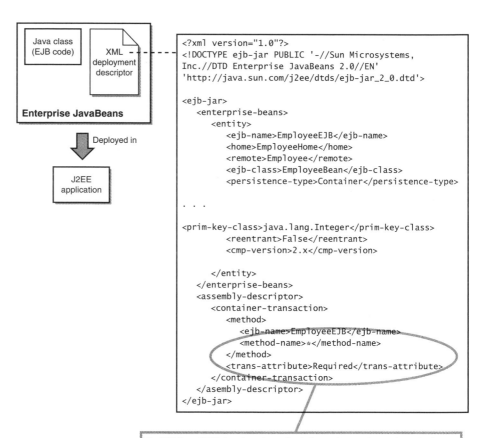

```
<?xml version="1.0"?>
<!DOCTYPE ejb-jar PUBLIC '-//Sun Microsystems,
Inc.//DTD Enterprise JavaBeans 2.0//EN'
'http://java.sun.com/j2ee/dtds/ejb-jar_2_0.dtd'>

<ejb-jar>
   <enterprise-beans>
      <entity>
         <ejb-name>EmployeeEJB</ejb-name>
         <home>EmployeeHome</home>
         <remote>Employee</remote>
         <ejb-class>EmployeeBean</ejb-class>
         <persistence-type>Container</persistence-type>

. . .

<prim-key-class>java.lang.Integer</prim-key-class>
         <reentrant>False</reentrant>
         <cmp-version>2.x</cmp-version>

      </entity>
   </enterprise-beans>
   <assembly-descriptor>
      <container-transaction>
         <method>
            <ejb-name>EmployeeEJB</ejb-name>
            <method-name>*</method-name>
         </method>
         <trans-attribute>Required</trans-attribute>
      </container-transaction>
   </asembly-descriptor>
</ejb-jar>
```

An XML-based EJB descriptor is used to indicate what services a piece of software requires of an EJB container. Here we see that the Java code must be run as part of a transaction. The code itself will have no knowledge of its use as part of the transaction.

❑ *EJB structural information:* EJB name, class, home and remote interfaces, bean type (session or entity), environment entries, resource factory references, EJB references, security role references, and other information based on the bean type

❑ *Application assembly information:* EJB references, security roles, security role references, method permissions, and container transaction attributes. Assembly descriptor information is optional.

SVG

Web designers have long struggled with getting graphics right on different browsers. Now they are challenged by a variety of new devices with a range of screen sizes and resolutions. What's needed is the ability to easily create rich graphics, responsive animation, and interactive behavior in a way that takes advantage of the growing XML infrastructure used in e-commerce, publishing, and business. SVG attempts to fill that bill.

SVG uses XML to render complex 2D graphics.

SVG is a W3C Recommendation that defines an XML grammar for creating vector-based 2D graphics for the Web and other applications. SVG is an alternative to delivering GIF or JPEG images to browsers. Because SVG is defined as an XML grammar, SVG graphics can easily be generated dynamically on Web servers using standard XML tools and delivered with a style sheet to a browser for rendering. For example, a Web server can generate a high-quality graphic from historical stock market data that requires minimal bandwidth.

SVG has several advantages over graphic image formats such as GIF or JPEG:

❑ *Readability:* SVG files can be read and modified by numerous tools. The files are typically much smaller and more compressible than comparable JPEG or GIF images.

❏ *Scalability:* Unlike bitmapped graphics formats such as GIF and JPEG, SVG is vector-based, meaning SVG images can be printed with high quality at any resolution, eliminating the "staircase" effect that occurs when expanding bitmapped images.

❏ *Ability to zoom:* You can magnify any portion of an SVG image without image degradation.

❏ *Searchable and selectable text:* It's possible to search an image library for the occurrence of specific text strings, like names in a map.

❏ *Scripting and animation:* SVG supports interactive graphics that allow complex animations.

As a W3C-sponsored XML vocabulary, SVG abides by the design requirement that it maintain compatibility with other W3C efforts. Table 3.2 illustrates the compatibility of SVG with other W3C initiatives.

Because the SVG Recommendation is fairly recent, it is expected that browser manufacturers will soon be releasing versions that support SVG. As of this writing several software packages can be used to display SVG images:

❏ *Adobe SVG Viewer:* Adobe supports a browser plug-in for Netscape 4.5 to 4.77, Microsoft Internet Explorer (IE) 4 or greater, RealPlayer 8 or higher, and Opera 5.x. There is also an ActiveX control for SVG display in Microsoft Office and Visual Basic.

❏ *Apache Batik SVG browser:* This open source browser uses XML technologies including an XML parser, an XSL Transformations (XSLT) engine, and a CSS parser to render SVG images.

❏ *CSIRO Pocket SVG Viewer:* Targeted for handheld devices, the Pocket SVG Viewer runs on the PocketPC operating system and requires only 390K of memory.

Table 3.2 How W3C Initiatives Integrate with SVG

Initiative	How Integrated with SVG
XML 1.0	SVG defined using XML 1.0
XLink	SVG uses XLink for URI referencing
XPointer	SVG is compatible with a subset of XPointer's ID referencing syntax
Cascading style sheets (CSS, CSS2) and Extensible Stylesheet Language (XSL)	SVG content can be styled by either CSS, CSS2, or XSL
Document Object Model (DOM) level 1	SVG includes a complete DOM and conforms to the DOM1 Recommendation
DOM level 2	SVG supports and incorporates many of the facilities described in DOM2, including the CSS object model and event handling
SMIL	SVG is designed to allow future versions of SMIL to use animated or static SVG content as media components; incorporates some features and approaches that are part of the SMIL 1.0 specification, including the `switch` element and the `systemLanguage` attribute
HTML/XHTML	SVG attempts to achieve maximum compatibility with both HTML 4 and XHTML 1.0
Web Accessibility	SVG is compatible with W3C work on WAI Initiative (WAI)

VoiceXML

VoiceXML is an example of using XML to encode instructions, in this case for software called a voice browser. Because VoiceXML is essentially a text document, it can be moved across the Internet just like any Web page, except that when VoiceXML text reaches a voice

The VoiceXML standard provides a platform for voice applications.

browser, that browser has the support of hardware to synthesize speech and do speech recognition. The goal is to leverage existing Web-based development and content delivery tools to build interactive voice applications.

VoiceXML documents describe conversations.

As Figure 3.6 shows, a VoiceXML document may be delivered to a server that converts text to voice and communicates over a telephone exchange, or it may be delivered directly to a device capable of performing speech processing. As the processing power of cell phones increases, it will be possible to perform VoiceXML conversions directly rather than relying on server-based transformations

Forms and Menus

VoiceXML supports forms and menus.

VoiceXML is centered around two kinds of conversational dialogs: forms and menus. Forms provide voice control for completing the equivalent of a Web form and contain sets of items to be completed

Figure 3.6 **VoiceXML is an example of using XML to control action. Conditions can be checked and branches can be followed to appropriate actions.**

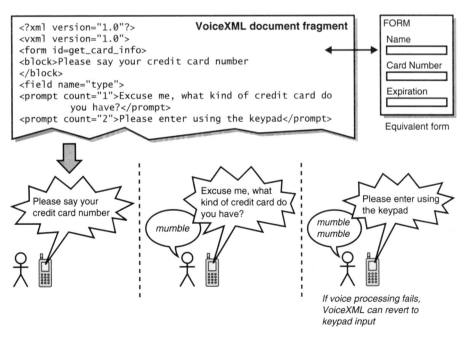

```
<?xml version="1.0"?>
<vxml version="1.0">
<form id=get_card_info>
<block>Please say your credit card number
</block>
<field name="type">
<prompt count="1">Excuse me, what kind of credit card do
       you have?</prompt>
<prompt count="2">Please enter using the keypad</prompt>
```

VoiceXML document fragment

FORM
Name
Card Number
Expiration

Equivalent form

Please say your credit card number

Excuse me, what kind of credit card do you have?

mumble

Please enter using the keypad

mumble mumble

If voice processing fails, VoiceXML can revert to keypad input during the dialog. Control items govern the gathering of the form's fields. Event handlers, which are blocks of procedural logic, are triggered when certain combinations of field items occur. For example, some fields may be specified as optional or required, and some responses may trigger the loading and execution of new forms.

Menus present users with a choice of options and have the ability to transfer control to other menu dialogs based on user response. A menu is a kind of form that gets information from a user and branches to different dialogs based on user response.

Figure 3-6 shows how VoiceXML may be used to collect credit card information from a VoiceXML form. The `form` element contains `field` elements that drive the dialog. When speech is not understood, `prompt` elements provide sequential alternatives. If keypads are available, input can revert to keypad data entry.

SMIL

SMIL is a broad-based effort to use XML to define instructions for the creation of Web-based interactive multimedia presentations. SMIL provides an XML alternative to technologies such as Flash or JavaScript that are widely used to control animation in browsers. SMIL allows an author to describe the temporal behavior of a multimedia presentation, associate hyperlinks with media objects, and describe the layout of a screen presentation. SMIL components may be used to integrate timing into XHTML and SVG. Like VoiceXML, SMIL is more action-oriented than purely data descriptive.

SMIL uses XML to build multimedia presentations.

SMIL 2.0 was approved as a W3C standard Recommendation in 2001. The advantages of SMIL include:

❑ Faster and easier development than with JavaScript or Dynamic HTML (DHTML) for programming animation and mouse events

❑ Web standard support in IE 5.5, RealPlayer, Windows Media Player, and Adobe's SVG plug-in

❑ No requirement that users enable JavaScript in their browsers

❑ Support for more complex actions than are possible with JavaScript or DHTML

❑ Animations faster than Flash for certain situations

SMIL Elements

XML elements are used to specify animation.

SMIL includes elements that describe not only how to draw graphics but also how to coordinate them over time. In SMIL, timing elements are used to specify animation. Fundamental to SMIL is the concept of a timeline. A timeline represents the amount of time that an element takes to run, from beginning to end. Timelines are used to map complex events, such as objects moving along an oval path or zigzag. SMIL timelines also support audio or video synchronization with an animation. Sound clips, QuickTime videos, or JPEG slide shows may be scheduled to run at different times during an animation.

There are three flavors of timeline elements:

❑ seq for animations that run in sequence, or one after another

❑ par for animations which run in parallel, or all the same time

❑ excl for exclusive elements, or animations which pause all other timelines when they run

SMIL Modularization

SMIL modules address the problem of integration.

One of the problems confronted by SMIL designers was how to design the language to handle the widest range of animation possibilities. Rather than create a long list of elements and attributes in a DTD, the designers opted to break SMIL into modules, each of which addresses different aspects of animation. Modules contain semantically related XML elements, attributes, and attribute values.

Through an approach known as profiling, designers can then combine modules to provide the functionality required by a specific application. Modularization enables language designers to specify dedicated markup intended for integration with other existing XML languages, such as MathML and XForms.

The use of modules in SMIL is based on work done with XHTML modularization (see Chapter 2). A "module" is a collection of semantically-related XML elements, attributes, and attribute values that represents a unit of functionality. Modules are defined in coherent sets in which all elements are associated with the same namespace.

A "language profile" is a combination of modules. Modules are "atomic," which means they cannot be partitioned when included in a language profile. Furthermore, a module specification may include a set of integration requirements, to which language profiles that include the module must comply.

From Action to Combination

XML's second wave of applications was the result of using XML to define elements that encode actions to be performed by some appropriately configured software engine. This treatment of instructions as data opened up possibilities for applying XML to a broad range of new problems centered on configuration and action.

The Third Wave: Power Through Combination

XML's third wave of application comes from XML's ability to combine with other technologies and give rise to new technologies that go beyond their constituent parts. Figure 3.7 illustrates XML's use in conjunction with other technologies. Systems engineers have long

XML's simplicity opens it up to combination.

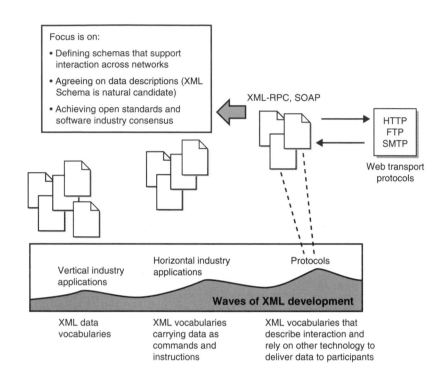

Figure 3.7 The third wave of XML applications: protocols for distributed interaction.

Focus is on:

• Defining schemas that support interaction across networks

• Agreeing on data descriptions (XML Schema is natural candidate)

• Achieving open standards and software industry consensus

XML-RPC, SOAP

HTTP
FTP
SMTP

Web transport protocols

Vertical industry applications

Horizontal industry applications

Protocols

Waves of XML development

XML data vocabularies

XML vocabularies carrying data as commands and instructions

XML vocabularies that describe interaction and rely on other technology to deliver data to participants

known that to understand and manage a working system requires an understanding of the dynamics that emerge when individual components interact, behaviors that are different from that those associated with individual parts.

XML protocols leverage the power of combination.

XML's emergence as a protocol language falls into this category. Because XML has limited itself to data description, it isn't constrained by programming language, platform, or transport considerations. It's open to combination with any number of different technologies. It is this combinatoric capability of XML that has propelled it into the world of protocols and distributed computing. Leveraging the power of HTTP and TCP/IP to deliver data anywhere across the Internet, XML in combination with HTTP (and other transport protocols) has been the basis for two important protocols:

XML Remote Procedure Call (XML-RPC) and Simple Object Access Protocol (SOAP).

Although we will cover XML-RPC and SOAP in detail in Chapter 4, it's helpful to look at how XML protocols are affecting XML's acceptance and use. XML protocols such as XML-RPC and SOAP are among the drivers behind a new model of distributed computing based on loosely coupled Web components and giving rise to the emergence of Web services (which we explore in Chapter 5). This use of XML across a broad spectrum of applications has created a groundswell of interest from both corporations and government. No longer viewed as an experimental emerging technology, XML is now accepted as a key technology, not just for data storage and exchange, but as a building block, underpinning the protocols that move data across networks. As we explore in the next section, this multifaceted use of XML has been one of the drivers of the British government's strategic vision for its next-century information system.

The British Government GovTalk Initiative

GovTalk is the name given to the British government initiative to use XML as the basis for exchanging information among government systems, between the government and its citizens and businesses worldwide, and between the UK and foreign governments. It is an initiative led by the Cabinet Office, designed to get UK public-sector organizations and private-sector companies to work together in agreeing on XML schemas and providing associated support to the UK public sector.

The main thrust of the specification has been to adopt the Internet and Web standards for all government systems. At the core of the standards effort is the strategic decision to adopt XML as the main standard for data integration. This strategy includes using XML schemas throughout the public sector based on agreed-upon governmental data standards.

Shaping this effort have been three important policy decisions:

❑ *Internet alignment:* The universal adoption of common standards used on the Internet and World Wide Web for all public-sector information systems

❑ *XML:* The primary standard for data integration and presentation tools for all public sector systems

❑ *Web browser as GUI:* All public information systems will be accessible through browser-based technology. Other interfaces are permitted but only after browser support has been implemented.

Figure 3.8 demonstrates how GovTalk provides implementation support through the availability of a central XML schema repository that can be reused throughout the public sector to reduce the costs and

Figure 3.8 The British Government's GovTalk initiative uses XML as the basis for data exchange across all aspects of government information technology. XML Schemas will be used to define data for all government ministries, and XML protocols will be used to exchange information between ministries.

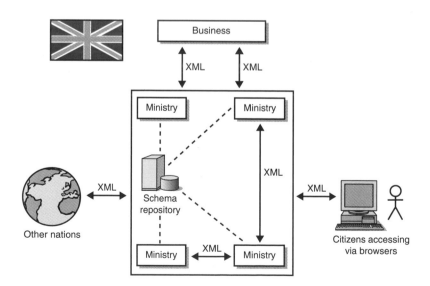

risks of developing data interchange systems. Before defining schemas for their data, ministries are encouraged to explore the online repository for relevant XML schema definitions, reports on best practices, and toolkits for developing interfaces and converting existing data.

Like ZwiftBooks, the British Government has found XML-related technologies useful to support interoperability and integration. Government policy is now officially to use XML and XML Schema for data integration; Unified Modeling Language, Resource Description Framework, and XML for data modeling; and the description language XSLT for data transformation.

GovTalk is also now being used for wide consultation on a number of other e-government frameworks and documents. It is intended to make adoption of XML-based policies and standards simple, attractive, and cost effective.

Resources

http://www.ofx.net

The OFX Web site. The OFX specification is publicly available for implementation by any financial institution or vendor, and is available for review.

http://www.w3.org/AudioVideo/

The W3C SMIL home page.

http://www.xml.org/xml/industry_industrysectors.jsp

XML and vertical industry vocabularies.

http://www.oasis-open.org

OASIS Web site. Industry portal for various XML vocabularies.

http://www/mismo.org
The MISMO Web site. Home of the MISMO DTD for mortgage transactions.

http://www.voicexml.org/
Web site for VoiceXML.

4

SOAP

In this chapter we go beyond XML's use in defining industry-specific data description languages to its use as a protocol language that has enabled communication and data exchange across the Web.

While XML has proven effective in promoting data exchange between partners and collaborators across a wide range of industries, it has surprised many in opening up a new perspective on middleware with XML protocols such as XML Remote Procedure Call (XML-RPC) and Simple Object Access Protocol (SOAP), that offer platform, language, and transport independence for data exchange between partners and suppliers.

XML accomplishes this through its simplicity of purpose and design, making no assumptions about Web transport. Critical to XML's success has been HTTP. The simple idea of transporting XML in the payload of an HTTP request has been the driving force behind Web-based distributed computing and the emergence of Web services. Because HTTP has been a catalyst for the Web and for XML, we'll look at how HTTP fits with strategies for delivering data and code across the Web and how XML-RPC and SOAP provide alternatives to conventional object-based distributed computing.

What Is SOAP and Why Is it Important?

SOAP is an XML-based protocol for exchanging information in a decentralized, distributed environment. It was literally made for the Web, a combination of XML and HTTP that opens up new options for distributed data exchange and interaction in a loosely coupled Web environment. As Figure 4.1 shows, SOAP is a technology that allows XML to move easily over the Web. SOAP does this by defining an XML envelope for delivering XML content and specifying a set of rules for servers to follow when they receive a SOAP message.

The fundamental change brought about by SOAP has been the ability to move data anywhere across the Web. Figure 4.2 illustrates that until SOAP there were only two main options for moving data between partners. One was to build a wide area network spanning a broad geographic region and let partners plug into it. This was the approach taken by Electronic Data Interchange (EDI), which defined messages and protocols for data transfer but left the network details up to the partners. The result was a collection of networks that pretty much locked the partners in and made it difficult and expensive to reach out to other EDI networks and costly to bring in new partners. The second approach for moving data between partners was

Figure 4.1 **SOAP has opened opportunities for extending the enterprise.**

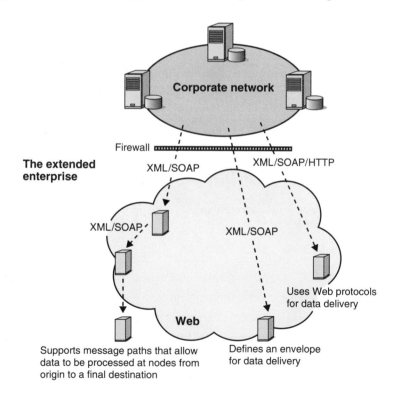

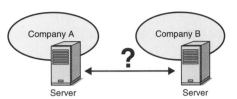

How to bridge the distributed computing gap?

Figure 4.2 **SOAP is one of several options for moving data across the Web.**

Option 1: EDI

• Begins with the definition of common data formats

• Uses a proprietary network for transport

• Delivers data across the network in agreed-upon formats

EDI starts with a data protocol and leaves the network to the implementation

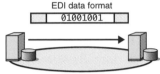

Proprietary wide area network

Option 2: CORBA, RMI, DCOM

• Begins with the definition of a transport protocol that can run on multiple platforms

• Uses an Object Request Broker to handle inter-object communication

• Delivers data as parameters of method calls

CORBA, RMI, and DCOM start from the ground up with common transport protocols

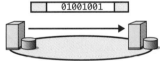

CORBA, RMI, or DCOM network

Option 3: SOAP

• Begins by defining an XML envelope for data

• Uses common Internet protocols (HTTP, FTP, SMTP) to deliver the SOAP envelope with XML content

• When using HTTP for transport, takes advantage of augmenting XML data with attachments

SOAP uses XML and HTTP, FTP, or SMTP to deliver the data

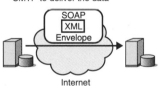

Internet

to build a distributed object infrastructure than ran over the Internet. This was the approach taken by Common Object Request Broker Architecture (CORBA), Remote Method Invocation (RMI), and Distributed Component Object Model (DCOM). The problem was that each had to decide on a protocol that could sit on top of TCP/IP and handle interobject communication. CORBA chose Internet Inter-ORB

Protocol (IIOP), DCOM chose Object Remote Procedure Call (ORPC), and RMI chose Java Remote Method Protocol (JRMP). While this approach reduced the need to share the same underlying network, the drawback was that CORBA could talk to CORBA, RMI to RMI, and DCOM to DCOM, but they could not talk to each other nor directly to the Web except through special sockets that required adding extra layers to an already complex architecture.

SOAP, the third option shown in Figure 4.2, combines the data capabilities of XML with the transport capability of HTTP, thereby overcoming the drawbacks of both EDI and tightly coupled distributed object systems such as CORBA, RMI, and DCOM. It does this by breaking the dependence between data and transport and in doing so opens up a new era of loosely coupled distributed data exchange.

Dave Winer, one of the authors of XML-RPC and a contributor to SOAP, describes the implications of working in this new loosely coupled space centered around XML.

> *[A]ll of a sudden you're not locked in. If you want to switch from Java to Python, for example, you can do it gradually, one component at a time. This kind of fluidity allows developers more choices, and relieves platform developers of the responsibility of being all things to all people. . . . Viewed another way XML-RPC turns the Internet itself into a scripting environment, much as Visual Basic turned Windows into a scripting environment, or AppleScript turned the Macintosh OS into one. It makes our worlds come together, makes the bigger world smaller and more approachable. And it's inclusive, no one need be left out.*[1]

---

[1] Dave Winer, foreword to *Programming Web Services with XML-RPC* by Simon St. Laurent, Edd Dumbill, and Joe Johnston (San Sebastopol, CA: O'Reilly, 2001). Also available at http://www.xmlrpc.com/stories/storyReader$1726.

Although Winer is talking about XML-RPC, a precursor to SOAP, his observation is applicable to the environment in which we now find ourselves, one where scripting languages are becoming important tools for assembling components and services. In the few short years since its inception in 1998, SOAP has gained wide acceptance across the software industry. Its impact is evident from the following observations:

❏ Web services frameworks use SOAP as the transport technology for delivering data and XML-RPC messages across distributed networks.

❏ Microsoft is committed to SOAP as part of its .NET initiative.

❏ Sun is using SOAP in its Sun Open Net Environment (Sun ONE) Web services framework.

❏ IBM, which has played a major role in the SOAP specification, has numerous SOAP support tools, including a SOAP toolkit for Java programmers. IBM has donated the toolkit to Apache Software Foundation's XML Project, which has published an Apache-SOAP implementation based on the toolkit.

❏ CORBA Object Request Broker (ORB) vendors such as Iona are actively supporting SOAP in the form of CORBA-to-SOAP bridges.

To understand SOAP's impact and how it has so quickly found a place in so many different software initiatives, from Web services to .NET to Java 2 Enterprise Edition (J2EE), it's instructive to look at how it evolved from a confluence of forces.

The Road to SOAP

There are many threads leading to SOAP. Let's begin with the long-standing need to automate the exchange of data between business partners and with EDI, an established technology for doing just that.

The notion of business-to-business data exchange was around long before the term "B2B" came into vogue. As far back as the 1960s, companies turned to computer automation to reduce the paperwork burden associated with purchase orders, bills of lading, invoices, shipping orders, and payments. Driven by a need to standardize the exchange of data between companies doing business with each other, in 1979 the American National Standards Institute (ANSI) chartered the Accredited Standards Committee X12 (ASC X12) group to develop uniform standards for interindustry electronic interchange of business transactions. The result was a collection of standards known as the Electronic Data Interchange, better known today as EDI.

EDI works by providing a collection of standard message formats and element dictionaries so that businesses can exchange data using networks of their choice. EDI's early success in the transportation industry led to its adoption by other industries, including health care insurance, management, financial services, and government procurement. Over the past two decades over 100,000 organizations have used EDI to conduct business with partners and suppliers.

However, despite its success, EDI suffers from the same problem faced by all pre-Web, tightly coupled technologies: network lock-in. As Figure 4.2 shows, EDI is built around point-to-point networks that require partners to use software that implements EDI's data and messaging specifications. Writing software for EDI is not trivial. It is expensive both to develop and to maintain. In addition, once an EDI system is in place, changes must be agreed upon and implemented by all participants. This makes it difficult to change alliances, since it's costly to begin exchanging information with new partners. For medium- and small-size businesses, EDI's cost is prohibitive.

The downside of EDI and other point-to-point solutions for doing B2B data exchange is that no matter how sophisticated the middleware,

ZwiftBooks Inc. and EDI

To help understand the issues behind EDI, consider our fictitious company ZwiftBooks in its efforts to use EDI to help find new sources of hard-to-get books. The CTO of ZwiftBooks has discovered that many of the major bookstores already use EDI to notify partners of books and prices. Each week the bookstores send data packets that contain listings of their latest inventories to partners. In order to participate in these exchanges ZwiftBooks must

- ❑ buy or write software to decode the messages and data in conformance with EDI specs for the industry
- ❑ pay for access to the wide area network used by the partners
- ❑ incur fees for data transfer

there will always be a need for a WAN wrapper, a network over which to deliver the data. Using the Internet as the global WAN wrapper and XML as the data format, the problem of data distribution is greatly simplified. The missing piece is how to get the data from point A to point B, which leads us to HTTP.

HTTP

HTTP is an important building block for using XML as a Web-based messaging protocol. Although the Internet and various protocols such as FTP and TELNET had been in existence since the 1970s for moving files, sending email, and allowing individuals to connect remotely, it wasn't until 1992 that the face of the Internet was changed through the use of a simple request-response protocol known as HTTP.

Figure 4.3 shows that HTTP works much like FTP except that the contents of a file are delivered to a browser instead of a filesystem. Add to the browser the ability to display specially designed HTML files, and we have the Web as we know it today.

To understand how XML is used as a protocol language it is instructive to take a look at how HTTP works. The first HTTP specification written by Tim Berners-Lee is a study in simple elegance. Clients request files from servers using a simple text string of the form:

GET filename

This command is interpreted as a request to a server listening on port 80. The response of the server is either the contents of the requested file or a string indicating an error. Like most Web technologies, HTTP gains its power from its simplicity and its explicit avoidance of transport lock-in. HTTP sits on top of TCP/IP, which is responsible for reliably moving data between Internet nodes. Figure 4.4 illustrates the simple request-response protocol that HTTP makes possible.

The most common scenario on the Web is for the requested file to contain text and HTML tags. When text and tags are returned to a browser, the tags are interpreted according to a browser's internal

Figure 4.3 **Both HTTP and FTP move data across the Internet. FTP delivers data directly to disk while HTTP delivers it to a browser. When the data is in HTML or a format the browser understands, we have the Web.**

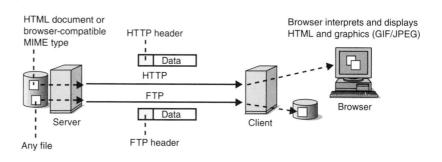

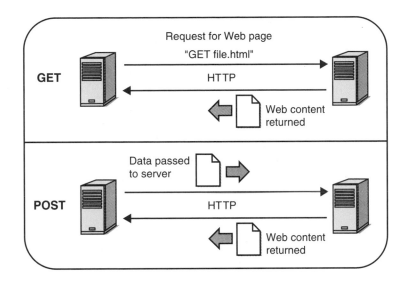

Figure 4.4 HTTP, a simple request-response Web protocol, has been the catalyst for XML's widespread use. The HTTP GET command requests a Web page. The HTTP POST command delivers information and receives information back.

programming model. The HTTP protocol says nothing about how tags are rendered, which is why different browsers often display the same Web page in very different ways. The HTTP GET command, however, allows data transfer only from server to client; to permit the transfer of data from client to server, the POST command was added.

POST Me Some Data

The POST command is a request for a server to do something with data delivered as part of the POST message. POST was included in the HTTP specification in order to deliver HTML form data to a server for processing by some server program. The structure of a POST request is similar to a GET, except that data intended for the server appears after the header and is referred to as the body or pay-load of the request.

Figure 4.5 illustrates the structure of an HTTP request showing the difference between GET and POST. When a POST request arrives at

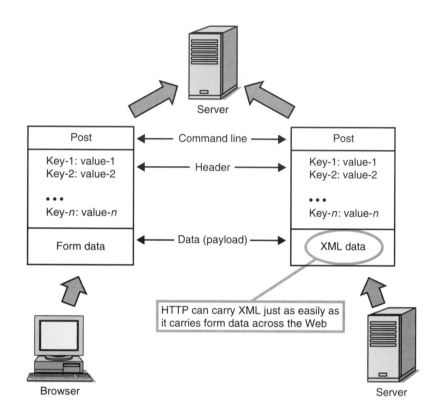

Figure 4.5 **The structure of an HTTP request provides an opportunity for delivering XML. As far as HTTP is concerned, it's just data.**

a server, the server looks for data following the blank line that signals the end of header information. This data delivery mechanism turns out to be the key element in moving XML across the Internet. Instead of supplying data from an HTML form, the payload slot of an HTTP request can just as easily be packaged with XML.

As Figure 4.6 shows, XML's transport independence means that it may be carried by any Internet protocol, including HTTP and FTP, or even sent via mail using Simple Mail Transfer Protocol (SMTP). This freedom to move data has opened the door to XML-RPC, SOAP, and the entire Web services initiative.

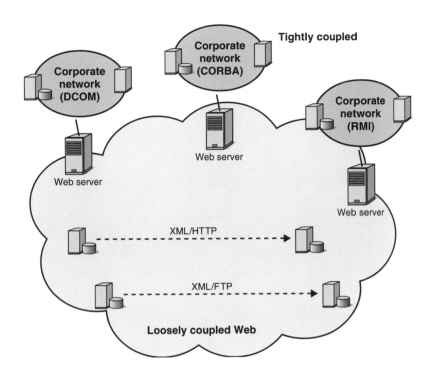

Figure 4.6 **XML and HTTP are loosely coupled, with no internal dependencies on each other. Distributed infrastructures such as CORBA, RMI, and DCOM are tightly coupled, with dependencies between data and transport.**

XML-RPC

XML-RPC, which does remote procedure calls over the Internet, is a great example of out-of-the-box thinking. In confronting the communication problem of how a program on machine A can get some code on machine B to run, XML-RPC ignores the difficulty entirely and delegates the transport to HTTP, focusing instead on the details of what to say, not how to get the message there.

Early work on XML-RPC was done by Dave Winer of UserLand Software. Winer had been working on one of the classic problems of distributed computing: how to get software running on different platforms to communicate. Shortly after XML came out in 1998, Winer demonstrated cross-platform communication by placing XML remote procedure commands in the body of an HTTP POST request. Because XML-RPC depends on HTTP to move data from one server to another, it only needs to define an XML vocabulary that specifies the name of some piece of code to execute remotely and any parameters the code might need.

Aren't Procedures Passé?

If you're from Object-land, you may wonder why we're not talking object methods instead of procedures. Isn't the term "procedure" rather antiquated, harking back to the days of procedural languages, structured programming, and data flow diagrams? There's actually a two-part answer here. First, RPC is a term that has been in use since before folks starting thinking objects and object-orientation, and XML-RPC carries forward in that tradition. Second, XML-RPC makes no assumptions about the kind of entity that will interpret the request for code execution. XML-RPC elements simply define a vocabulary to communicate information about a piece of code to be executed on some remote server. When a server receives an XML-RPC message packaged in an HTTP POST request, the XML is used to trigger a remote procedure and the result is sent back to the originator as XML.

As for data flow diagrams, they're back. Because data is free to move about the Web unencumbered by code, data flow has now returned as an important technique for modeling the flow of data across networks. One important aspect of SOAP is its ability to specify message paths and intermediaries for handling SOAP messages. Data flow is an excellent design technique to model these interactions.

Data Typing

In keeping with the spirit of Web reuse, XML-RPC uses XML Schema data types to specify the parameter types of the procedure call. Data types include scalars, numbers, strings, and dates, as well as complex record and list structures. Table 4.1 lists the possible scalar data types for XML-RPC parameters and return values.

ZwiftBooks and XML-RPC

To understand how a company might make use of XML-RPC, let's look at how ZwiftBooks Inc. might use it to allow other computer systems to query the ZwiftBooks server about the availability and delivery time of a badly needed book. The basic idea is that the user supplies an ISBN and a zip code and ZwiftBooks returns the guaranteed delivery time.

Figure 4.7 illustrates the use of XML-RPC over HTTP to trigger the execution of a procedure called `getGuaranteedDeliveryTime` based on ISBN number and zip code. As can be seen in the diagram, a

Table 4.1 Scalar Parameter Types for XML-RPC

Tag	Type	Example
`<i4>` or `<int>`	four-byte signed integer	-7247
`<boolean>`	0 (false) or 1 (true)	1
`<string>`	ASCII string	XML for all
`<double>`	double precision signed floating-point number	-72.47
`<dateTime.iso8601>`	date/time	20010524T20:08:45
`<base64>`	base64-encoded binary	7WegYR24048

Figure 4.7 **An XML-RPC request from a ZwiftBooks server showing the request, the response, and an XML-RPC fault if the server does not understand the request.**

XML-RPC request

```
POST/RPC2 HTTP/1.0
-----
<?xml version="1.0"?>
<methodCall>
    <methodName>getGuaranteedDeliveryTime</methodName>
        <params>
            <param>
                <value><string>0-13-18188-222-2</string></value>
            </param>
            <param>
                <value><string>75240</string></value>
            </param>
        </params>
</methodCall>
```

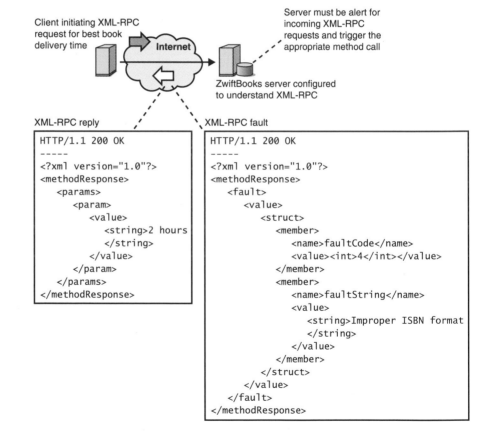

Client initiating XML-RPC request for best book delivery time

Internet

Server must be alert for incoming XML-RPC requests and trigger the appropriate method call

ZwiftBooks server configured to understand XML-RPC

XML-RPC reply

```
HTTP/1.1 200 OK
-----
<?xml version="1.0"?>
<methodResponse>
    <params>
        <param>
            <value>
                <string>2 hours
                </string>
            </value>
        </param>
    </params>
</methodResponse>
```

XML-RPC fault

```
HTTP/1.1 200 OK
-----
<?xml version="1.0"?>
<methodResponse>
    <fault>
        <value>
            <struct>
                <member>
                    <name>faultCode</name>
                    <value><int>4</int></value>
                </member>
                <member>
                    <name>faultString</name>
                    <value>
                        <string>Improper ISBN format
                        </string>
                    </value>
                </member>
            </struct>
        </value>
    </fault>
</methodResponse>
```

well-formed XML document is getting a free ride over the Internet in the payload of the request that would normally contain the data from a Web form. To make this work, the server must be in on the deal, notice that XML is arriving, and be able to process the XML-RPC elements in order to execute whatever procedure is specified in the `methodCall` element.

There are several items of interest in this example. The XML-RPC specification places a number of minimal requirements on the XML, including the following:

❑ The XML payload must be well-formed XML and contain a single `methodCall` structure.

❑ The `methodCall` element must contain a `methodName` sub-item consisting of a string that names the method to be called.

❑ If parameters are required, the `methodCall` element must contain a `params` sub-item that contains individual `param` elements, each of which contains a single `value`.

XML-RPC Responses

The job of the server is to process the XML-RPC request for the execution of some piece of code and return a value to the client. According to the rules of XML-RPC, a server must return either the result of the procedure execution or a `fault` element.

Figure 4.7 also illustrates the return value of an XML-RPC packaged in the data area of an HTTP reply. Again, as far as HTTP is concerned, it's just data.

XML-RPC specifies that the response to a procedure call must be a single XML structure, a `methodResponse`, which can contain either the return value packaged in a single `params` element or a `fault` element which contains information about why the fault occurred.

Figure 4.7 also illustrates returning a `fault` element as the payload of an HTTP response. As we'll see with SOAP, the specification for describing failure is an important aspect of XML-based protocols.

SOAP

SOAP carries on the XML-RPC tradition by defining an XML language for packaging arbitrary XML inside an XML envelope. Although SOAP does not depend on HTTP, the momentum behind SOAP is attributable to the fact that HTTP will usually be used as the transport protocol for SOAP messages.

Understanding SOAP is important for seeing how XML can be used to move information across the Web and how it fits in the grand vision of making XML-based distributed computing a reality. Dave Winer, whom some consider the godfather of XML-RPC, and who publishes a widely read forum called "DaveNet,"[2] wrote about his work with RPC and caught the attention of some folks at Microsoft who asked Winer if he'd be interested in working with them on XML-over-HTTP. As Winer recounts it:

> I flew up to Redmond, met with Bob and met Mohsen Al-Ghosein and Don Box for the first time. We sat in a conference room, I had a projected laptop. I opened Notepad with an example call from our earlier protocol. As people expressed their ideas I changed the example. It was one of the most productive brainstorming sessions of my career. . . . A few weeks into the process I wanted to release the software to our users, so we forked a release, called it XML-RPC, and continued working with Microsoft on what would become SOAP 1.1.[3]

---

[2] http://davenet.userland.com/.

[3] See note 1 on p. 112.

On Coupling

In discussions about SOAP, the term "coupling" is often used with different shades of meaning depending on context. One meaning, taken from the software engineering literature, refers to coupling as the degree of connectedness between modules in a software system.

In a classic 1972 software engineering paper, Dave Parnas argued that the criteria for creation of modules should center around their capacity to insulate themselves through a focus on core functionality.[4] Later, Glenford Myers extrapolated on Parnas' ideas, identifying "High Module Independence" as one of the most important characteristics of quality software and using the term "coupling" to mean the degree of connectedness between modules.[5]

In the late 1980s and 1990s, another related meaning of the word "coupling" emerged based on the relationship between sending and receiving processes in distributed networks. In tightly coupled networks, senders and receivers rendezvous with each other, requiring that both processes exist at the same time and maintain knowledge of each other's identity and location. Loosely coupled networks, on the other hand, ease these constraints. Through the use of messaging middleware, loosely coupled systems do not require that sender and receiver be operational at the same time, nor do they require identity or location to be known in advance.

---

[4] David L. Parnas, "On the criteria to be used in decomposing systems into modules," *Communications of the ACM, 1972*, 15(12): 1053–58.

[5] Glenford Myers, *The Art of Software Testing* (New York: John Wiley & Sons, 1979).

(continued)

On Coupling (continued)

With SOAP, we find both meanings of the word "coupling"
applicable. SOAP is decoupled from any underlying transport
software *and*, through its message structure, enables the creation of loosely coupled networks that don't require tight binding between processes in order to communicate.

SOAP Background

The SOAP 1.0 specification was developed by Microsoft, Develop-
Mentor, and Dave Winer of UserLand Software and released in the
spring of 1998. Figure 4.8 illustrates the influences on SOAP. Prior to

Figure 4.8 The SOAP specification and its influences.

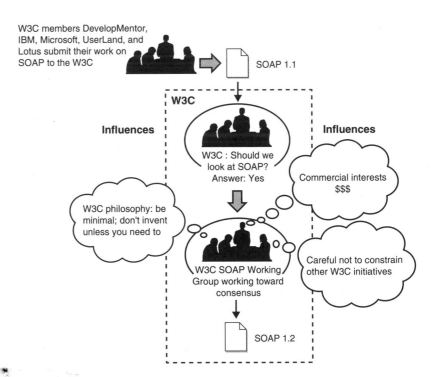

the release of SOAP 1.0, Winer released his work on RPC as the XML-RPC specification (http://www.xmlrpc.com), which is very close to SOAP 1.0. Following the release of SOAP 1.0, IBM and Lotus joined the original developers, along with a group of partners including Ariba, Commerce One, Compaq, IONA, Intel Corp., ObjectSpace, Rogue Wave, and others. SOAP 1.1 was published by the W3C as a Note in May 2000. In July 2001, the W3C released the first public Working Draft for SOAP Version 1.2 based on the work of the W3C's XML Protocol Working Group.

The SOAP Protocol

As Figure 4.9 illustrates, SOAP is a transport protocol similar to IIOP for CORBA, ORPC for DCOM, or JRMP for RMI. SOAP differs from CORBA, RMI, or DCOM in several ways:

❑ IIOP, ORPC, and JRMP are binary protocols, while SOAP is a text-based protocol that uses XML. Using XML for data encoding makes SOAP easier to debug and easier to read than a binary stream.

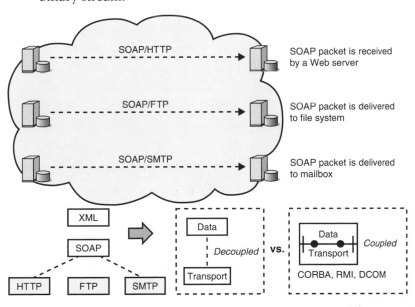

Figure 4.9 **The SOAP protocol opens up new options for data exchange across the Web.**

❑ Because SOAP is text-based, it is able to move more easily across firewalls than IIOP, ORPC, or JRMP.

❑ SOAP is based on XML, which is standards-driven rather than vendor-driven. Potential adopters are less likely to fear vendor lock-in with SOAP.

The net effect is that SOAP can be picked up by different transport protocols and delivered in different ways. For example, when used with HTTP it can be delivered to a Web server; when used over FTP it can deposited directly into a file system; and when used with SMTP it can delivered to a user's mailbox.

Figure 4.10 illustrates that SOAP can be used for direct connection between sender and receiver, or, with the use of messaging middleware, SOAP messages can be stored for subsequent delivery and/or broadcast to multiple receivers.

It should be noted that for many companies, using SOAP as protocol for exchanging data between established partners is proving a totally satisfactory way to leverage the benefits of XML and the Web. In this scenario all that is required is an agreed-upon schema, either a DTD or an XML Schema, for the XML data being exchanged and a SOAP server capable of handling the incoming XML as it arrives over the Web. Details about what kind of schemas to expect and who will check that the XML conforms to the schemas are decided offline by individuals participating in the process. On the software side, senders need to be involved in packaging their data in an XML document. For those companies already storing data in XML, this should require only minimal effort. If the stored XML data is not in the form required by the agreement, an XSL Transformations (XSLT) style sheet can be programmed to automate the transformation.

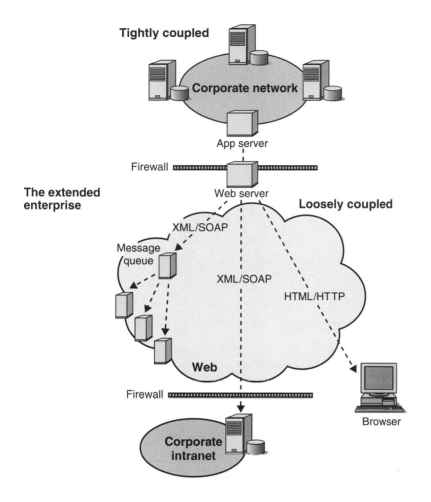

Figure 4.10 SOAP extends the Web from server-to-browser to server-to-server interaction.

SOAP Overview

SOAP consists of three parts:

- ❏ Encoding rules that control XML tags that define a SOAP message and a framework that describes message content
- ❏ Rules for exchanging application-defined data types, including when to accept or discard data or return an exception to the sender
- ❏ Conventions for representing remote procedure calls and responses

SOAP messages define one-way data transmission from a sender to a receiver. However, SOAP messages are often combined to implement patterns such as request-response. When using HTTP bindings with SOAP, SOAP response messages can use the same connection as the inbound request.

SOAP Message Structure

Figure 4.11 illustrates the structure of a SOAP message, consisting of three parts:

❑ *The SOAP Envelope:* The outermost element of a SOAP message. The Envelope element is the root of the XML document that defines a SOAP message.

❑ *The SOAP Header:* An optional, yet key element in architecting a distributed system around XML. The Header element provides a

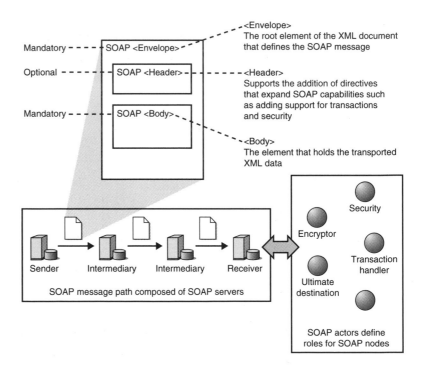

Figure 4.11 SOAP messages have a common format that includes a SOAP Envelope, an optional Header, and a Body section that contains the message content. SOAP also defines a message path and set of roles that SOAP nodes can adopt along a path.

modular way of directing SOAP servers to do processing before passing the SOAP message on. For example, it is possible to add SOAP header information that instructs a server to add transaction or authentication information. Headers are also important in building piped architectures where processing is done in stages and data is modified as it is passed from handler to handler.

❑ *The SOAP Body:* An element that must appear in a SOAP message. The Body element is where the transported XML is loaded. SOAP makes no assumptions about the kind of XML transported in the body of a SOAP message. The data may be domain-specific XML or it may take the form of a remote procedure call.

SOAP Messaging Example

In the previous section we looked at sending XML-RPC over HTTP to execute specific procedures on our ZwiftBooks server. With SOAP we may still use XML-RPC to trigger specific methods on the server, or we may simply define XML elements that get processed by our SOAP server.

To understand how SOAP works, let's continue our ZwiftBooks example and look at how SOAP may be used to expand business functionality by opening our server up to collectors who wish to notify ZwiftBooks about books they have for sale. ZwiftBooks will then add the providers and their books to the ZwiftBooks database.

To make this happen, several things must be done by ZwiftBooks:

1. Define a top-level element and related subelements that will trigger processing of the book availability data by the SOAP server.
2. Define a schema (DTD or XML Schema) that dictates the form of the XML that will arrive from collectors and book providers.

3. Specify a namespace that is unique to ZwiftBooks. This may be the ZwiftBooks Web site or any URI.
4. Configure the server to return a fault if the incoming SOAP message is not one of the special elements defined in step 1.

Figure 4.12 illustrates a SOAP request for the ZwiftBooks guaranteed delivery time for a specific book, specified by ISBN number. Note that the SOAP `Envelope` element is the top-level element in the body of the SOAP message and within the SOAP `body` element is found the request for `GetGuaranteedDeliveryTime`, packaged as an element including the ISBN number.

Figure 4.12 **A SOAP request sent to the ZwiftBooks server.**

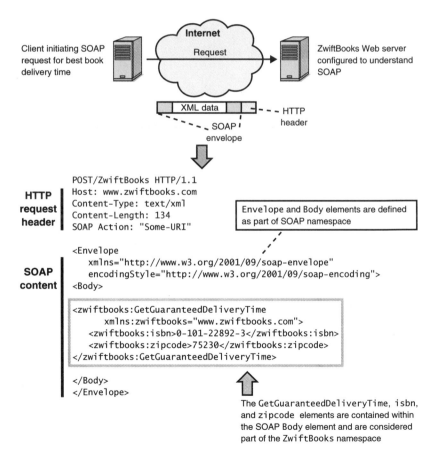

A SOAP response takes the form illustrated in Figure 4.13. Here the XML response indicating the best delivery time is packaged in a SOAP message that is delivered using the standard HTTP response protocol. As far as HTTP is concerned, it's just data being returned to the client that initiated the request. However, for a client that understands SOAP, the data becomes useful information.

Message Paths

An important aspect of SOAP is the provision for message paths. Independent of the transport protocol used to send SOAP messages, messages may be routed from server to server along a so-called message path. As we saw in Figure 4.11, message paths support message processing at one or more intermediate nodes in addition to the ultimate destination.

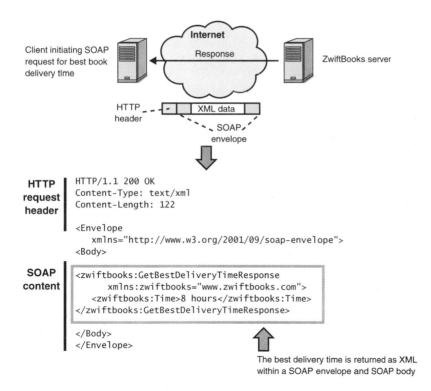

Figure 4.13 **A SOAP response to a request to the ZwiftBooks server.**

SOAP Intermediaries

SOAP intermediaries are an essential aspect of building scalable Web-based distributed systems. Intermediaries can act in different roles, including proxies, caches, store-and-forward hops, and gateways. Again, experience with HTTP has shown that intermediaries cannot be implicitly defined but must be provided as an explicit part of the messaging path model. Thus, one of the key motivations of the Working Group is to ensure that an XML protocol supports composability between peers.

A SOAP-compliant server must be able to act as a SOAP intermediary capable of processing and forwarding a SOAP message on a path from its origin to a final destination. SOAP intermediaries may be explicitly specified by providing their URIs as the value of the SOAP `actor` attribute within a SOAP `header`, for example:

```
<SOAP-ENV:Header
SOAP-ENV:actor=http://yourServer.com
. . .>
```

Alternatively, a SOAP message can specify that the header should be processed by the first SOAP application that processes the message, as in this example:

```
<SOAP-ENV:Header
SOAP-ENV:actor="http://schemas.xmlsoap.org/soap/actor/next"
  . . .>
```

SOAP and Actors

If the SOAP `actor` attribute is not present in a header, then the recipient of the message is considered the final destination. The following list covers the rules a well-behaved SOAP server must follow when receiving a SOAP message:

❏ Identify the parts of the SOAP message intended for that application. This means checking the header for an `actor` attribute that is either the URI of the application or the URI http://schemas.xmlsoap.org/soap/actor/next, which means that the application must process the header.

❏ Verify that all parts of the header intended for the application and associated with a `mustUnderstand="true"` attribute are supported by the application. If the application cannot process the message, then it must discard the message and return a SOAP fault (see section on SOAP faults on page 137).

❏ Process the parts of the header intended for the application. If there are elements that include the attribute `mustUnderstand="false"` or that do not specify the `mustUnderstand` attribute, then the application may ignore those elements.

If the application is not the ultimate destination of the message, then it must remove all header elements intended for it before forwarding the message.

SOAP Design Patterns

Architectural design patterns capture the proven experience of software architects in the form of architectural patterns, each with distinct properties that address different architectural design problems. To a business strategist, software architecture patterns provide a high-level conceptual view of a software system independent of the specific implementation's details. To a software engineer, patterns provide a structure within which components can be designed and integrated. To those tasked with moving from requirements to design, patterns provide a starting point for developing implementation strategies.

Figure 4.14 illustrates two of the architectural patterns in wide use today: the Layers Pattern, and the Pipe and Filter Pattern. The

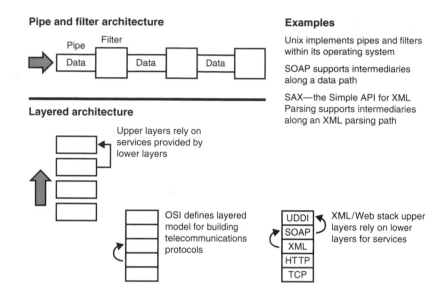

Figure 4.14 Architectural design patterns: The Layers Pattern and the Pipe and Filter Pattern.

Layers Pattern is one of the earliest successful architectural patterns and is the basis for the design of telecommunications infrastructures such as TCP/IP. Layers describe a solution to a problem by partitioning the problem into subtasks that are assigned to individual layers. Each layer draws on services from the layer below and provides services to the layer above.

A variant of the Layers pattern, the Multitier Pattern, is used to build tiered systems. For example, two-tier client-server systems partition display functionality to the client tier and business logic to the server tier. Three-tier systems add another tier for managing data.

The Pipe and Filter Pattern is another architectural approach to systems construction that assumes a stream of data moving through a series of pipes and filters and being transformed as it travels from origin to destination. In addition to serving as transforming agents, stages in the Filter Pattern can be used to buffer data and help deal with issues that arise in working with interruptible network connections.

The SOAP specification provides support for the filters through its ability to specify intermediary processing agents along a path from an XML document's origin to a final destination.

Filters are also supported by the Simple API for XML (SAX), a Java application program interface for processing XML. SAX makes use of a filter class that can act as an intermediary in a complex chain of processing. The filter class is passed as the event handler to another class that generates SAX events, forwarding all or some of those events to the next handler or filter in the processing chain.

Filters may be used to prune the document tree by not forwarding events for elements with a given name (or that satisfy some other condition), or a filter can generate new events to add parent or child elements to an existing document stream. Filters can also be used to add or remove element attributes or modify the character data.

The Filter is related to UNIX's capability to take simple processing functions and pipe them together to perform complex tasks. The power of SOAP and SAX filters derives from the fact that simpler, easy-to-maintain filters may be chained together to produce complex XML data transformations.

SOAP Faults

SOAP faults occur when an application cannot understand a SOAP message or when an error occurs during the processing of a message. SOAP defines an XML `fault` element that carries error and/or status information back to the message sender.

Faults are intended to provide detail to the sender as to why the fault occurred. The information that can be returned as part of a fault includes the following:

- ❏ *faultcode:* SOAP defines a set of faultcodes for basic SOAP errors, although an application may provide its own codes.
- ❏ *faultstring:* This element provides a readable explanation as to why the fault occurred.
- ❏ *detail:* The value of the detail element is that it provides information about the problem that occurred while processing the Body element. If not present, it indicates that the problem did not occur in the body of the SOAP message.

SOAP with Attachments

SOAP provides a protocol to deliver XML across the Internet. However, requirements often dictate that not just XML needs to be transported but also other related documents such as DTDs, schema, Unified Modeling Language diagrams, faxes, public and private keys, and digests that may be related to the XML. In keeping with the spirit of the Web not to introduce new technologies when existing ones are available, SOAP relies on the existing rules for HTTP attachments to deliver auxiliary data with a primary SOAP message, allowing a SOAP message to reference the attachments.

The SOAP with Attachments (see Figure 4.15) document defines a binding for a SOAP message to be carried within a Multi-Purpose Internet Mail Extensions (MIME) multipart/related message in such a way that the processing rules for the SOAP message are preserved. The MIME multipart mechanism for encapsulation of compound documents can be used to bundle entities related to the SOAP message, such as attachments.

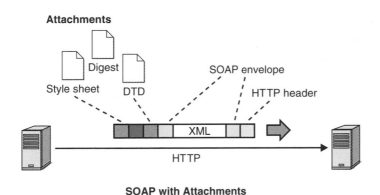

SOAP with Attachments

Figure 4.15 **SOAP with Attachments lets additional documents travel with SOAP-based XML content using HTTP as the transport protocol.**

SOAP and Firewalls

SOAP's global reach is made possible by its alliance with HTTP, the Internet protocol that is the basis for moving data back and forth from Web servers to browsers. HTTP works by accessing Web servers on port 80, which is kept open for Web traffic. Most servers shut down other ports for security purposes.

SOAP's use of port 80 is a double-edged sword. While an open port 80 makes SOAP messaging possible, it also makes system managers nervous about incoming SOAP traffic, since SOAP messages traveling on port 80 bypass the protection afforded by firewalls. SOAP messages can contain XML-RPC commands to execute code on the server, which requires caution to protect the server from unwanted attacks, the form of which is difficult to anticipate.

It should be noted that while XML-RPC calls can easily pass through firewalls, XML-RPC distinguishes itself from other server traffic by including a header element that specifies `content-type` as `text/xml`. This at least alerts the server and associated firewall software that XML is being POSTed to the server.

The W3C and SOAP

The XML Protocol Working Group is the W3C group formed in response to the submission of the SOAP 1.1 specification as the basis for a universal XML-based protocol. The formation of the Working Group signals the W3C's willingness to consider extending the Web from a network that delivers documents and links to human users, to a network that supports communication between applications.

The goal of the XML Protocol Working Group is the creation of simple protocols that can be deployed across the Web and easily programmed through scripting languages, XML, and Web tools. It is important to note that the goal of the Working Group is not to provide a complete infrastructure for Web communication, but to build a foundational layer that can be incrementally extended to support the security, scalability, and robustness required for more complex applications.

A key aspect of the XML Protocol Working Group is that, like all other W3C initiatives, the group effort must fit within the broader W3C goals of modularity and simplicity. In defining a protocol for the Web, it is important that the final version of the envelope and any serialization mechanisms developed by the Working Group should not preclude any programming model nor assume any particular mode of communication between peers. In addition, it should also support distributed extensibility where the communicating parties do not have a priori knowledge of each other.

By limiting the scope of its effort to include neither transport nor application-specific features, the Working Group is better positioned to achieve its goal of producing a simple mechanism for encapsulating and representing data that is transferred between communicating peers. In keeping with the foundational W3C design principle of avoiding constraints if at all possible, the XML Protocol Working Group carries on the W3C philosophy of fostering interoperability.

Much of the work on SOAP has been influenced by the experience of developing HTTP, which has demonstrated how difficult it is to retrofit support for evolution and how important extensibility is as a feature of an infrastructure.

Taking SOAP to the Next Level

Going beyond the simple use of SOAP to exchange data, several options are emerging that use SOAP as their base protocol. As can be seen in Figure 4.16, other options include Electronic Business XML (ebXML) and Web services. Although we examine ebXML and Web services in more detail in Chapter 5, it's important to realize that both these technologies impose some structure on the freewheeling

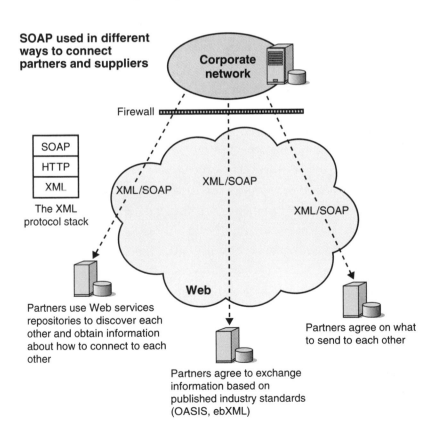

SOAP used in different ways to connect partners and suppliers

Corporate network

Firewall

| SOAP |
| HTTP |
| XML |

The XML protocol stack

XML/SOAP

XML/SOAP

XML/SOAP

Web

Partners use Web services repositories to discover each other and obtain information about how to connect to each other

Partners agree to exchange information based on published industry standards (OASIS, ebXML)

Partners agree on what to send to each other

Figure 4.16 **SOAP offers an envelope for sending XML data across the Web. Technologies such as Web services and ebXML add structure and process to the B2B dialog.**

world of SOAP-based communication. As we'll see, ebXML is useful in defining messages and processes for common B2B transactions, and Web services is an infrastructure for discovering and connecting to services anywhere on the Web. Thus rather than spending time and money defining a schema for purchase orders, a company can turn to ebXML or a Web services framework to provide a structure for communication. However, using SOAP alone is a completely satisfactory approach with minimal risk that gets the job done.

Summary

SOAP and XML-RPC are XML languages that represent the third wave of XML in practice: the use of XML with other technologies to create new functionality through the power of combination. XML-RPC specifies remote procedure calls that aren't tied to a particular programming language, component model, or platform. SOAP builds on this capability, adding an XML message envelope, header, and body, as well as a set of rules for the senders and receivers of SOAP messages. In combination with HTTP, SOAP can deliver XML content anywhere across the Internet. However, SOAP does not address how to locate others across the growing expanse of the Web, nor does it concern itself with how to communicate securely in a transaction-based environment. For these issues we need other technologies and protocols that build on SOAP's foundation. As we'll see in the next chapter and beyond, Web services provides a way to handle discovery and conversation with other SOAP-enabled servers, while .NET and J2EE provide an infrastructure for adding transactions, security, and identity to the SOAP world.

Resources

Web

http://www.w3.org/TR/SOAP/

The SOAP 1.1 specification.

http://www.w3.org/TR/2001/WD-soap12-20010709/

SOAP version 1.2.

http://www.develop.com/soap/soapfaq.htm

DevelopMentor's SOAP FAQ.

http://www.webservices.org

Webservices resource center Web site.

http://msdn.microosft.com/webservices

Microsoft's Web services Web site.

http://www.linuxdoc.org/HOWTO/XML-RPC-HOWTO/

XML-RPC Howto.

http://davenet.userland.com/1998/07/14/xmlRpcForNewbies

XML-RPC for Newbies.

http://frontier.userland.com/stories/storyReader$101

How to write and call an XML-RPC handler.

http://www.itworld.com/nl/java_entrp/

Java in the Enterprise Newsletter Archive.

http://www.xmledi-group.org/

XML EDI group.

http://www.w3.org/TR/SOAP-attachments
SOAP Messages with Attachments—W3C Note 11 December 2000.

Book

Simon St. Laurent, Joe Johnston, and Edd Dumbill, *Programming Web Services with XML-RPC* (San Sebastopol, CA: O'Reilly, 2001).

5

Web Services

Web services is an effort to extend the Web from an infrastructure that provides services to humans to one that provides services to software looking to connect with other software. Web services builds on Simple Object Access Protocol (SOAP), taking it to the next level by adding a process and set of protocols that businesses can use to find each other and interact over the Web instead of over preestablished networks. The key ingredient in Web services is a repository that adds another player to the traditional client-provider equation. It's an effort to realize the object-oriented dream of component assembly, except now in a loosely coupled global Web where the vocabulary is about services instead of objects.

To understand Web services we'll look at two XML initiatives, Universal Description, Discovery, and Integration (UDDI) and Web Services Definition Language (WSDL), to see how they underpin the vision of the Web as a software distribution medium. We'll also look at Electronic Business XML (ebXML) as an example of adding a process model to Web interactions. As we examine the Web services model, it's important to realize that the Web services vision is not a done deal. Although all the major industry players are investing heavily in Web services, it remains to be seen how this vision of discovery and interaction will play out.

What Is Web Services?

Web services is at once a technology, a process, and a phenomenon. As a technology it is a set of protocols that builds on the global connectivity made possible by SOAP and the synergies of XML and HTTP. As a process, it is an approach to software discovery and

Web services builds on SOAP and HTTP.

connection over the Web. As a phenomenon, it's an industry-wide realization that the decentralized, loosely coupled, synergistic Web can't be ignored.

As Figure 5.1 shows, Web services builds on SOAP's capability for distributed, decentralized network communication by adding new protocols and conventions that expose business functions to interested parties over the Internet from any Web-connected device. As we discussed in Chapter 1, we're moving into a new computing paradigm based on the assembly of constituent parts. SOAP, for example, is not a stand-alone technology, but the result of synergies between XML and HTTP. This phenomenon of emergence has not been lost on the major industry players, who are actively working to

Figure 5.1 Web services provides a framework for communication across the Web. It is both a set of protocols and a process for discovery and connection.

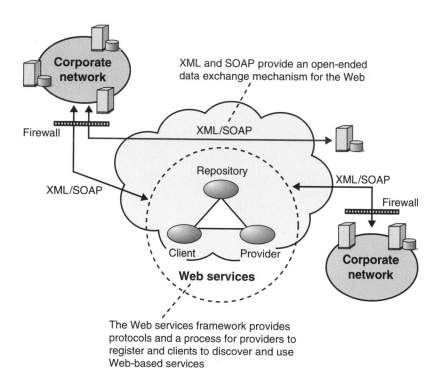

The Web services framework provides protocols and a process for providers to register and clients to discover and use Web-based services

update their existing infrastructures to keep pace with the changes wrought by SOAP-based messaging for the global Web.

Web services is a technology and process for discovery and connection.

Web services represents an industry-wide response to the need for a flexible and efficient business collaboration environment. Technically, it is a way to link loosely coupled systems using technology that doesn't bind them to a particular programming language, component model, or platform. Practically, it represents a discrete business process with supporting protocols that functions by describing and exposing itself to users of the Web, being invoked by a remote user, and returning a response. It includes:

- ❏ *Describing:* Web services describes its functionality and attributes so that other applications can figure out how to use it.
- ❏ *Exposing:* Web services register with a repository that contains a white pages holding basic service-provider information, a yellow pages listing services by category, and a green pages describing how to connect and use the services.
- ❏ *Being invoked:* When a Web service has been located, a remote application can invoke the service.
- ❏ *Returning a response:* When a service has been invoked, results are returned to the requesting application.

The driving force behind Web services is the desire to allow businesses to use the Internet to publish, discover, and aggregate other Web services using the global underpinning of SOAP. The fact that the delivery of Web services requires only the Internet means that legacy code and data as well as object systems can plug into the Web services framework. This capability is expected to result in new products, business processes, and value chains with global scope, deliverable over wired or wireless networks. How these will emerge is anyone's guess. But the track record of the Web, XML, and now SOAP indicates that new technologies will rapidly emerge.

What Qualifies as Web Services?

A Web service is anything that can define itself via an interface.

Any software components or application can be exposed as Web services so that it can be discovered and used by another component or application. Web services may be as simple as a movie review or weather forecast or as complex as a complete travel package that includes hotel and airline bookings and restaurant reservations. What Web services brings to the table is a technical infrastructure that ensures that services, even from different vendors, will interoperate. While this idea of component assembly has long been the dream of object technology, Web services takes the object vision to the next level by adding capabilities that don't require advance knowledge of how services fit together.

Opportunity and Risk

Web services offers new opportunities for profit and efficiencies.

Web services represents a new model of software distribution and interconnection based on the notion of services globally available over the Web rather than object-to-object connections over limited networks. Because of the global scope of Web-based services, the potential financial upside is extremely attractive. Financial incentives include new revenue opportunities through creation of private trading networks, increased revenue through expanded distribution channels, and reduced inventory and transaction costs.

Web services also promises improved collaboration with customers, partners, and suppliers. It provides opportunities for reducing integration time and expense compared to existing enterprise application integration and business-to-business (B2B) solutions. There is also opportunity for improved supply-chain efficiencies, quick response to changing market conditions and customer preferences by utilizing loosely coupled modular services, and improved customer service by allowing customers and trading partners access to core systems.

However, the Web services vision is still new and not without risk. Despite the significant potential, it remains to be seen how Web services will play out on a large scale. It's expected that Web services will begin to play a role in the delivery of simple services but, until the technology matures, complex trading partner interactions will still require an up-front human element to solidify agreements. As we look into the details of the Web services protocols UDDI and WSDL, we will revisit the issue of risks.

Early adopters run the risk of any new technology.

Web Services: A ZwiftBooks Perspective

To understand how companies might take advantage of Web services, let's look at how ZwiftBooks, the must-have, instant book delivery service, might take the plunge.

ZwiftBooks uses a Web services repository to list its offerings.

There are several decisions ZwiftBooks must make as a provider to take advantage of Web services technology. It must

1. Decide on the service it wants to provide
2. Pick a registry (or registries) for uploading its information
3. Decide how to list its service at the registry
4. Define explicitly how users can connect to its service

Let's explore each a little further.

Deciding on a Service

The first step is to decide what aspects of the business ZwiftBooks wants to expose to potential clients. Remember, Web services is about *services,* and ZwiftBooks could very easily begin by publishing its telephone service instead of its newly developed SOAP-based service. Let's assume, though, that ZwiftBooks has its server act together and is ready to accept SOAP requests, so it decides to go with the automated book query service.

Picking a Registry

There are currently several registries implemented by various software vendors. ZwiftBooks selects SuperReg, a registry run by a major Web services company that is known to get lots of traffic.

Deciding How to List

An important issue for ZwiftBooks is how is get discovered on the registry. Table 5.1 outlines the options for storing information in a UDDI repository. Web services registries support white, yellow, and green pages. Of course, ZwiftBooks will be in the white pages under "Z," but that's probably not going to bring thousands of book lovers to its SOAP server. What ZwiftBooks needs is to list itself by category, just like in the conventional yellow pages. A logical place would probably be "Books." But is that enough?

Individuals and software agents will search repositories.

Remember, Web services is intended for computer-to-computer interactions. Now while there may be a human on the other end of the computer trying to find a book service, ZwiftBooks needs to think about how to make itself attractive to computer-based agents trolling the Web for business partners. These computer systems will be more concerned with whether ZwiftBooks can plug into their B2B framework. Is ZwiftBooks prepared to deliver book information based on industry standards? If so, then maybe ZwiftBooks is worth a further look; if not, it's time for the robot to move on.

Web services yellow pages will list companies according to conformant standards.

This brings us to a new way of thinking about yellow pages. What will be important in attracting software agents that represent potential customers and partners in the freewheeling world of Web services is whether a company is prepared to participate in data interchange using standard processes and procedures. Thus, instead of listing itself just under "Books" in the yellow pages, ZwiftBooks may also want to list itself as conformant to the International Book Exchange Consortium or whatever standards it is prepared to abide by. If it

Table 5.1 The Organization of UDDI

Directory	Operation	Information
White pages: Name, address, telephone number, and other contact information of a given business	**Publish:** How the provider of Web services registers itself	**Business information:** A businessEntity object contains information about services, categories, contacts, URLs, and other things necessary to interact with a given business.
Yellow pages: Categories of businesses based on existing (nonelectronic) standards	**Find:** How an application finds a particular Web service	**Service information:** Describes a group of Web services. These are contained in a businessService object.
Green pages: Technical information about the Web services provided by a given business	**Bind:** How an application connects to and interacts with Web services after it's been found	**Binding information:** The technical details necessary to invoke Web services. This includes URLs, information about method names, argument types, and so on. The bindingTemplate object represents this data.
		Service specification detail: This is metadata about the various specifications implemented by a given Web service. These are called tModels in the UDDI specification.

does so, potential customers and partners can at least know in advance that it is possible to do business with ZwiftBooks according to their own processes and procedures.

Defining How to Connect

The final step for ZwiftBooks is to place an entry into the green pages that describes how to connect to and query the ZwiftBooks server. To do this ZwiftBooks prepares a WSDL document using WSDL's XML syntax.

Web Services Technologies

An architecture built around a client, a provider, and a registry.

Web services depends on several enabling technologies including XML, SOAP, UDDI, and WSDL. In the following sections we examine UDDI and WSDL, key pieces in the Web services framework.

The Web Services Architecture

As Figure 5.2 illustrates, there are three major aspects to Web services:

❑ A *service provider* provides an interface for software that can carry out a specified set of tasks.

❑ A *service requester* discovers and invokes a software service to provide a business solution. The requester will commonly invoke a remote procedure call on the service provider, passing parameter data to the provider and receiving a result in reply.

❑ A *repository* or *broker* manages and publishes the service. Service providers publish their services with the broker, and requests access those services by creating bindings to the service provider.

Key Technologies

Web services builds on SOAP, UDDI, and WSDL.

Web services relies on several key underlying technologies, in particular, UDDI, WSDL, and SOAP.

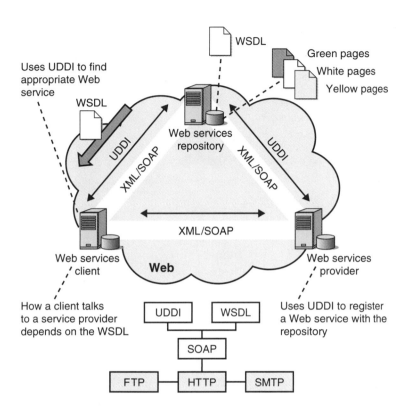

Figure 5.2 The Web services triad includes a broker, a service provider, and a service requester.

UDDI is a protocol for describing Web services components that allows businesses to register with an Internet directory so they can advertise their services and companies can find each other and carry out transactions over the Web.

WSDL is the proposed standard for describing a Web service. WSDL is built around an XML-based service Interface Definition Language that defines both the service interface and the implementation details. WSDL details may be obtained from UDDI entries that describe the SOAP messages needed to use a particular Web service.

SOAP is a protocol for communicating with a UDDI service (see Figure 5.3). SOAP simplifies UDDI access by allowing applications to

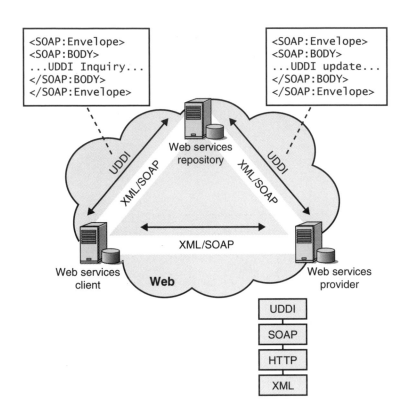

Figure 5.3
Communication involving UDDI uses SOAP to package UDDI requests and replies to a Web services repository.

invoke object methods or functions residing on remote servers. The advantage of SOAP is that it can use universal HTTP to make a request and to receive a response. SOAP requests and responses use XML not only to target the remote method but to package any data that is required by the method.

UDDI

UDDI is the protocol for communicating with registries.

At the core of UDDI is the UDDI Business Registry, a global, public, online directory that provides businesses a uniform way to describe their services, to discover services from other companies, and to understand the details of how to connect and interact with the software that implements a service.

UDDI stems from a cooperative agreement among Microsoft, IBM, and Ariba on an XML-based specification for establishing a registry of businesses and services on the Internet. Since the initiative began in August 2000, the project has expanded to over 260 UDDI community members.

UDDI defines a layer above SOAP in an interoperability stack that builds on TCP/IP, HTTP, and XML. UDDI defines an XML-based infrastructure for software to automatically discover available services on the Web, using SOAP as the protocol to invoke services.

UDDI: Public versus Private Registries

A UDDI-compliant registry provides an information framework for describing the services of a Web entity or business. The Web services vision uses UDDI registries as the focal point for registering and locating services. It is expected that some registries will be public and others private. Microsoft, IBM, and HP have agreed to provide a public UDDI registry, open for search and connection across the entire Internet. But private registries will also be available either internally within companies or among a closely knit family of trusted partners and collaborators.

Registries may serve different public and private functions.

In Version 2 of the UDDI specification there is support for deploying both public and private Web service registries, allowing enterprises to deploy private registries to manage internal Web services using the UDDI specification. As a result many IT companies are beginning to use Web services technologies behind their firewalls for application-to-application integration. By starting small on less critical projects, managers and developers can gain the experience needed to migrate to more ambitious projects beyond their corporate boundaries.

The UDDI Family of Specifications

The UDDI framework consists of several specifications that describe how a program can interact with a registry, including the following.

❑ The UDDI Programmer's API Specification defines approximately 30 SOAP messages that are used to perform inquiry and publishing functions against any UDDI-compliant business registry. This specification outlines the details of each of the XML structures associated with these messages.

❑ The UDDI Data Structure Specification defines the four major data structures used by Programmer API. These include businessEntity, businessService, bindingTemplate, and tModel.

Using UDDI to Make the ZwiftBooks Connection

The following is a scenario of interaction for connecting to our ZwiftBooks server using UDDI discovery:

1. A company is interested in writing software that connects to several book-service providers and comparing price and delivery times for each. It needs a program that can connect to the UDDI business registry via either a Web interface or a tool that uses the Inquiry API. After a lookup based on an appropriate yellow pages listing, the company obtains a businessEntity that represents ZwiftBooks.

2. Using the businessEntity, the client can either drill down for more detail or request a complete businessEntity structure. In either case, the objective is to obtain a bindingTemplate

that provides the information about how to connect to Zwift-Books Web service.

3. Based on the details of the specification provided by the `bindingTemplate`, the company sets up its program to interact with the ZwiftBooks Web service. The semantics of the service may be obtained by accessing the `tModel` contained in the `bindingTemplate` for the service.

4. At runtime, the program invokes the Web service based on the connection details provided in the `bindingTemplate`.

If the remote Web services and the calling program each accurately implement the required interface conventions (as defined in the specification referenced in the `tModel`), calls to the remote service will be successful. However, if there is a problem with the interaction between client and Web service, UDDI specifies details for failure and recovery.

UDDI Failure and Recovery

Web businesses making use of Web services for e-commerce need to be able to detect and manage communication problems and other failures. Because distributed systems have more failure points than standalone systems, it is important for clients to be able to detect and/or recover from failures that occur during interaction with remote partners. UDDI addresses quality-of-service issues by defining a calling convention that involves the use of cached `bindingTemplate`s. When a failure occurs, the cached information is refreshed based on current information from a UDDI Web registry.

UDDI failure is part of the protocol.

The following scenario describes how error recovery fits into Web services:

1. A developer prepares a program to use a Web service, caching the appropriate `bindingTemplate` for use at runtime.

2. During program execution, the program calling the remote Web service uses the cached `bindingTemplate` that was earlier obtained from a UDDI Web registry.

3. If the call fails, the program uses the `bindingKey` value and the `get_bindingTemplate` API call to acquire a new copy of a `bindingTemplate` for this unique Web service.

4. The program compares the new `bindingTemplate` information with the cached version and, if they are different, retries the failed call using the new `bindingTemplate`.

5. If both versions are the same, the client retries the call. This approach, called "retry on failure," is more efficient than acquiring a new copy of `bindingTemplate` data prior to each call. It also proves useful when a business needs to redirect traffic to a new site; it need only activate the new site and change the published location information for the affected `bindingTemplate`s.

WSDL

WSDL: how to connect to providers.

WSDL is the piece of the Web services framework that describes how to connect to Web services providers. WSDL is an XML format for describing how one software system can connect and utilize the services of another software system over the Internet. The WSDL specification supports the building of Web-based computing services that target computer programs rather than human users. WSDL uses an XML-based syntax to describe the specifics of accessing a Web service, such as the type and number of parameters passed to a service and the type and structure of the result returned.

Once a Web service has been discovered (via UDDI), WSDL provides the details of how to actually bind and interact with that service. WSDL supports direct client interaction with a Web service provider by building on the infrastructure provided by HTTP and SOAP.

However, it is important to note that WSDL is not directly dependent on SOAP and HTTP. The WSDL specification also provides
example mappings of WSDL descriptions onto a number of other
Web protocols that can be used for passing parameters and results,
including URL-encoded parameter passing in HTTP and multipart
Multi-Purpose Internet Mail Extensions transported via HTTP.

WSDL defines services as collections of network endpoints or ports.
Figure 5.4 illustrates that in WSDL the abstract definition of endpoints and messages is separated from their concrete network-based
data bindings. Abstracting away specific connection details allows
reuse of abstract definitions of messages, which themselves are
abstract descriptions of the data being exchanged. Also in this picture are port types, which are abstract collections of operations.

*WSDL ports define
data bindings.*

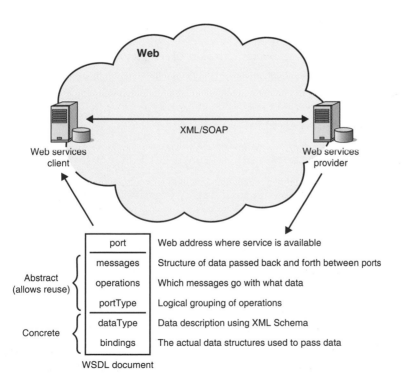

Figure 5.4 **The
structure of a
WSDL document.**

In WSDL, the concrete protocol and data format specifications for a particular port type constitute a reusable binding. A port is defined by associating a network address with a reusable binding. In this way, the reusable abstraction is brought together with a concrete implementation allowing for implementation details to change while keeping the service abstraction the same.

A ZwiftBooks WSDL Example

ZwiftBooks defines its WSDL so clients can connect.

ZwiftBooks has decided to move its service offering into the realm of Web services and to develop a WSDL description that others can use to connect to a ZwiftBooks server to find the time of delivery for a book within a specific zip code. For ZwiftBooks, the basic idea is to describe not just the messages used in a communication exchange but to tie them together as request-response pairs.

Port Types and Operations

In WSDL, the messages between client and server are described by defining an `operation` element that specifies which message serves as the input and which message acts as the output, as in the following example:

```
<operation name='GetDeliveryInfo'
    parameterOrder='zipcode isbn'>
    <input message='wsdlns:ZBooks.GetDeliveryInfo'/>
    <output
    message='wsdlns:ZBooks.GetDeliveryInfoResponse'/>
</operation>
```

Note that the `operation` element specifies the request and response as `input` and `output` elements. Each refers to a corresponding message by its fully qualified name, such as `wsdlns:ZBooks.GetDeliveryInfo`.

In WSDL, the collection of all operations (that is, methods) exposed by the ZwiftBooks service is called a portType and is defined using the WSDL `portType` element, which packages the `operation` element.

```
<portType name='ZBooksSoapPort'>
<operation name='GetDeliveryInfo'
    parameterOrder='zipcode isbn>
    <input message='wsdlns:ZBooks.GetDeliveryInfo'/>
    <output
    message='wsdlns:ZBooks.GetDeliveryInfoResponse'/>
</operation>
<!-- other ZwiftBooks operations would be listed here -->
</portType>
```

From Abstraction to Reality

In the above example we've described in abstract terms what a ZwiftBooks service does. However, nothing has been said about how a client is expected to deliver an ISBN number or a zipcode. Should they be in the form of integers, strings, or special data types? Because WSDL messages rely on SOAP for delivery, and because SOAP uses XML Schema for data types, WSDL also relies on XML Schema. Thus, to define the concrete aspects of an operation, we use the WSDL `binding` element:

WSDL bindings represent concrete connections.

```
<binding name='ZBooksSoapBinding'
    type='wsdlns:ZBooksSoapPort' >
. . .
</binding>
```

The binding name is arbitrary, but the name for the binding attribute on the `port` element must match whatever name we use here. Inside the `binding` element there is a WSDL SOAP extension element called `soap:binding` that is used to specify the transport protocol—such as HTTP, Simple Mail Transport Protocol (SMTP), or FTP—and whether we want clients to invoke a remote procedure call (RPC) at our site or just send an XML document.

For example, to indicate to potential clients that they should invoke a method on our ZwiftBooks server, we add the `style='rpc'` attribute and value to the `soap:binding` element:

```
<soap:binding style='rpc'
        transport='http://schemas.xmlsoap.org/soap/http'/>
```

To define an operation, we add an `operation` element with the same name as the previously defined operation. Within this `operation` element, we now add a `soap:operation` element with the `soapAction` attribute. Finally, we must specify how the input and output messages of this operation are encoded. The complete binding looks like this:

```
<binding name='ZBooksSoapBinding'
        type='wsdlns:ZBooksSoapPort'>
 <soap:binding
     style='rpc'
     transport='http://schemas.xmlsoap.org/soap/http'/>
 <operation name='GetDeliveryInfo'>

 <soap:operation
   soapAction='http://zbooks.org/action/ZBooks.
                Get-DeliveryInfo'/>
  <input>
    <soap:body
      use='encoded'
      namespace='http://zbooks.org/message/'
      encodingStyle='http://schemas.xmlsoap.org/soap/
                        encoding/'/>
  </input>
  <output>
    <soap:body
      use='encoded'
      namespace='http://zbooks.org/message/'
      encodingStyle='http://schemas.xmlsoap.org/soap/
                        encoding/'/>
```

```
  </output>
 </operation>
</binding>
```

Within the operation we add input and output elements and a
soap:body element to specify the actual data encoding. The URI
http://schemas.xmlsoap.org/soap/encoding/ indicates the SOAP
encoding style as described in the SOAP specification. Now the
WSDL file is complete and ZwiftBooks clients can begin to use it to
figure out how to connect to the ZwiftBooks SOAP server and begin
to use ZwiftBooks services. While there are many steps and pieces
involved in defining a WSDL descriptor of a service, much of the
complexity is handled by support tools that are part of Web Services
delivery environments.

Web Services Caveats

The Web services effort to take the Web to new levels of server-to-
server interaction is generating significant excitement across the
software industry. Web services is a unique venture that sees competitive rivals coming together to evolve a technology in parallel,
with vendors pushing the technology and setting standards. However, as with any technological innovation, while it addresses some
immediate problems of the past, it comes with new problems of its
own that we must recognize and understand, lest we rush in blindly.
For Web services there are a number of risks (see Figure 5.5).

Web services risks.

Maturity

There is always risk in being an early adopter of any new technology. The key building blocks underlying Web services—UDDI,
SOAP, and WSDL—are based on written English-language specifications, and there is risk that implementations from different vendors
will suffer incompatibilities.

*Different
implementations
may not work
together.*

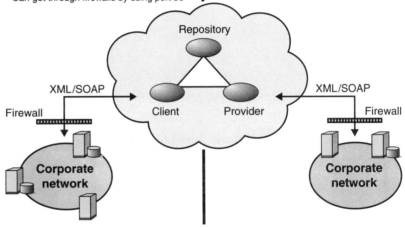

Figure 5.5 **The pros and cons of Web services.**

Web services

Pros

- Global method for describing and finding Internet-based business services
- Packaging and publishing of applications in a readily understandable format
- New revenue streams made possible through syndication of existing application as Web services
- Capability for customized connections between business partnerships
- Can get through firewalls by using port 80

Cons

- New technology
- Tracking changes (configuration management)
- Transactions not addressed
- Security not addressed
- Can get through firewalls by using port 80

Security

SOAP messages on port 80 bypass firewalls.

Security is essential to a thriving e-commerce world and, while Web services does not specifically address security issues, the fact that it operates over the Web means that it can utilize existing Web secure communication capabilities such as the Secure Sockets Layer and X.509 protocols. However, because SOAP running over HTTP will use the standard Web server port 80, it places new burdens on system administrators to deal with traffic that easily moves through firewalls.

Another issue related to security involves XML, which is at the heart of all Web services communication, via SOAP, UDDI, WSDL, and the delivery of XML data. While at one level XML is just data, there are special security issues that are particular to XML that must be addressed by both users and providers of Web services. For example, I may want to encrypt or digitally sign only part of a SOAP message because I want a SOAP intermediary to be able to add something to the message but not read a small part I want to keep secret. These new issues arise with Web services because of XML and SOAP. (See Chapter 7 for details.)

Transactions

The ability to wrap Web services in transactions is critical to its success. Without the all-or-none property of complex interactions, it's not possible to do serious e-business on the Web. While Web services does not itself address transactions as part of the Web services initiative, transactional capabilities are available by integrating Web services with the opportunities provided by middleware frameworks—such as .NET or Java 2 Enterprise Edition—or by connections to mainframe-based transaction monitors such as Customer Information Control System. These issues are discussed in more detail in Chapter 6.

Transactions must be specified outside the Web services framework.

Configuration Management

Configuration management has been a nasty problem for software since the first commercial program went from release 1.0 to release 1.1. For complex software products, keeping compatible versions of constantly evolving modules in sync with each other is a continual, nagging problem. Many of the frustrations with the Windows operating system come after installing new software and experiencing the agony of "DLL Hell," as it's affectionately referred to in the industry. The dynamic link library (DLL) problem occurs when installing new software that requires updates to one or more system DLLs. After the updates are made, existing software that requires

Change management is not addressed.

the older DLL no longer works because it has not been updated to handle the new DLL. It's a tricky problem with no easy solution.

There is a similar potential problem lurking behind Web services. For example if company X provides a Web service that depends on a Web service from company Y, and company Y changes the interface to its service, then unless company X receives notice of the change in time to adjust its own software, company X's Web service will fail.

ebXML

ebXML adds process to e-business interaction.

As we've seen, the Web services architecture is based on repositories that allow businesses to find each other and begin to interact over the web. Using a repository as a central information source is an effective way to reduce the difficulty clients and businesses have in finding each other. However, the Web services approach isn't the only way to organize interactions around a repository. Another approach that also uses repositories to line up business partners is ebXML. Electronic Business XML represents a global initiative to define processes around which business can interact over the Web. It is a technology aimed at bringing the benefits of B2B data exchange to a global audience of small, medium, and large businesses. The broad effort of ebXML includes multiple specifications that define standard ways of exchanging business messages, conducting trading relationships, communicating data in common terms, and defining and registering business processes.

UN/CEFACT and OASIS are key players behind ebXML.

The key players behind ebXML are the United Nations Centre for Trade Facilitation and Electronic Business, the technical and e-business group responsible for developing and promoting global business processes and tools, and the Organization for the Advancement of Structured Information Standards (OASIS), the international, non-profit consortium of technology companies formed to promote open, collaborative development of interoperability specifications based on standards such as XML and Standard Generalized Markup Language.

The first phase of the ebXML initiative, having met its 18-month deadline in May 2001, has received wide industry support. It continues to gain support from a variety of sources and other standards organizations, including the following groups:

❑ RosettaNet, a consortium of more than 400 companies in information technology, electronics, and semiconductor manufacturing, plans to integrate the ebXML Messaging Services Specification into future releases of its XML-based B2B initiative.

❑ Two Electronic Data Interchange (EDI) standards groups—the Accredited Standards Committee X12 and the United Nations Directories for Electronic Data Interchange for Administration, Commerce and Transport Working Group—have announced support for the ebXML effort to establish a set of core components for global business-process integration.

❑ The Global Commerce Initiative, representing manufacturers and retailers, has selected ebXML as the basis for its trading exchanges and B2B communications.

❑ The Open Applications Group Inc. has announced that it will incorporate the ebXML specifications into more than 180 business transaction standards it now supports.

❑ Other industry groups that have embraced ebXML include the Automotive Industry Action Group, Health Level Seven, and the Open Travel Alliance.

ebXML Technologies

Electronic Business XML is based on a set of building blocks that makes use of existing standards wherever possible. The ebXML specifications have been developed through a worldwide volunteer effort in a

ebXML is inclusive of small and large businesses.

process that is open and transparent. Anyone, anywhere with a computer and Internet connection may participate in the ebXML initiatives.

The technical architecture consists of several pieces:

❑ *Messaging:* ebXML uses SOAP to send messages.

❑ *Business processes:* ebXML distinguishes itself from other XML frameworks through its emphasis on business processes. Modeling languages and charting tools such as the Unified Modeling Language (UML) are used to standardize and capture the flow of business data among trading partners.

❑ *Trading partner profiles and agreements:* ebXML defines an XML-based Collaboration Protocol Profile (CPP) to list supported industries, business processes, messages, and data-exchange technologies.

❑ *Registries and repositories:* Registries contain the industry processes, messages, and vocabularies that define the transactions that occur between trading partners.

❑ *Core components:* Core components operate at the data level to provide interoperability among industries and identify the data items that businesses use most often across industries, assigning them neutral names and unique identifiers.

ZwiftBooks and ebXML

ZwiftBooks uses ebXML to define a process for doing business.

As we can see in Figure 5.6, ZwiftBooks first reviews the contents of an ebXML registry to determine the requirements for an ebXML implementation appropriate for the publishing industry. Having determined the appropriateness of relevant ebXML transaction definitions, ZwiftBooks decides to buy rather than internally generate the software needed to support the anticipated ebXML transactions.

The next step is for ZwiftBooks to create and register a CPP with the ebXML registry. If ZwiftBooks has found a suitable Business Process

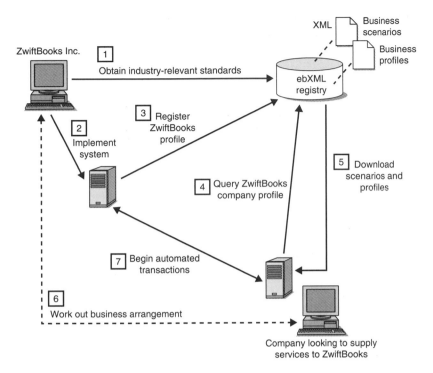

Figure 5.6 The steps in an ebXML-driven business process.

in the registry, it will use it; otherwise it will define a process peculiar to its way of doing business and register it in the registry. The net effect will be sufficient information in the CPP for potential partners to determine the business roles in which ZwiftBooks is interested and the type of protocols it expects from its potential partners.

When ZwiftBooks has registered its CPP, other companies can query the ebXML repository to determine compatibility. If the potential partner determines that partnering is feasible, negotiation can proceed based on conformance to the CPPs. While it may be ideal to have all this occur automatically online, the reality of partnering will likely involve person-to-person interaction before final deals are signed. Once agreement has been reached, the two companies can begin doing business and engaging in transactions.

ebXML Terminology

Registry: A central server that stores a variety of data necessary to make ebXML work. Among the information a registry makes available in XML form are Business Process and Information Meta Models, the Core Library, Collaboration Protocol Profiles, and the Business Library. Basically, when a business wants to start an ebXML relationship with another business, it queries a registry in order to locate a suitable partner and to find information about requirements for dealing with that partner.

Business Processes: Activities that a business can engage in and for which it would generally want one or more partners. A Business Process is formally described by the Business Process Specification Schema (a World Wide Web Consortium [W3C] XML Schema and also a document type definition), but may also be modeled in UML.

Collaboration Protocol Profile (CPP): A profile filed with a registry by a business wishing to engage in ebXML transactions. The CPP will specify some Business Processes of the business, as well as some Business Service Interfaces it supports.

Business Service Interface: The ways that a business is able to carry out the transactions necessary in its Business Processes. The Business Service Interface also includes the kinds of Business Messages the business supports and the protocols over which these messages might travel.

Business Messages: The actual information communicated as part of a business transaction. A message contains multiple layers. At the outside layer, an actual communication protocol must be used, such as HTTP or SMTP. SOAP is an ebXML recommendation as an envelope for a message payload. Other layers may deal with encryption or authentication.

Core Library: A set of standard parts that may be used in larger ebXML elements. For example, Core Processes may be referenced by Business Processes. The Core Library is contributed by the ebXML initiative itself, while larger elements may be contributed by specific industries or businesses.

Collaboration Protocol Agreement (CPA): In essence, a contract between two or more businesses that can be derived automatically from the CPPs of the respective companies. If a CPP says "I can do X," a CPA says "We will do X together."

SOAP: The W3C protocol for exchange of information in a distributed environment endorsed by the ebXML initiative. Of interest for ebXML is SOAP's function as an envelope that defines a framework for describing what is in a message and how to process it.

Summary

Web services is an effort to take the Web from a content delivery network for server-human interaction to a network for server-to-server interaction where software packaged as services can be registered, discovered, and connected to. At the heart of Web services is a repository for maintaining information about services and two key protocols, UDDI for registration and discovery and WSDL for figuring out how to connect to existing services. But UDDI and WSDL are not the only ways to give structure to the decentralized, distributed Web space made possible by SOAP. For example, ebXML builds on UDDI and SOAP to structure business data exchange around business processes and semantics that allow companies of all sizes to leverage the power of the Web. Also, as Web services mature and proliferate, intermediaries acting as Web service hubs will emerge that will insert themselves between service consumers and providers. Such hubs will act as agents and brokers, utilizing UDDI and WSDL while presenting a simple service interface to their clients.

Resources

http://www.webservicesarchitect.com/
"Web Services Architect" is an electronic journal focusing on the concerns of technical professionals designing systems based on Web services. The goal is to help develop the Web services community and contribute to the collective noise as that community finds its voice. The site includes insightful articles that focus on Web services and how the technology is being implemented and received by businesses.

http://www.uddi.org/
The official UDDI Web site.

http://www.ebxml.org/
The official ebXML Web site promoting XML and process-driven interaction for organizations of all sizes.

http://www.w3.org/TR/wsdl
WSDL as understood by the W3C.

http://www.devxpert.com/tutors/wsdl/wsdl.asp
A tutorial on WSDL.

**http://www.internetnews.com/wd-news/article/
0,,10_789091,00.html**
"OASIS Forges ebXML Technical Committees," by Clint Boulton.

**http://www.javaworld.com/javaworld/javaone00/
j1-00-ebxml.html**
"How ebXML plays in global trade," by Brett McLaughlin.

**http://www-106.ibm.com/developerworks/xml/library/
x-ebxml/**
"Understanding ebXML," by David Metz.

http://www.itworld.com/nl/xml_prac/
XML Newsletter Archive.

http://www.xmethods.com/
"X Methods" lists publicly available Web services and their SOAP
access interfaces.

http://www-106.ibm.com/developerworks/webservices/
IBM's Web Services Zone.

6

.NET, J2EE, and Beyond

*The Web services battle lines are shaping up along two fronts: Microsoft
on one side with its .NET initiative centered around Microsoft server technology, and Sun on the other side with Java 2 Enterprise Edition (J2EE)
architecture, backed by competing implementations from Sun, IBM, Oracle,
HP, BEA, and others. To understand the dynamics of the industry, it's
important to understand that while the key Web services protocols, including Simple Object Access Protocol (SOAP), Universal Description, Discovery,
and Integration (UDDI), and Web Services Definition Language (WSDL),
provide transport, discovery, and connections, they do not address other
critical requirements for the electronic enterprise: transactions, security,
and identity. Transactions allow multiple interactions to be treated as a
single atomic all-or-none operation, security enables privacy and authentication for those transactions, and identity provides a means for verifying
who's who over the Internet.*

*In the following sections we look at Microsoft's .NET initiative as well as
the Web services-related strategies of Sun Microsystems, IBM, Oracle, and
BEA Systems. As the battle for developer mind share in the Web services
market continues, each of the major software companies is attempting to
play to its strength and deliver SOAP-based Web services products that
deliver transactions, security, and identity while playing to their own
particular corporate strengths.*

SOAP, Web Services, and E-Commerce

The widespread use of SOAP as a distributed protocol for communicating across the Web and the emergence of Web services as a technology that adds structure to the open space of the Web have added

*SOAP opens up new
options for distributed
computing.*

a new dimension to the traditional enterprise computing model, based on middleware and application servers tied to tightly coupled networks. As Figure 6.1 shows, the opening up of the Web frontier to server-to-server SOAP-based interactions has fundamentally changed the computing landscape through the addition of loosely coupled message-based architectures.

Web-based e-commerce needs transaction capability.

However, making this loosely coupled Web space commercially viable for service-based interaction requires transactional capabilities to ensure consistency across networks, security to protect transactions, and some way to manage identity in open networks. What makes the

Figure 6.1 SOAP and Web services open up new possibilities for interaction.

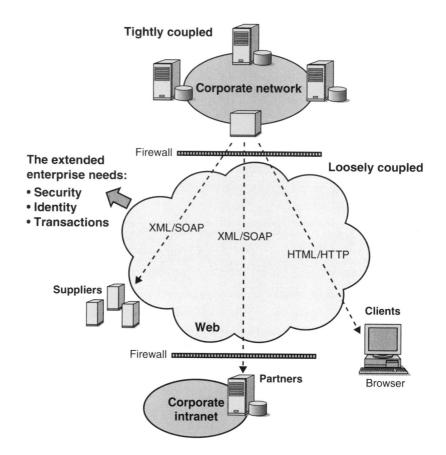

scramble to get aboard the SOAP and Web services train interesting is that much of the capability for insuring a secure, transaction-aware Web comes from middleware that has its roots in tightly coupled object systems.

To help understand the forces at play in the emerging world of SOAP and Web services it's important to explain why transactions, security, and identity are critical to the success of the new Web environment where we now find ourselves.

Transactions

Transactions are a key aspect of any electronic commerce endeavor. A transaction is a set of software operations that share what is known as the ACID properties of transactions: atomicity, consistency, isolation, and durability.

The ACID properties of transactions.

- *Atomicity* requires that all operations of a transaction be performed successfully in order for the transaction to be considered complete. If all of a transaction's operations cannot be performed, then none of them may be performed.

- *Consistency* refers to data consistency: a transaction must transition the data from one consistent state to another while preserving the data's semantic and physical integrity.

- *Isolation* requires that each transaction appear to be the only transaction currently manipulating the data. Other transactions may run concurrently, but other transactions should not see the intermediate data resulting from other concurrent transactions until they have successfully completed and committed their work. Isolation protects a transaction from working with changes to data that can be rolled back.

- *Durability* means that updates made by committed transactions persist in the database regardless of failures that occur after the commit operation. Thus, if a system crashes after a transaction has committed, the data changes associated with that transaction are always recoverable.

Because transactions are essential for any Web-based e-commerce infrastructure, all the major software vendors are lining up behind transaction monitors, the software that provides runtime services such as thread and connection pooling, object creation and storage services, state management, and standard interfaces to a variety of back-end databases.

Security

The Internet relies on several security protocols.

Secure communication is another essential aspect of any Web-based enterprise computing architecture. For Web-based e-commerce, the Secure Sockets Layer and Transport Layer Security protocols have been successful in verifying the authentication of Web sites, encrypting the transfer of data, and ensuring the integrity of information exchange.

XML has specialized security requirements.

However, transporting XML over SOAP creates new challenges for managing secure communication over loosely coupled networks, particularly when only parts of an XML message need to be encrypted or verified. Such is the case, for example, when multiple SOAP agents must interact with a document in different ways on its path from sender to receiver. Since neither SOAP nor Web services protocols address security issues, it falls to implementations relying on .NET or J2EE to add security. Chapter 7 deals with security in more detail, so we'll defer our treatment of security discussion until then.

Identity

Web-based networks need a way to validate users.

The shift from a tightly coupled application model to distributed Web-based computing means a change in focus away from the computer and toward the user. When the machine is the central focus, software licenses that allow a certain piece of software to run legally on a certain machine are the keys to commerce. Without such licenses, the software may not be installed, or if installed, would run illegally.

However, when dealing with users connecting via the Web, it is now the user and not the hardware that needs to be validated. In this new model user authentication becomes a key issue. Thus there is a shift from asking whether a particular software package is licensed to run to asking whether the software is licensed to run for a particular user. To do this requires that the system validate the user based on permissions stored in some database to determine what the user can and can't do.

Currently there are two alternatives for managing user identity: Microsoft's Passport technology and the Sun-backed Liberty Alliance.

Passport

Passport is Microsoft's single-sign-on authentication service that allows users access to participating Web sites. Passport has been integrated with Microsoft's Hotmail email service and is the entry point for Microsoft's .NET My Services (formerly HailStorm), an initiative that targets Web services to consumer applications. Passport also can store credit card and address information as part of a user's account. With access to Passport, users can participate in express purchasing over the Web without having to manually enter their addresses and payment information.

Microsoft's Passport maintains identity across a variety of applications.

However, the central control of user information via Passport has many privacy advocates alarmed and has triggered reaction from other industry players concerned about Microsoft's possible misuse of the potential power wielded by Passport. In response to these concerns, Microsoft has agreed to consider handing over management of Passport to a federated group made up of rivals and corporate partners; details are being worked out as of this writing. The battles shaping up are indicative of the challenges now faced by players in the new Web space.

The Liberty Alliance Project

The Liberty Alliance: an alternative to Passport.

The Liberty Alliance Project is an initiative to provide an alternative to Passport. The goal is to create a single-sign-on, decentralized authentication system for online services, accessible from any Internet-enabled device. With Liberty, the objective is to create a universal digital identity service based on open standards. Users will be able to log in once on a given Web site and be authenticated for all online services supporting the Liberty standard. The plan is for customer data, such as phone numbers, addresses, credit records, and payment information, to be secure.

.NET and J2EE

.NET and J2EE are frameworks for enterprise puting.

Figure 6.2 illustrates the relationship between the loosely coupled environment of the Web and the tightly coupled object-based frameworks that have been subsumed by .NET and J2EE. For example, bringing transactional integrity to SOAP-based data interchanges across Web space requires connections to transaction engines running under tightly coupled networks. Thus, the challenge for next-generation systems is to bridge the gap between the two worlds: the Web with its promise of global connectivity and more conventional middleware that holds the key to transactions, security, and identity. This is in essence the battle of titans that we now see shaping up between Microsoft's .NET and a host of rivals with implementations based on Sun's J2EE.

J2EE and .NET offer options for transactions, security, and identity.

While they are often compared with each other, .NET and J2EE have fundamental differences that make direct comparison difficult. Microsoft's .NET represents the implementation of a complete enterprise architecture tuned to the Windows platform. J2EE, on the other

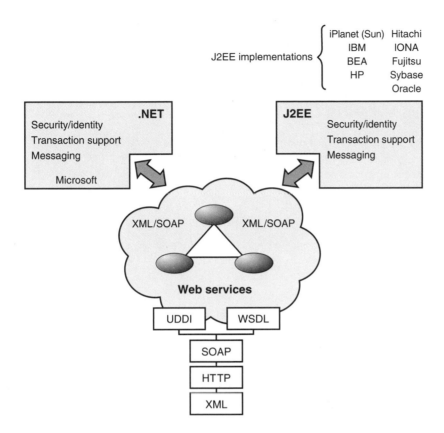

Figure 6.2
Microsoft's .NET and Sun's J2EE are the main architectural rivals for bridging the gap between loosely coupled Web services and more tightly coupled middle-tier services. One challenge is how to reconcile the global reach of the Web with the requirement for transactional integrity provided by more conventional middleware.

hand, is a specification of architectural components designed to work together to define a complete enterprise architecture. However, because J2EE is a specification, it requires implementation from vendors such as Sun, IBM, BEA, Oracle, and HP. These companies turn the Java-based J2EE specification into code and, not surprisingly, provide additional functionality based on the strengths of their individual product lines.

To better understand the forces at play in the battle for the enterprise heartland, let's look at Microsoft's .NET implementation and J2EE as implemented by Sun, IBM, BEA, Oracle, and HP.

.NET

.NET: a Microsoft framework.

Microsoft's .NET is an umbrella term that describes Microsoft's strategy for delivering software as services across the Web. Microsoft realized early the importance of XML for the Web and began adjusting its corporate focus from a Windows-centric view of the world to a more outward-looking Web perspective. Its early B2B BizTalk initiative used XML to move data between partners, which may explain its early interest in XML Remote Procedure Call (XML-RPC) and SOAP (see Chapter 5).

.NET is based on earlier Microsoft technology.

The .NET initiative represents a development framework that integrates earlier Microsoft technologies with newer technologies built around XML. The result is an integrated framework focused on the Internet that packages the component services of the earlier extension to the Component Object Model known as COM+ and the Active Server Pages (ASP) Web development framework with XML and support for XML protocols such as SOAP, WSDL, and UDDI.

An important aspect of .NET is that it allows developers to build a service-oriented consciousness into software up front rather than as an afterthought. Microsoft is also repackaging many of its Web-based applications—such as the Hotmail email service, Passport Internet authentication technology, and MSN Messenger instant messaging client—as Web services building blocks.

The .NET architecture includes several technology components:

❑ *Development tools:* A set of languages, including C# and VB.NET; a set of development tools, including VisualStudio.NET; a comprehensive class library for building Web services and Web and Windows applications; as well as the Common Language Runtime (CLR) to execute objects built within this framework

❑ *Specialized servers:* A set of .NET Enterprise Servers that provide specialized functionality for relational data storage, email, and B2B commerce

❑ *Web services:* Support services such as Passport and .NET My Services that let developers build applications that require knowledge of user identity

❑ *Devices:* New .NET-enabled non-PC devices, from cell phones to game boxes. Microsoft is devoting considerable resources to the development and success of .NET and related technologies; their bets are on .NET as the next big thing in computing.

The .NET Platform

Figure 6.3 illustrates the Microsoft .NET Platform, which consists of five main components. At the lowest layer lies the operating system, which can be one of a variety of Windows platforms, including Windows XP, Windows 2000, Windows ME, or Windows CE. As part of the .NET strategy, Microsoft is planning to deliver more .NET device software to facilitate a new generation of smart devices.

.NET is designed for Windows platforms.

Sitting on top of the operating system is a series of .NET Enterprise Servers as well as a number of building-block services available for applications and developers. Services include Passport and .NET My Services, which support authentication and personalization while providing a consistent user experience. Microsoft appears committed to add other services, including calendar, directory, and search, to its Web services offerings. It is expected that third-party vendors will follow suit and provide Web services of their own.

At the top layer of the .NET architecture is VisualStudio.NET (also called VS.NET). VS.NET is designed to support the rapid development of Web services through an Integrated Development Environment

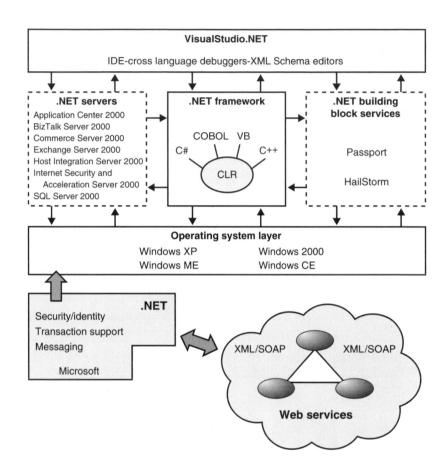

Figure 6.3 The Microsoft .NET Platform.

(IDE) that supports multiple languages, cross-language debugging, and an XML Schema Editor for defining XML vocabularies.

The .NET Framework

A Common Language Runtime supports different languages for .NET development.

At the center of .NET is the .NET Framework, a development and run-time environment for developing business applications on the Windows platform. Key ingredients of the .NET Framework are CLR and a common framework of classes that can be used by all .NET languages. The .NET Framework is architected around a unified hub-and-spoke programming model designed to make different languages interchangeable. This allows development organizations to mix and match languages based on the availability of skills, expertise, and task requirements. In VisualStudio.NET, developers can automate the deployment of applications or components as Web services by simply marking a check box in the development environment. Additionally, all programming documentation is generated as XML documents, making project information and metadata easy to share with other developers, departments, or external business partners.

The Common Language Runtime

The .NET approach to software integration is based on a hub-and-spoke configuration where a variety of languages are translated into a CLR. Figure 6.3 illustrates how multiple languages may be used to generate a common Intermediate Language (IL) that is at the core of the CLR framework. The .NET IL is similar to Java's platform-neutral byte codes that can be ported across platforms.

With .NET all languages translate into a CLR.

For example, during the development of a complex application that involves the use of legacy systems, part of the application could be written in a .NET-compliant version of COBOL while other pieces might be written in C# and Visual Basic. The entire application, using a mix of languages, could be translated into IL, a compiled language at the heart of the CLR framework. Then the IL could be compiled to native code using a just-in-time compiler that precompiles frequently used code fragments. The developer could then check off whether the application would be deployed as a Web service. If so, the logic would be communicated automatically via SOAP and would be able to use emerging Web services standard application program interfaces (APIs) such as WSDL and UDDI.

COBOL may be used to develop .NET applications.

What about Transactions?

Microsoft has long understood the importance of transactions for enterprise computing. In the early 1990s, Microsoft began working

MTS is the Microsoft transaction engine.

on its own transaction software for its middleware effort. The result was the Microsoft Transaction Server (MTS), designed to carry out basic runtime services such as ensuring all parts of a transaction occur in an all-or-none fashion, managing thread and connection pooling, and handling state management. Their transaction software was based on a Object Transaction Monitor, integrating the capabilities of a Transaction-Processing Monitor with distributed object services. The result was a transaction engine that serves as a container for components running in the middle tier of a three-tier application. This is also the approach followed by Sun in the design of their J2EE middleware.

Unlike early programming with transaction monitors, MTS does not require developers to insert complex transaction-processing code directly into their programs. Developers do not have to write the classic `begin transaction, end transaction`. Instead, the programmer adds a `transaction` attribute of `component`'s class.

J2EE

J2EE is the Java-centric enterprise platform specification.

J2EE is a standard for building robust enterprise applications based on an evolving vision of application-server technology centered around the Java programming language. It has historically been used to build Web sites and applications around Enterprise JavaBeans (EJB). Recently it has been extended to include support for XML and Web services.

J2EE is now part of a collaborative process.

While J2EE originated with Sun, changes to the J2EE specification are under the collaborative umbrella of the Java Community Process with input from vendors who have J2EE-compliant server products. Also as part of the Java Community Process, Sun is rolling out its Web Services Pack, a combination of applications and APIs designed to integrate Sun's Java programming language with XML and Web services. The Web Services Pack, illustrated in Figure 6.4, includes the following APIs:

❑ *Java API for XML Processing (JAXP):* JAXP gives developers flexibility by letting them easily swap out XML parsers, which they may want to do if a parser that performs better for their application becomes available. Without JAXP, it's easy to get locked into one vendor's XML parser.

❑ *Java Architecture for XML Binding (JAXB):* JAXB is a Java API and toolset for creating two-way mapping between XML documents and Java objects. JAXB simplifies the task of going from an XML document type definition or schema and creating a program to process a conformant XML document. For example, an XML schema for mortgage banking created by the Mortgage Industry Standards Maintenance Organization (MISMO) is used by the mortgage industry to exchange loan information.

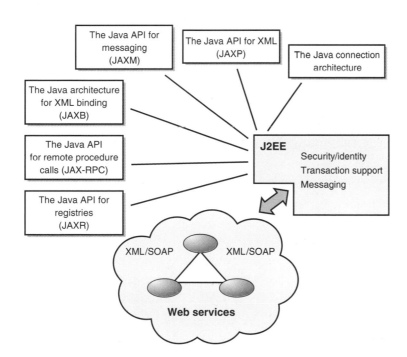

Figure 6.4 **The Web services pack.**

JAXB enables the creation of Java classes from the schema that will support the processing of XML data encoded in the MISMO format. Prior to JAXB, programmers were required to write Java code to format the parsed XML data into Java objects based on the XML schema. JAXB greatly simplifies the process, which was complex, error prone, and often not portable.

❏ *Java API for XML Messaging (JAXM):* JAXM is designed to allow access to emerging XML messaging standards such as Electronic Business XML (ebXML) Transport/Packaging and Routing. It typically will be used along with JAX-RPC, which will give Java programmers a single interface to any XML-based Remote Procedure Call (RPC) mechanism, including the SOAP standard. Although SOAP is the acknowledged XML transport standard for Web services, developers using JAX-RPC will be better able to switch to any future XML-based RPC mechanism.

❏ *Java API for XML Remote Procedure Calls (JAX-RPC):* JAX-RPC is the API for doing XML-based procedure calls via XML-RPC in Java. XML-RPC allows one network node to execute code on another node by transferring XML data. XML-RPC is discussed in detail in Chapter 4.

❏ *Java API for XML Registries (JAXR):* JAXR provides a uniform standard interface to registries of XML business data such as the UDDI protocol. JAXR simplifies the development of e-business applications that can register and extract data from various registries, including those used with the ebXML modular business framework for global e-commerce.

Different vendors implement J2EE.

Vendors with server products that are based on J2EE include Sun, IBM, BEA, Oracle, and HP. Each vendor provides additional features not found in the J2EE specification, which may create problems for organizations looking to switch J2EE vendors. In the following sections, we'll look at how some vendors have used J2EE to integrate their application server offerings with the world of Web services.

Sun ONE and Web Services

Sun has been quick to respond to Microsoft's embrace of XML and Web services (although it can be argued that Sun's initial cautious attitude toward XML is attributable to its solid positioning on the code side of the code-data divide discussed in Chapter 1). Sun's answer to Microsoft's .NET is Sun ONE, the Sun Open Net Environment, a framework for creating and deploying Web services from Sun's J2EE framework. Sun ONE is intended to be a template for interoperability between various devices and networks, bridging the gap between the loosely coupled Web and more tightly coupled object frameworks. To bring things together it relies on XML, SOAP, and Java to add Web services extensions from within J2EE. For developers, this means that from a Sun perspective Web services will be built using servlets, Java Server Pages, and EJB technology.

Sun ONE: Sun's J2EE implementation

The integration of Web services with more conventional middleware offerings is based on Sun's iPlanet integration platform that incorporates Java, SOAP, and XML and supports message queuing for asynchronous message routing between disparate applications.

IBM

IBM, an early player in the Web services arena, was an original partner with Microsoft and Ariba in the rollout of the UDDI specification that is used for the registration and discovery of Web services. IBM has also been a longstanding proponent of XML and has been extremely active in the development of XML support tools. The IBM AlphaWorks Web site contains numerous tools for working with XML and Web services. IBM was one of the first companies to make its Java XML4J parser widely available, and its UDDI4J Java-based toolkit for working with UDDI has been made open source. IBM also has implemented a UDDI registry at http://www.ibm.com/services/uddi.

IBM is active in Web services.

Unlike Microsoft's .NET or Sun ONE, IBM does not have an umbrella term that it uses to describe its Web services offerings. IBM's Web services initiative centers around its middleware and development tools. Its centerpiece Web services offering is its WebSphere application server that includes the Web services protocols and standards. Associated with WebSphere are tools that facilitate the creation of Web services.

IBM has based its Web services–aware WebSphere application server around J2EE.

The WebSphere software platform, built around J2EE, delivers a full set of APIs for XML, enterprise Java, and Web services. IBM's experience and background with mainframe computing lets them provide these services across a range of platforms, including Microsoft Windows NT, Linux, HP-UX, and IBM S/390.

IBM's WebSphere middleware server supports the development, deployment, and integration of e-business applications from Web publishing to transaction processing. Within WebSphere, IBM leverages its longstanding experience in transaction processing with its Customer Information Control System (CICS) to provide high transaction throughput in its MQSeries middleware that integrates Java's EJB, CORBA, and Web services technologies.

ECLIPSE

IBM's Web services integration centers around WebSphere Studio, a toolset built using Eclipse, an open-source, Java-based software platform designed for building IDEs. Eclipse is an effort to reduce the complexity associated with building applications that rely on other applications and services. With Eclipse, a specialized IDE can be constructed that draws on the services of other toolsets from different vendors. Developers can build more complex applications by working with only one IDE rather than having to master multiple tools and travel up the learning curves associated with each.

From a collaborative Web perspective, IBM's Eclipse effort is very much in keeping with the underlying software philosophy of the Web that says, in effect, "keep it simple and assemble complexity." The Eclipse effort is supported by more than 150 toolmakers so that Web-service development with the WebSphere Studio toolset can be integrated with a variety of different tools that will be built using Eclipse technology standards.

BEA

BEA is an application service provider that targets businesses seeking complete e-business solutions. Their flagship product is the BEA WebLogic server, a Java J2EE-based middle-tier server that integrates Web-based front ends with back-end data stores.

BEA brings application server expertise to Web services.

BEA addresses transactions up front, using the terms "complex" and "simple" to distinguish between Web services that do or do not require transactional and security support. The BEA WebLogic E-Business Platform has the following components:

❑ *BEA WebLogic Server:* The WebLogic Server can access and expose simple, single call-and-response Web services using SOAP and XML. It will also support UDDI and WSDL.

❑ *BEA WebLogic Integration:* This BEA component integrates its tightly coupled middleware with complex Web services that require transactional integrity and security. Support is also available for ebXML.

❑ *BEA WebLogic Personalization Server:* The BEA WebLogic Personalization Server will focus on personalization and customization of content and services based on user preferences, prior experience, or preestablished business rules.

HP

HP has long been active in e-services.

HP uses the term "E-Services" for its Web services initiative. HP's work in the Web services arena began in the mid-1990s with a research project known as e-speak, an effort to formulate service-centric computing requirements. HP has been actively involved in many of the Web services standards, including UDDI, the World Wide Web Consortium's XML Protocol initiative, SOAP 1.1, RosettaNet, and ebXML.

The HP Web Services Platform is a software infrastructure for developing and deploying loosely coupled Web services. Such services can be a mixture of internal and external services and may include applications, business processes, computing resources, or data stores. The HP Web Services Platform leverages its early e-speak technology to provide standards-compliant architecture for creating and deploying Web services.

An important component of the HP Web Services Platform is the HP Web Services Registry, which may be used to publish and discover both public and private registries. Services may be composed from existing Java classes, EJBs, or Cocoon applications. Their objective is an interoperable platform that is compatible with multiple messaging infrastructures, including Microsoft's BizTalk and ebXML.

The HP Web Services Platform sits on top of a J2EE-compliant Web server. In 2000, HP purchased Bluestone to position itself in the XML world and is using Bluestone's Web server as the core technology in its Web services initiative.

HP's modular Web services infrastructure runs on top of the J2EE-compliant HP Bluestone application server, providing both tightly coupled J2EE interaction as well as loosely coupled connectivity with a variety of systems including the Microsoft .NET environment.

The HP Web Services Platform is compliant with open standards, allowing users to develop, register, and discover Web services published in UDDI-compliant public registries. HP's offerings are compatible with the main emerging Web services standards, including SOAP, WSDL, and UDDI.

Oracle

Oracle has adapted its database products to fit the demands of the Web services world. The Oracle9*i* Web Services Framework provides an infrastructure that supports the development, management, and deployment of Web services to portals, exchanges, and other Internet and mobile applications. It uses XML as a common access method.

Oracle brings its database expertise to Web services.

The Oracle9*i* Web Services Framework uses a Web services client library written in Java. The client library includes connection drivers for linking to Web services repositories. Oracle9*i* Web-service descriptors can be published as WSDL in other UDDI registries to support Internet-wide service discovery, and services described using WSDL can be imported into the Oracle9*i* Web Services Registry.

Adapters

Oracle uses adapters to extend the basic framework. For example, specialized adapters may be created to build connections with legacy systems. Some of the adapters include

- ❑ *Input and output adapters* for specifying XSLT style sheets to transform service requests to the XML format required by a service
- ❑ *Protocol adapters* to connect with Web services using HTTP, HTTP over Secure Socket Layers, Java Database Connectivity, Simple Mail Transfer Protocol, and SOAP

❑ *Execution adapters* to execute service requests in a particular flow, minimally relaying a request to contact a resource provider, and relaying the response. Standard adapters include simple, compound, failover, and conditional.

Summary

With XML and SOAP providing the data and transport, and Web services providing the protocols for discovery and connection, there still remains the need to incorporate transactions, security, and identity into Web-based, service-oriented applications. For enterprises looking to move into this space there are two main options: Microsoft's .NET framework and the Sun-led J2EE initiative. However, making direct comparisons between .NET and J2EE is a bit like comparing apples and oranges. Microsoft's .NET is a Web services framework that works well on Windows platforms with Windows-based technologies. Sun's J2EE, on the other hand, is a Java-based specification based on the EJB framework, with implementations available from Sun, IBM, BEA, HP, Oracle, and others. While J2EE proponents criticize .NET for its Microsoft lock-in, the competitive marketplace reality is such that different J2EE implementers will inevitably offer complementary services and interfaces that play to individual corporate strengths. This will limit, to some extent, the portability between J2EE solutions. The bottom line is that the choice between .NET and J2EE will always be a choice between product platforms, driven by the services a vendor can provide and a company's vision of its future.

Resources

http://www.microsoft.com/windows2000/technologies/web/default.asp
Microsoft and Web services.

http://java.sun.com/xml/
Sun's Web site for Java and XML technologies.

http://java.sun.com/j2ee/webservices/
Sun's Web site for Java and Web services.

http://www-4.ibm.com/software/solutions/webservices/
IBM's Web services Web site.

http://www.ibm.com/developerworks/webservices
IBM's DeveloperWorks Web Services Zone.

http://www.bluestone.com/products/hp_we_services
HP's Web services site.

**http://www.bea.com/products/weblogic/server/
paper_webservices.shtml**
A BEA white paper discussing their Web services offerings.

**http://technet.oracle.com/products/dynamic_services/
content.html**
A discussion of Oracle's Web services strategies.

http://www.webservices.org
A vendor-neutral site.

http://www.webservicesarchitect.com/
Another vendor-neutral site.

7

XML Security

XML is a flexible data framework that allows applications to communicate across the Internet. In order for XML to be used for e-commerce applications, there must be support for security and trust. Requirements for XML security include confidentiality, authentication, and data integrity. The World Wide Web Consortium (W3C) addresses these issues through XML Encryption and XML Signature, for authenticating merchants, suppliers, and buyers, and for digitally signing and encrypting XML documents. These initiatives make use of public and private keys but do not address the issue of how to trust key providers.

Although security mechanisms such as HyperText Transfer Protocol over Secure Socket Layer (HTTPS) are already in place to provide confidentiality, authentication, and data integrity across the Web, XML transport over Simple Object Access Protocol (SOAP) raises security issues that pertain to XML and its processing. For example, both XML namespaces and entities entail substitutions that are not actually carried out until an XML document arrives at its destination, meaning that the XML in transit is not the same as the XML at its final destination. Issues such as these are addressed through the use of XML canonical forms that capture the essential aspects of an XML document and make it possible to apply security constructs. Issues of trust are handled by XML Key Management Specification (XKMS), which builds on the services of XML Signature and XML Encryption and relies on established certificate authorities (CAs).

Security Overview

Before we examine the issues related to XML security, it's important to understand the basics of e-commerce–based security so we can take note of the special issues introduced by XML. Figure 7.1 illustrates the three basic security requirements for e-business:

- ❏ *Confidentiality:* Ensuring that information is not made available or disclosed to unauthorized individuals, entities, or processes. Someone eavesdropping on a conversation or tapping into a data stream should not be able to understand the communication.
- ❏ *Authentication:* The ability to determine that a message really comes from the listed sender. Closely associated with authentication is nonrepudiation: preventing the originator of a document or communication from denying having sent it. For a business transaction to be valid, neither party should later be able to deny participation.
- ❏ *Data integrity:* Ensuring that when information arrives at its destination it hasn't been tampered with or altered in transit from its original form, either accidentally or deliberately.

These three dimensions of secure e-commerce rest on a foundation of cryptography. All cryptography operates according to the same

Figure 7.1 **The three pillars of secure e-commerce.**

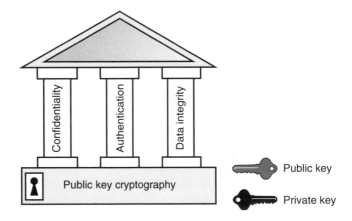

basic principle: some algorithm or formula is used to scramble or encipher information so that it is difficult to determine its meaning without an appropriate key to unscramble or decipher the information. Approaches to cryptography fall into two main categories: single-key encryption, which relies on a single secret key to encode and decode information, and public-key cryptography, which uses two keys, one private and the other public, to encode and decode data.

Single-Key Cryptography

In the past, most encryption systems used a single secret key for encoding and decoding information. However, single-key encryption systems face the problem of making the single key known to the message recipient. During World War II, a similar but more sophisticated scheme was used when letter sequences from pages in popular novels were used as the basis for encrypting messages. However, schemes employing a single key exhibit one fundamental weakness: the decoding key must be somehow communicated from sender to receiver.

Single-key cryptography is the basis for classic encryption.

Whether one uses a letter-offset technique such as replacing "a" with "b," "b" with "c," and so on, or a state-of-the-art 1024-bit encryption key to mathematically compute a substitute letter, there is still the problem of making the key known to the message recipient.

In electronic commerce, single-key systems are effective for secure communication between fixed devices such as ATM machines and servers, since encryption keys can be determined in advance and stored on both the server and the ATM machine. However, single keys don't work well on the Web, where commerce depends on individuals just showing up to do business. For the Web, the answer lies in public-key cryptography.

Single-key cryptography does not scale to the Web.

Public-Key Cryptography

Public-key cryptography is based on complementary public and private keys.

Public-key cryptography enables secure communication between parties *without the need to exchange a secret key*. It is the basis for privacy, authentication, data integrity, and nonrepudiation, the basic elements for any Web-based e-commerce system. Public-key cryptography uses a complex mathematical formula to generate two separate but related keys, one open to public view and the other private, known only to one individual. The complementary public and private keys can be used to handle confidentiality and authentication. Each requires key usage in a slightly different way.

Confidentiality

Encrypting with a public key ensures confidentiality.

Confidentiality in digital communication can be accomplished by using someone's public key to send a message. As Figure 7.2 shows, messages encoded with a public key can be decoded only by the corresponding private key, ensuring that the message is kept confidential. The owner of the private key never has to reveal that key to anyone.

Figure 7.2 Public-key (asymmetric) cryptography uses mathematically generated public and private keys.

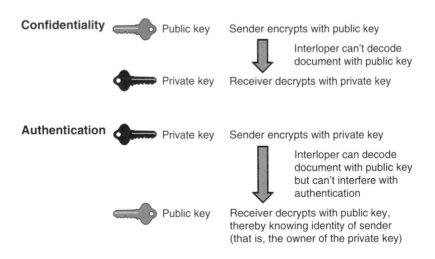

Confidentiality   Public key   Sender encrypts with public key

Interloper can't decode document with public key

Private key   Receiver decrypts with private key

Authentication   Private key   Sender encrypts with private key

Interloper can decode document with public key but can't interfere with authentication

Public key   Receiver decrypts with public key, thereby knowing identity of sender (that is, the owner of the private key)

Authentication

Keeping messages secret is only one aspect of electronic communication. Although a public key guarantees secrecy, it is impossible to authenticate the sender of the message encoded with a public key. However, messages encoded with the private key can be decoded only by the public key, thereby ensuring authentication.

Encrypting with a private key ensures authentication.

Data Integrity

Data integrity ensures that the message received is the message sent. The technology for validating messages is called digital hashing. A digest or digital hash is an algorithmically generated short string of characters that uniquely characterizes a document. As Figure 7.3 shows, if the document changes in any way, recomputing the digest will yield a different result; if the document is copied verbatim, the digest will be exactly the same. Thus, to test the integrity of a document, one compares the digital hash of the original document with that of the version received; if the hashes do not match, the data integrity of the document has been compromised. Although it's theoretically possible

A digest or digital hash represents a unique snapshot of a document.

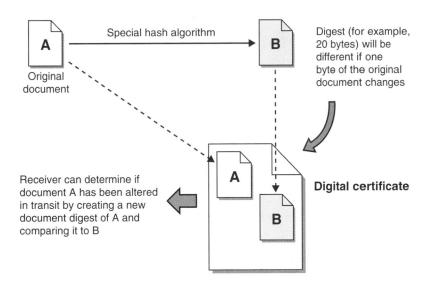

Special hash algorithm

A — Original document

B — Digest (for example, 20 bytes) will be different if one byte of the original document changes

Receiver can determine if document A has been altered in transit by creating a new document digest of A and comparing it to B

Digital certificate

Figure 7.3 A document digest is an algorithmically generated, abbreviated, unique representation of a document. If one character of the document is altered, the document digest will be different.

for two different documents to generate the same digital hash, it's practically impossible to use this fact to defeat the comparison procedure.

Digital Signatures

A digital signature guarantees document authenticity.

A digital signature is like writing your name across the face of a document. A digital signature in combination with public-key encryption is used to authenticate the identity of the sender by encrypting with a private key and to validate the content of the message by transmitting a copy of the digital hash of the message.

Digital signatures can be used in a range of applications from online credit card purchases to the verification of complex legal documents. For example, if you send your will electronically to your attorney in another city, you want the assurance that someone can't intercept it along the way and make changes to it; you want a guarantee that the document that goes into your attorney's file is identical to the one you actually sent, and you want your attorney to have the assurance that the will actually came from you. To accomplish this, you must

1. Write the will
2. Create a digital hash of the will
3. Encrypt both the original will and the digital hash with your private key
4. Send the encrypted document to your attorney

Upon receiving the will, your attorney will

1. Decode the document with your public key, thereby guaranteeing that the will was actually sent by you
2. Compute a digital hash of the document received
3. Compare the resultant digital hash with the hash contained in the message

If the hashes match, the will can safely be recorded; if the hashes do not match, the will has been tampered with.

Managing Certificates and Private Keys

While digital signing is an important technology for ensuring secure e-commerce, keeping certificates and private keys secure remains one of the biggest security challenges. Unlike short passwords, which are usually easy to memorize, private- and public-key pairs are very difficult to memorize because they are mathematically generated. Certificate authorities address the problem of how to be sure that, when your lawyer retrieves your public key, it's really your public key and not someone else's. Certificates are issued by a CA, a trusted entity that manages certificate distribution. If each party in a transaction has a certificate issued from a trusted CA, the transaction can be completed.

Certificate authorities represent trusted entities in Web security.

Once a CA is chosen, certificates from companies signed by that authority are trusted. However, trusting a CA is a matter of choice. Netscape Navigator and Microsoft Internet Explorer come with a list of certificates for some trusted CAs (like Verisign and Entrust). Current versions of both browsers let you manage that list, adding certificates for CAs you trust and removing those you choose not to trust.

When issued, a certificate is given a set life span, for example, 365 days. When it expires, a new certificate must be issued. However, the question of certificate revocation must also be addressed. There are many reasons why a certificate might need to be revoked long before it expires. For example, an e-commerce site may close down, in which case the certificate should be revoked so that it can't be used for improper purposes.

Certificates have limited life spans to allow for changes in circumstance.

Why Is XML Special?

XML's use in Internet e-commerce applications demands the essential ingredients of all electronic security systems: confidentiality, authentication, and data integrity. While public-key cryptography

HTTPS is not sufficient.

provides techniques for meeting all three requirements, there are issues peculiar to XML and SOAP that require approaches that go beyond the basic capabilities provided by existing and widely accepted transport-layer security mechanisms, such as Secure Sockets Layer (SSL) and Transport Layer Security (TLS). The problem is that solutions such as SSL and TLS address only part of the requirements for confidentiality, authentication, and data integrity when an XML-SOAP combination is in use. The following sections describe several scenarios in which the security provided by the various transport-layer mechanisms may not be sufficient.

XML Document Security Issues

XML requires special treatment when encrypting or signing.

The rules of XML allow for some special scenarios that make it difficult to simply encrypt or digitally sign XML, such as the following:

❑ Missing attributes declared to have default values are provided to the application as if present with the default value.

❑ Character references are replaced with the corresponding character.

❑ Entity references are replaced with the corresponding declared entity.

❑ Attribute values are normalized by replacing character and entity references.

❑ Attribute values are also normalized, unless the attribute is declared to be an XML CDATA type (see Appendix A for more on CDATA). When normalized, all leading and trailing spaces are stripped, and all interior runs of spaces are replaced with a single space.

SOAP Security Issues

SOAP messaging raises new issues concerning digitally signing XML.

Just as XML processing brings up special issues related to digitally signing XML documents, SOAP, the common transport protocol for XML, also raises some issues:

❏ SOAP security must illustrate how data can flow through an application and network topology to meet the requirements set by the policies of the business without exposing the data to undue risk.

❏ SOAP security must not mandate specific technology or infra-structure, but must provide for portability, flexibility, interoperability, and heterogeneity.

Digital signatures only work if the calculation of a digital hash is performed on exactly the same bits as the signing calculations. Since noncontent white space can be added to an XML document without changing its meaning, some way to standardize a document must be used before signing and verification. For example, in ASCII text there are three commonly used line endings; we need to permit a signed text to be modified from one line-ending convention to another between the time of signing and signature verification and still be treated as the same document for verification purposes. The solution is to convert the document to some standard canonical form before signing so that surface changes in the document will not break the signature.

XML white space may change while XML content remains the same.

Canonicalization

XML Canonicalization is the use of an algorithm to generate the canonical form of an XML document to ensure security in cases where XML is subject to surface representation changes or to processing that discards some information not essential to the data represented in the XML. Canonicalization addresses the fact that when XML is read and processed using standard XML parsing and processing techniques, some surface representation information may be lost or modified.

A canonical form represents the underlying content of an XML document.

The document that results from XML Canonicalization ensures that all internal entities and XML namespaces are expanded: entities are replaced with their definitions and the canonical form explicitly represents the namespace that an element would otherwise inherit. The steps that take place during the creation of a core canonical form include

❑ Encoding the document in the Universal Character Set UTF-8

❑ Normalizing line breaks before parsing

❑ Normalizing attribute values as if by a validating processor

❑ Replacing character and parsed entity references

❑ Replacing CDATA sections with their character content

❑ Removing the XML declaration and document type declaration (DTD)

❑ Converting empty elements to start-end tag pairs

❑ Normalizing white space outside of the document element and within start and end tags

❑ Retaining all white space in character content (excluding characters removed during line-feed normalization)

❑ Setting attribute value delimiters to quotation marks

❑ Replacing special characters in attribute values and character content by character references

❑ Removing superfluous namespace declarations from each element

❑ Adding default attributes to each element

Once an XML canonical form is obtained, confidentiality, authentication, and data integrity are handled by the XML Security Framework.

The XML Security Framework

The W3C security framework.

The W3C is driving three XML security technologies:

❑ XML Digital Signature

❑ XML Encryption

❑ XML Key Management Services

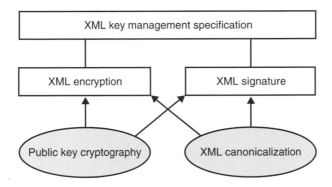

Figure 7.4 **The building blocks of the XML security architecture**

Figure 7-4 and the following paragraphs illustrate how the building blocks interrelate to form the XML security architecture.

XML Encryption

XML Encryption supports the encryption of all or part of an XML document. The specification is flexible enough to allow the encryption of any of the following:

XML Encryption supports encrypting specific parts of an XML document.

❑ The entire XML document

❑ An element and all its subelements

❑ The content of an XML element

❑ A reference to a resource outside the document

Because XML Encryption is not locked into any specific encryption scheme, additional information is provided on

❑ *Encrypted content:* the information itself or a reference to the location of the data

❑ *Key information:* information or a reference to information via a Uniform Resource Identifier (URI) about the keys involved in the encryption

The steps for XML Encryption include:

- ❑ Selecting the XML to be encrypted (all or part of a document)
- ❑ Converting to canonical form if using entities or namespaces with prefixes
- ❑ Encrypting the resulting canonical form using public-key encryption
- ❑ Sending the encrypted XML to the intended recipient

Encrypting XML Data

A credit card example.

The following examples show different ways we can use XML Encryption to encrypt an XML document. Let's take for our example the following XML containing credit card information related to one of John von Neumann's purchases.

```
<?xml version='1.0'?>
<PaymentInfo xmlns='http://globalbank.org'>
  <Name>John von Neumann<Name/>
  <CreditCard Limit='5,000' Currency='USD'>
    <Number>4654 2445 0277 5567</Number>
    <Issuer>World Bank</Issuer>
    <Expiration>04/05</Expiration>
  </CreditCard>
</PaymentInfo>
```

As we'll see in the following examples, the important element in the XML Encryption specification is `EncryptedData`, which contains the `CipherValue` element that holds the actual encrypted value. However, how we use these elements will depend on what part of the XML document we wish to encrypt. The following scenarios illustrate different ways of applying XML Encryption to the XML credit card information.

Scenario 1: XML Subelement and Content Encryption

Our XML example shows that John von Neumann is using a credit card with a limit of $5,000 USD. In this example, because von Neumann's credit card data is sensitive but his name is not, an application can selectively keep only the critical information confidential by encrypting the `CreditCard` element. The resultant XML looks like the following.

```
<?xml version='1.0'?>
<PaymentInfo xmlns='http://globalbank.org'>
   <Name>John von Neumann<Name/>
   <EncryptedData
       Type='http://www.w3.org/2001/04/xmlenc#Element'
           xmlns='http://www.w3.org/2001/04/xmlenc#'>
       <CipherData>
          <CipherValue>
              A23B45C56
          </CipherValue>
       </CipherData>
   </EncryptedData>
</PaymentInfo>
```

By encrypting the entire `CreditCard` element from its start to end tags, the identity of all the elements and the data are hidden. An eavesdropper cannot determine whether von Neumann used a credit card, a check, or a wire transfer. The `CipherData` element contains the `CipherValue` element that encompasses the entire `CreditCard` element including tags and data. Note that the use of the version namespace `http://www.w3.org/2001/04/xmlenc#` is required and that the attribute specification of `Type='http://www.w3.org/2001/04/xmlenc#Element'`, while not required, is recommended so that the recipient can ascertain that an entire element has been encrypted.

Scenario 2: Partial XML Element Encryption

In different circumstances, it may be useful for intermediate agents handling the data along a SOAP message path to know that John von Neumann used a credit card with a particular limit, but they may not need to know the card's number, issuer, and expiration date. In this case, the subelements and content of the CreditCard element are encrypted but not the CreditCard element name nor the attributes. The resultant XML would look like the following:

```
<?xml version='1.0'?>
<PaymentInfo xmlns='http://globalbank.org'>
  <Name>John von Neumann<Name/>
  <CreditCard Limit='5,000' Currency='USD'>
  <EncryptedData
      Type='http://www.w3.org/2001/04/xmlenc#Content'
              xmlns='http://www.w3.org/2001/04/xmlenc#'>
      <CipherData>
       <CipherValue>C23455CB6</CipherValue>
      </CipherData>
  </EncryptedData>
  </CreditCard>
</PaymentInfo>
```

Scenario 3: Encrypting XML Element Content Only

In this example, we consider a scenario in which all the information except the actual credit card number is made public, including the Number element itself.

```
<?xml version='1.0'?>
<PaymentInfo xmlns='http://globalbank.org'>
 <Name>John von Neumann<Name/>
 <CreditCard Limit='5,000' Currency='USD'>
  <Number>
   <EncryptedData
    xmlns='http://www.w3.org/2001/04/xmlenc#'
```

```
   Type='http://www.w3.org/2001/04/xmlenc#Content'>
    <CipherData>
      <CipherValue>A2345C66</CipherValue'
    </CipherData>
   </EncryptedData>
  </Number>
  <Issuer>World Bank </Issuer>
  <Expiration>04/02</Expiration>
 </CreditCard>
</PaymentInfo>
```

Here, both CreditCard and Number are made public, but the character data content of Number is encrypted. Note that we use the attribute Type='http://www.w3.org/2001/04/xmlenc#Content' to indicate to the receiver that element content is being encoded.

Scenario 4: Encrypting Arbitrary Data and XML Documents
If the situation requires that the entire XML document beginning at the root note be encrypted, all the elements are encrypted as a single encrypted string.

```
<?xml version='1.0'?>
<EncryptedData xmlns='http://www.w3.org/2001/04/xmlenc#'>
  <CipherData>
    <CipherValue>A23B45223C56</CipherValue>
  </CipherData>
</EncryptedData>
```

XML Digital Signature

XML Digital Signature elements.

The XML Digital Signature specification defines both the syntax and rules for processing XML digital signatures. Signatures provide integrity, message authentication, and signer authentication services for data either contained within an XML document or referred to by such a document.

Digital Signature Elements

The XML Digital Signature specification defines a series of XML elements for describing details of the signature. Some of these elements and what they signify are as follows:

❑ **SignedInfo:** The required `SignedInfo` element holds the information that is actually signed.

❑ **CanonicalizationMethod:** This element indicates the algorithm used to canonicalize the `SignedInfo` element before it is digested as part of the signature operation.

❑ **SignatureMethod:** This element specifies the algorithm used to convert the canonicalized `SignedInfo` into the `Signature-Value`. It is a combination of a digest algorithm and a key-dependent algorithm. The algorithm names are signed to resist attacks based on substituting a weaker algorithm.

❑ **Reference:** Each `Reference` element includes the method used to compute the digital hash and resulting digest value calculated over the identified data object. It also may include transformations that produced the input to the digest operation. A data object is signed by computing its digest value and a signature over that value. The signature is later checked via reference and signature validation.

❑ **KeyInfo:** This element indicates the key to be used to validate the signature. Possible forms for identification include certificates, key names, and key agreement algorithms and information. `KeyInfo` is optional since the signer may not wish to reveal key information to all document processing parties.

❑ `Transforms`: This element is an optional ordered list of processing steps applied to the resource's content before the digest was computed. Transforms can include operations such as canonicalization, encoding/decoding, compression/inflation, and the application of Extensible Stylesheet Language (XSL) or XPath. XPath transforms permit the signer to derive an XML document that omits portions of the source document. As a result, excluded portions may be changed without affecting signature validity.

❑ `DigestMethod`: This element is the algorithm applied to the data after `Transforms` is applied to yield the `DigestValue`. The signing of the `DigestValue` is what binds resource content to the signer's key.

❑ `DigestValue`: This element holds the value computed based on the data being signed. Changing one character of the data being signed will result in an entirely different digest value.

Steps in Signature Generation

To digitally sign an XML document using XML Signature, you must carry out the following steps:

1. Create a `SignedInfo` element with `SignatureMethod`, `CanonicalizationMethod`, and `Reference`(s).
2. Canonicalize the XML document.
3. Calculate the `SignatureValue` based on algorithms specified in `SignedInfo`.
4. Construct the `Signature` element that includes `SignedInfo`, `KeyInfo` (if required), and `SignatureValue`.

XKMS

XKMS works with public-key infrastructures.

XKMS is a W3C initiative that targets the delegation of trust processing decisions to one or more specialized trust processors, to give businesses an easier way to manage digital signatures and data encryption. Instead of relying on proprietary public-key infrastructure (PKI) implementations, companies can use standard interfaces to work with different vendors to handle issues surrounding digital certification checking, revocation status checking, and validation. XKMS allows these functions to be performed through standard interfaces so that financial institutions, for example, won't have to care what type of PKI system a company has implemented in order to do business with them.

XKMS was submitted to the W3C by Microsoft, VeriSign, and webMethods and is backed by a range of companies including Baltimore Technologies, Entrust, HP, IBM, Iona Technologies, Reuters, and RSA Security. As Figure 7.4 shows, XKMS is one of the three W3C specifications that define the XML security architecture.

XKMS Structure

XKMS

XKMS specifies protocols for distributing and registering public keys and is suitable for use in conjunction with the proposed standard for XML Signature and as a companion standard for XML Encryption. XKMS has two parts: the XML Key Information Service Specification (X-KISS) and the XML Key Registration Service Specification (X-KRSS).

X-KISS

X-KISS

X-KISS defines a protocol for a trust service that resolves public-key information contained in documents that conform to the XML Signature specification. The X-KISS protocol allows a client of such a service to delegate part or all of the tasks required to process the XML Signature `ds:KeyInfo` element. A basic objective of the protocol design is to minimize the complexity of application implementations by allowing them to become clients and thereby to be shielded from the complexity and syntax of the underlying PKI used to establish trust relationships. The underlying PKI may be based upon a different specification, such as X.509, the international standard for public-key certificates, or Pretty Good Privacy (PGP), the widely available public-key encryption system.

By design, the XML Signature specification does not mandate use of a particular trust policy. The signer of a document is not required to include any key information but may include a `ds:KeyInfo` element that specifies the key itself, a key name, X.509 certificate, a PGP Key Identifier, and so on. Alternatively, a link may be provided to a location where the full `ds:KeyInfo` information may be found.

XML Signature makes no assumptions about PKI.

X-KRSS

X-KRSS defines a protocol for a Web service that accepts registration of public-key information. Once registered, the public key may be used in conjunction with other Web services, including X-KISS. A client of a conforming service may request that the registration service bind information to a public key. The information bound may include a name, an identifier, or extended attributes defined by the implementation.

X-KRSS.

The key pair to which the information is bound may be generated in advance by the client or, to support key recovery, may be generated on request by the service. The registration protocol may also be used for subsequent recovery of a private key. The protocol provides for authentication of the applicant and, in case the key pair is generated by the client, proof of possession of the private key. A means of communicating the private key to the client is provided in cases where the private key is generated by the registration service.

Guidelines for Signing XML Documents

Rules for digitally signing XML.

Just as in nonelectronic life, a user should only sign what is seen. Because XML relies on transformations and substitutions during the processing of an XML document, special care needs to be taken when working with the XML Security Framework. For instance, if an XML document includes an embedded style sheet (such as when XSLT is used), it is the transformed document that should be represented to the user and signed rather than the document without the style sheet. In addition, when a document references an external style sheet, the content of that external style sheet should also be signed.

Content presentation may introduce changes.

If signing is intended to convey the judgment of a user about document content, then it is important that what gets signed is the information that was presented to that user. However, when content is presented on a screen or viewed in a printout based on some XML source, the signer must be careful to sign not only the original XML but also any style sheets or other information that may affect the presentation.

Transformations may alter content.

Some applications might operate with the original or intermediary data, but a signer should be careful about potential weaknesses introduced between the original and transformed data. This is a trust decision about the character and meaning of the transforms that an application needs to make. Consider a canonicalization algorithm that normalizes character case (lower to upper) or character composition ("e and accent" to "accented-e"). An adversary could introduce changes that are normalized and thus inconsequential to signature validity but material to a Document Object Model processor. For instance, by changing the case of a character one might influence the result of an XPath selection, introducing a serious risk if that change is normalized for signature validation but the XML processor operating over the original data returns a different result than intended. Care should be taken that all documents associated with a core XML document be part of the signature process.

Similarly, care must be taken by applications executing algorithms specified in an XML signature when additional information is supplied as parameters such as XSLT transforms. The algorithms specified in the document will often be implemented via a trusted library, yet perverse parameters might cause unacceptable processing or memory demand. As in any security infrastructure, the security of an overall system will depend on the security and integrity of procedures and personnel as well as procedural enforcement.

Summary

Security is one of the important aspects of Web commerce that is not addressed directly by SOAP or Web services. While it is possible to use standard security protocols to encrypt and authenticate XML, there are matters relating to the structure and definition of XML and its use in SOAP that require specialized security solutions. For example, when XML travels along message paths it may be necessary for various receiving agents to view selected parts of an XML document while keeping other parts secure. To address this issue, the W3C has developed XML Encryption and XML Signature to provide for the selective signing and encryption of XML elements and content. Also important with respect to XML security is XML Canonicalization, an algorithmic technology that generates the canonical form of an XML document so that nonessential parts of the document are discarded. Issues of trust are handled by XKMS, which builds on the services of XML Signature and XML Encryption and relies on established certificate authorities.

Resources

http://www.w3.org/TR/xml-encryption-req
The design principles, scope, and requirements for XML Encryption.

http://www.w3.org/Signature/Drafts/xml-exc-c14n.html
XML Canonicalization, working draft.

http://www.w3.org/TR/xmldsig-core/
W3C Proposed Recommendation for XML Signature.

http://www.xmltrustcenter.org
A software development kit for XKMS.

http://www.xml.com/pub/a/2001/08/08/xmldsig.html
"An Introduction to XML Digital Signatures" by Ed Simon, Paul Madsen, and Carlisle Adams.

http://www.oasis-open.org/committees/security/
OASIS security page with links to SAML, the XML-based Security Assertion Markup Language.

8

Back to the Future

This chapter is about the future. Not the future in the guise of the next great technological breakthrough, World Wide Web Consortium Recommendation, or powerful application program interface (API), but the future of technologies and systems that are already with us, waiting to find their place in the space of the Web and to combine with other technologies to open up new opportunities and new applications. The two technology families we're referring to are peer-to-peer (P2P) and legacy applications, one very new, hot, and in vogue, the other older, traditional, and a bit stodgy.

P2P represents a new way of communicating and sharing using the Web as an infrastructure. The recent past has seen the power of P2P in the form of Napster, the music sharing system that has shaken the music industry. Other applications of P2P include Groove Networks, which has initiated new ways of building collaborative applications that target small virtual groups over the Web.

Legacy is at the other end of the spectrum of newness. By "legacy" we refer to software with a long shelf life that was built around mainframes and was commonly written in COBOL. During the past decade mainframe-based legacy systems have struggled to find a place in the rapidly evolving world of client-server middleware and component frameworks. Now with the arrival of the Web, a renewed interest in data, and the capability to move that data around using common Web protocols, mainframes have taken on a new luster. In a strange twist of technological fate, mainframes are finding themselves more suited to the P2P world than are the client-server systems that, only a short time ago, were seen as mainframe replacements.

Change

XML is a driver of change.

The overriding theme of this book has been change: change brought about by XML and its capacity to describe data not only in the conventional IT sense of the word, but in the more general sense that includes directives for action also known as "code." Yet XML is more than just a technology for delivering data or code as data; it is a part of a broader effort to build applications out of constituent parts rather than to construct hard-wired solutions.

SOAP is the product of XML and HTTP.

The Web itself—a product of HTTP, HTML, and the browser—is an example of this power of convergent assembly. SOAP is another example, itself a product of the Web (as transport) and XML (as data). What these technology combinations give us is a freewheeling Web space of loosely coupled asynchronous communicating servers that are finding their place amid existing object systems and legacy applications.

Convergence

The Web is fertile ground for convergence.

The computing world where we now find ourselves is an amalgam of players and technologies, all trying to find synergies through interconnection. As Figure 8.1 illustrates, the main pieces coming together include the loosely coupled Web riding on waves of SOAP and XML, more traditional tightly coupled object systems bound by their own transport protocols but able to support critical transactional capability, and the even more traditional legacy applications, many of them running on large mainframe environments. The irony here is that the central repository model made possible by the mainframe and once thought to have been made obsolete by client-server network computing is now experiencing a renewed interest due to several factors, including delivery of services to critical applications, high-bandwidth throughput, and more recently the need to manage collaborative P2P efforts over the loosely coupled Web.

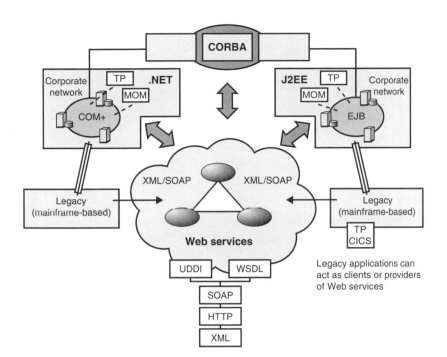

Figure 8.1 The three major pieces of application space.

The challenge for the software industry is to work out the details of the interplay between tightly coupled object systems and the loosely coupled Web. As we saw in Chapter 5, the force bringing these two entities together is the need to add transaction and messaging to the Web. The result (as we've seen in Chapter 6) is Java 2 Enterprise Edition (J2EE) and .NET. However, there are other kinds of interaction that play a role in the future shape of the new Web. These include

❑ Integrating legacy mainframe applications between tightly coupled object frameworks and the Web

❑ Identifying clients plugging in from the loose space of the Web to traditional tightly coupled networks

❑ Understanding how the loose space of the Web is opening up new ways of P2P and collaborative interaction and how these

The challenge is to bring tightly coupled and loosely coupled systems together.

new models of interaction fit with the more conventional computing models

Thus we've now got three very different subsystems looking to find each other and interconnect in new ways to arrive at new synergies. So while it's unwise to try to predict, it is at least reasonable to expect the immediate future will be based on the interactions between the three forces of mainframe legacy applications, tightly coupled client server systems, and the new more open space of the Web.

In the following sections we explore each of these interactions to get a glimpse of what may be in store in the near future.

Collaborative and P2P Computing

One of the things made possible by loosely coupled networks is ad hoc interaction between network nodes, which has opened the door to P2P computing that takes advantage of the possibility of connection between any two Web devices.

What Is P2P?

P2P is about connection in a loosely coupled environment.

P2P is less a technology than the concept that, because we no longer need servers to interconnect us, we're free to focus on data and not the infrastructure to get the data from point A to point B. Given that P2P doesn't *need* servers, it's important to realize that servers actually come in quite handy, not for controlling the flow of data but as repositories of shared data. It turns out to be simpler to keep data in one place than to worry about distributed data management, cache control, and all the hard problems that computer science has been trying to solve for the past few decades. In the end, storing data in one place is much easier and more convenient. And what's really good at storing data in a central repository with lots of access? The mainframe.

Napster

Napster began in 1999 as an idea in the head of a teenager, and with the synergic power of the Web it has forced the music industry to rethink its distribution mechanisms and treatment of intellectual property. Napster centers around the distribution of MP3 files. MP3 is a digital music format that can be downloaded from the Internet and played on your computer, listened to on a portable player, or even burned on your own private CD. The advantage of MP3 is that song files are small enough to move easily around the Internet, even with limited bandwidth.

The original MP3 craze was fueled by sites like www.mp3.com, where users could upload songs to a Web site and other users could log in and download the songs. In 1999 Shawn Fanning, frustrated by some of the technical difficulties in finding music he liked on the Web, spent several months writing the code that would become the utility Napster.

Napster (actually Fanning's nickname in high school because of his "nappy" hair) altered the model so that instead of songs being stored on a central server, they were stored on individual users' machines. With Napster's P2P sharing, when someone downloads a song, it is actually downloaded from another person's computer, which could be in the same city or elsewhere around the globe. The purpose of the central Napster server is to monitor all Napster users currently online and connect them to each other. The server itself does not contain any MP3 song files.

The music industry, very upset with Napster, has taken steps to close it down. The Recording Industry Association of America

(continued)

Napster (continued)

filed a lawsuit based on copyright infringement and the fact that thousands of people were making thousands of copies of copyrighted songs, with no money going to the record labels or the artists. Napster claims that the music files are personal files that people maintain on their own machines and that Napster does not traffic in the songs.

In a settlement with the record industry, Napster has agreed to charge users for its music service and to pay $26 million to music publishers and songwriters. From user fees, owners of music-publishing rights will receive one-third of the royalties, leaving two-thirds of those royalties for record labels. How this all will play out remains to be seen, since many of the legal issues are unresolved as of this writing. However, no matter which side you may be on in this debate, the reality is that P2P computing has incredible potential to change how data is distributed. And it's a high-impact software endeavor that was assembled by a kid in his garage in a few months, using the power of the Web.

So now in many ways we've come full circle. After a decade-long fling with client-server middleware, we're now back to seeing the advantage of the mainframe model. As Figure 8.2 illustrates, the Web as a network running standard protocols such as HTTP, SOAP, and TCP/IP gives us either pure P2P with no intermediaries, a Web services model where peers find each other through registry lookup, or a mainframe model where peers find each other through a registry that stores data of common interest.

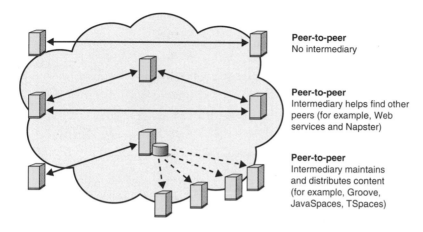

Peer-to-peer
No intermediary

Peer-to-peer
Intermediary helps find other peers (for example, Web services and Napster)

Peer-to-peer
Intermediary maintains and distributes content (for example, Groove, JavaSpaces, TSpaces)

Figure 8.2
Three options for adding order to loosely coupled, asynchronous Web-based interactions: peers freely associating, using a third party registry to locate peers, and using a third party registry to locate peers and to store common data.

P2P Software

The option in which peers find each other through a registry that stores data of common interest is the basis for the success of Groove Networks, an open, real-time, P2P communication platform that is based on data sharing rather than a common tightly coupled infrastructure. Groove is the brainchild of Ray Ozzie, the creator of Lotus Notes, who has successfully leveraged the loose space of the Web by giving end-users a way to work together in a secure, shared virtual workspace, either connected or disconnected from a corporate network.

Groove is based on data sharing.

Groove provides basic collaborative functionalities that include

- ❏ File sharing
- ❏ Discussion boards
- ❏ Chat (text-based and voice-based)
- ❏ Whiteboard
- ❏ Picture sharing
- ❏ Calendar
- ❏ Organizer

In an interview with the trade publication CRN, Ozzie describes Groove as

> *[a] platform layer as a component management service. If they [developers] write tools or solutions within the Groove environment, they can package up their code, and they don't have to worry about delivering that code to all the workstations that are using it. They can host that code on our component servers, and the moment that any one of those users accepts an invitation to one of the shared spaces, the code comes down and gets installed automatically. The framework lets you program in any number of languages, any dotcom compliant language in the Windows environment. Once they build the app, we provide the synchronization of how that app interacts with itself. We transparently provide storage services so that anything someone does automatically gets stored in a secure XML object store. We do the communications services transparently. They don't have to worry about how to get the information from one workstation to another.*[1]

For application developers, the Groove platform serves as the base for building collaborative applications. Groove has created domain-specific tools that enable application-specific collaboration. For example, there is a "Team Sports Groove" that consists of pieces for coaches, players, and players' parents to manage a sports team and track its progress. Other examples include "Family Groove" for families to share news, post events, and share pictures, and an "Educational Groove" that uses the Web to structure online classroom support for both faculty and students.

---

[1] Kelley Dalmore, "An Interview with Ray Ozzie," http://www.crn.com/sections/Interview/Interview.asp?RSID=CRN&ArticleID=21070.

This move toward collaborative computing has not been lost on the major industry players. Microsoft, for example, has taken a stake in Groove Networks to round out its push into Web space. The addition of a P2P component to Microsoft's existing .NET infrastructure means that users can gain access to critical documents across a range of devices. Similarly, Sun has come out with a P2P framework called JXTA,[2] which is a set of open P2P protocols that allows any network-connected device including cell phones, PDAs, PCs, or servers to communicate and collaborate. What remains to be seen is how the synergy between P2P and Web services will play out, since industrial-strength collaborative software requires secure messaging, the ability to archive data, and solutions to the nasty problems of version control and configuration management.

Both .NET and J2EE have P2P initiatives.

Other P2P Initiatives

The move to embrace P2P is not limited to Microsoft; both Sun and IBM also have major P2P initiatives. Sun's effort is known as JavaSpaces, and IBM's project is called TSpaces. Both TSpaces and JavaSpaces are a kind of network middleware that supports synchronous communication among diverse systems. Both have their origins in the Linda distributed operating system proposed by David Gelernter at Yale in the 1980s. As Figure 8.3 illustrates, the idea behind Linda, JavaSpaces, and TSpaces is an open asynchronous network space into which client software deposits work requests that are extracted by servers able and willing to accept the work. When the work is done, results are deposited back into the shared space for retrieval by the client.

JavaSpaces and TSpaces.

In Linda, the shared memory space is called TupleSpace, where results of a computer's processes or the processes themselves are stored and

Linda = TupleSpace.

---

[2] JXTA is short for "juxtapose," reflecting the fact that P2P computing is juxtaposed to the conventional client-server computing model.

Figure 8.3 **The P2P concept of a shared space for loosely coupled asynchronous interaction has its origins in David Gelernter's Linda system of the 1980s. Both Sun's JavaSpaces and IBM's TSpaces are based on Linda's TupleSpace and use entries and templates to deposit and retrieve data and code.**

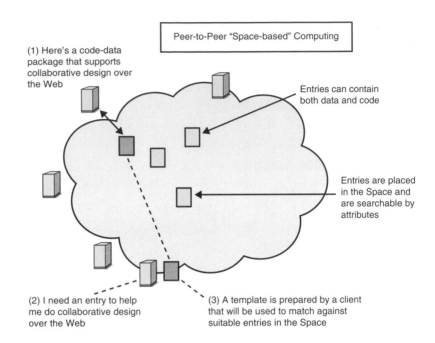

Peer-to-Peer "Space-based" Computing

(1) Here's a code-data package that supports collaborative design over the Web

Entries can contain both data and code

Entries are placed in the Space and are searchable by attributes

(2) I need an entry to help me do collaborative design over the Web

(3) A template is prepared by a client that will be used to match against suitable entries in the Space

can be accessed by multiple CPUs. All of the contents of a TupleSpace are marked with self-describing tags that help match processes with CPUs looking for tasks, essentially functioning the way a bulletin board might in the physical world.

For example, a student seeking a ride to Florida over spring break could pin an envelope labeled "need ride" to a bulletin board on campus. Another student looking for riders could take down the envelope and check the required destination. If there was a match, the driver could slip his or her phone number into the envelope and return it to the bulletin board. If their destinations did not match, the driver could leave the envelope untouched for other drivers to see.

JavaSpaces and TSpaces can move data and code.

Both Sun's JavaSpaces and IBM's TSpaces are structured along the lines of Linda except that instead of just data being made available, code in the form of serialized objects can be posted which can be run on any platform capable of running Java. The effect is that code and data can be passed around in a distributed environment in a way that preserves state. The goal is to raise the level of abstraction for programmers so they can create completely distributed applications that run regardless of hardware and location. Just as file utilities in operating systems free users from having to know exactly where on the disk their data resides, so the JavaSpaces and Tspaces frameworks take developers to a level where the entities representing data, applications, and even computers themselves are abstracted away in the cloud of "tuple-space." Users don't need and may not care to know where their computational resources reside; they simply access them by abstracted addresses.

ZwiftBooks and P2P

P2P computing provides an opportunity for ZwiftBooks to leverage the power of collaboration in its effort to deliver books as rapidly as possible. Working out of a conventional Web-server-based infrastructure (which could be based on .NET or J2EE), ZwiftBooks also acts as a peer in P2P network space that offers both wireless and wired connectivity. Individuals interested in acting as couriers for ZwiftBooks use their cell phone or PDA to post their availability in the P2P network. Availability takes the form of an entry that includes name, city, and contact information. Couriers register long-standing entries that describe their general availability as well as short-term entries that indicate immediate availability.

ZwiftBooks at the cutting edge with P2P.

When ZwiftBooks receives a request for a book, it submits a template into P2P space that matches against delivery city and returns all the potential delivery people who have submitted short-leased availability entries within the past hour. A ZwiftBooks who operator then selects a delivery person and either manually or programmatically contacts the individual, providing details about the book delivery. If no one has submitted a matching city entry when a request enters the P2P space, a match is made against the more permanent entries. These entries include software objects that send wireless messages to registered ZwiftBooks couriers that a new entry has been posted. Couriers then have an opportunity to submit an "immediately available" entry that indicates availability. In this way, ZwiftBooks extends its own service capability with minimal cost and overhead by leveraging the capability of an existing P2P network.

Legacy Systems

Legacy systems are revitalized by XML and the Web.

Legacy is an inevitable part of the technology curve: the new becomes old, and the software a company has relied on for years becomes cumbersome and difficult to integrate with newer systems.

Beginning in the 1960s and 1970s, mainframes were the workhorses of computing. Built around processors that were weak in comparison to today's gigahertz servers, mainframes brought to the table two things that still make them players today: the ability to traffic in large volumes of data thanks to powerful, separate input/output processors and the ability to manage large volumes of transactions by running complex transaction processing software known as Transaction Monitors.

During the 1980s, the increasing power of the microprocessor coupled with the emergence of local area networks gave rise to

Bridging the Legacy Gap

XML's hierarchical data structure means that there is a close connection between XML and many COBOL-based legacy applications. For example, the following excerpts illustrate the similarity between XML and COBOL data description.

```
<ShoeOrder>
  <OrderNumber>3832</OrderNumber>
  <color>Brown</color>
  <size> 9 </size>
  <width> AA </width>
</ShoeOrder>

01 ShoeOrder.
    05 OrderNumber pic 9(04) value "3832".
    05 Color       pic x(10) value "Brown".
    05 Size        pic x(02) value "9".
    05 Width       pic x(04) value "AA".
```

In this example, the top-level COBOL 01 level corresponds to the XML start element tag <ShoeOrder>, which is closed with the corresponding end tag </ShoeOrder>. Similarly, the Cobol 05 elements appear within the ShoeOrder element as color, size, and width and their corresponding elements. This similarity means that developers can establish COBOL legacy applications as Internet components simply by transforming COBOL data descriptors into XML tags.

XML's ability to liberate data from code also means that it could easily become the basis for data exchange across the Web without changing current Web protocols. Middleware based on data rather than component interfaces would permit even greater legacy integration, since middle-tier servers could transform appropriately tagged XML into whatever form an application requires.

client-server computing and challenged the power of the main-frame. Amid assertions that "the mainframe was dead," client-server systems did make significant inroads into the mainframe market.

The attempt to connect legacy mainframe applications gave rise to Common Object Request Broker Architecture (CORBA), an effort to unify languages in a common object format.

The 1990s gave us something totally different: the Web. Built out of constituent parts, the Web brought computing to everyone, not just workers attached to client-server networks. But the Web brought more than just a network; it brought with it a philosophy of open standards and collaborative interaction among both software components and the information workers who actively designed reusability into parts by limiting their scope.

Connection Challenges

COBOL is a major legacy component.

A decade ago the problem was how to connect mainframe applications—which were typically written in COBOL, data intensive, and transaction-based—to client-server systems. Today, the problem is how to make both mainframe applications *and* client-server systems work with the Web.

Thanks to e-commerce, legacy data and applications have taken on a new importance. As the Web opens up to both wired and wireless devices and connections, the killer applications will be those that can get the data to the customers, employees, and partners anywhere, anytime.

Both the year 2000 (Y2K) and the Web revolution have set the stage for an unprecedented shift in thinking about legacy. Ironically, although the threat of Y2K problems put most software development on hold, the intense code assessment and cleanup also culminated in an up-to-date inventory of systems and applications. As a result, many companies are in better shape than before Y2K to exploit the Web environment.

For mainframe-based legacy applications, the solution to the integration problem has been component technology—CORBA, Enterprise JavaBeans, or Distributed Component Object Module—to move data across the enterprise. The problem is that all variations of this technology are code-centric, meaning that the software must fit into a specific, often proprietary, program infrastructure before integration can take place.

Distributed object systems are no longer the only option for legacy.

Suggestions for dealing with the legacy problem have included the "scrap and rewrite" approach and the suggestion to build bridges into multilanguage object systems such as CORBA, which define language-neutral bindings for passing data between procedures and object methods. With options such as these, it's no wonder pundits were proclaiming "the mainframe was dead" in the late 1980s and early 1990s.

Legacy's New Position

Now, however, legacy finds itself in an interesting position. Long outsiders in the client-server realm, mainframe legacy applications and mainframes themselves are seeing a renewed interest because of changes in the shape of the Web. As Figure 8.4 shows, XML-based SOAP messaging and Web services connectivity based on .NET and J2EE have opened up new options for extending legacy systems.

SOAP opens up new options for legacy.

One option is to offer services or use other Web services through direct SOAP connections to customers, partners, and suppliers. Another option is to use the .NET framework to integrate legacy code directly. For example, existing COBOL applications can be recompiled to operate as part of the .NET Common Language Runtime and be made to interoperate with any of the other .NET languages. On the J2EE side, the Java Connection Architecture driven by the Java Community Process defines a standard for connecting

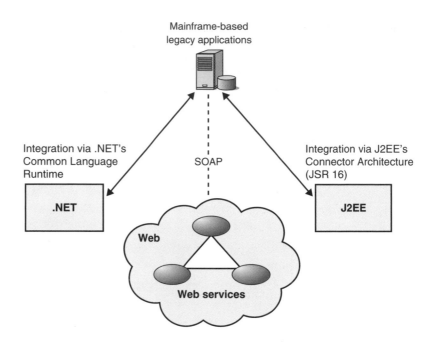

the J2EE platform to heterogeneous non-Java applications, including mainframe transaction processing, database systems, and legacy applications written in COBOL and other languages.

Summary

The future of distributed computing may very well be an interesting mix of the old and the new. Older legacy systems that include mainframe-based transaction, database, and COBOL applications are finding new opportunities for interconnection based on XML data descriptions, SOAP messaging, and Web services frameworks that allow legacy systems to package functionality either as Web services or to extend capabilities by acting as a client for other Web services. Similarly, newer P2P applications are emerging that offer innovative ways to leverage the loosely coupled space of the Web for collaboration and sharing. How these newer P2P technologies play with existing object systems and older legacy applications remains to be seen, but with data free to move across the Web and open to the forces of combinatoric interaction, we can expect the unexpected as the XML-driven data revolution takes us into the future.

Resources

Article

David Gelernter, "Generative Communication in Linda," *ACM Transactions on Programming Languages and Systems* 7(1): 80-112.

Web

http://www.napster.com/

The Napster Web site. Napster continues as a driving force in an evolving music industry.

http://www.groove.net

Groove Networks.

http://www.jxta.org/

The Project JXTA Web site.

http://www.openp2p.com/

The O'Reilly Web site devoted to P2P technologies.

http://www.adtools.com

The Fujitsu Web site dedicated to COBOL and Web services.

http://java.sun.com/products/javaspaces/

Sun's JavaSpaces Web site.

http://www.almaden.ibm.com/cs/TSpaces/

IBM's TSpaces Web site.

Appendix A

XML Language Basics

This section is meant to provide a short, high-level overview of XML. For a more detailed treatment of XML see the references at the end of this appendix.

XML stands for "Extensible Markup Language," a language developed by the World Wide Web Consortium (W3C). It is considered a meta-language because it is used to define other languages through the use of markup tags, which add structure and meaning to documents. While XML markup tags look like HTML tags, they allow designers to describe the content rather than the format of the text they enclose. When describing data, developers are free to name their tags in whatever way best describes their content. This flexibility is what makes XML an extensible language.

XML Fundamentals

Although XML includes several language components, most individual XML vocabularies can be read and understood by focusing on three commonly used XML structures, which we will explore in this overview: elements, attributes, and entities. Elements and attributes are used to describe content while entities are substitutes for special or commonly used character strings.

Elements

Elements are the primary means for describing data in XML. The rules for composing elements are flexible, allowing for different combinations of text content, attributes, and other elements. However, there are three ways elements are used in XML documents.

Simple Content

Text or other data appears between start and end tags. The start tag has the same name as the end tag except that the end tag begins with a slash. The following element has a start tag, content, and an end tag.

```
<author>Stephen Hawking</author>
```

Element as Container for Other Elements

An element may contain other elements, providing a hierarchical or tree data structure. The following book element contains the author and title elements.

```
<book>
    <author>Stephen Hawking</author>
    <title>A brief history of time</title>
</book>
```

Empty Element as Container for Attributes

When an element has no content but only attributes, there is a shorthand way of writing the element that bypasses the need for both a start and end tag. An element written with a slash following the tag name indicates an empty element, as in

```
<book/>
```

which is shorthand for

```
<book></book>
```

The most common use of empty elements is to hold attribute data.

```
<book title="A brief history of time" author="Stephen
Hawking"/>
```

Technically, an element can contain it all—other elements, text, and attributes—but packing both elements and text into a single element is considered poor style because, as the following example shows, it makes it difficult for a reader to understand what the author is trying to express.

```
<book isbn="0-102-9393-3">
  A brief history of time
  <author>Stephen Hawking</author>
</book>
```

Because readability is an important aspect of XML design, many industry groups charged with defining XML vocabularies specify naming conventions to make it easier to read the XML and distinguish data elements from structure elements.

For example, the Mortgage Industry Standards Maintenance Organization uses all capitals to distinguish elements that contain other elements and initial capitals for words in element names that contain only data. Applying this convention to our book example would give us

```
<BOOK>
    <Author>Stephen Hawking</Author>
    <Title>A brief history of time</Title>
</BOOK>
```

Element Naming Rules

While the decision to capitalize or not is up to the XML language designer, there are official naming rules for XML which must be followed.

- ❑ Names can contain letters, numbers, and other characters.
- ❑ Names must not begin with a number or punctuation.
- ❑ Names must not start with the string "xml" in any upper- or lowercase form.
- ❑ Names must not contain spaces.

Also, when designing element names, one should not use the colon, since it is reserved for use with XML namespaces.

Attributes

Attributes provide additional information about elements. In HTML, for example, attributes are used to specify the name of an image file when loading an HTML document.

```
<img src="computer.gif">
```

Attributes are often used to indicate information that is not part of the data described within an element. Often an attribute is used to describe something about the data itself. For example, in the following XML the attribute use might tell a program handling the data that the file is not required.

```
<file use="optional">computer.gif</file>
```

In XML, attribute values must always be enclosed in quotation marks, either single or double.

Elements versus Attributes

The question whether to use elements or attributes to represent data has been widely debated. XML allows data to be stored either as the content of an element or as an attribute. The following two examples show the same data represented in different ways.

```
<book isbn="092373637">
    <title>Anna Karenina</title>
    <author>Tolstoy</author>
</book>

<book>
    <isbn>092373637</isbn>
    <title>Anna Karenina</title>
```

```
    <author>Tolstoy</author>
</book>
```

In the first example isbn is an attribute; in the second, isbn is a child element of book. There are no official rules about when to use attributes. The general consensus is to use elements if the information seems like data and to use attributes when describing something *about* the data. Reasons for not using attributes to store data include the following:

❏ Attributes cannot contain multiple values, while elements can have multiple subelements.

❏ Attributes are not easily expandable to account for future changes.

❏ Attributes are more difficult than elements to manipulate with programs.

❏ Attribute values are not easy to check against a document type definition (DTD).

Entities

Entities are used to substitute one string for another in an XML document. For example, if a phrase such as "XML and the Data Revolution" is repeated frequently in a document, one can define a short-cut entity declaration in the DTD.

```
<!ENTITY xdr " XML and the Data Revolution ">
```

Then, when you want to use the full phrase, you use &xdr; and it will be substituted in the XML document. Using entities can help avoid misspellings and the tediousness of typing the same thing over and over.

Predefined Entities

XML has adopted five predefined entities from the HTML world. The ampersand (&), greater-than (>), lesser-than (<), double-quote ("), and apostrophe (') characters are represented within XML documents as "&", "<", ">", """, and "'", respectively.

If the entities are long, it's possible to store the information separately in another file. This can be accomplished through an external entity reference, which uses the XML keyword SYSTEM between the entity name and URL of the file.

```
<!ENTITY text SYSTEM "http://my.url.here">
```

Parameter Entities

While entities are useful for creating substitution strings within XML documents, it's often useful to define shortcuts in a DTD to make writing a DTD easier. This is where parameter entities come in. A parameter entity is defined by inserting a percent sign prior to the entity name. Once defined, a parameter entity can be substituted by surrounding the parameter name with a percent sign and semicolon.

CDATA

The XML CDATA section is used to prevent the processing of a portion of data. When an XML document is parsed, all the XML is processed except the data inside a CDATA section. This allows the inclusion of content that may confuse an XML processor.

For example, if an XML document contains greater-than or ampersand characters, as many programs or scripts do, one can define a CDATA section to contain this data. A CDATA section starts with "<![CDATA[" and ends with "]]>". The following example shows how a CDATA section may be used to include script code within an XML element named script.

```
<script>
<![CDATA[
  function compare(a,b) {
```

```
    if (a < b) then {
      return 1
    }
    else {
     return 0
    }
  }
]]>
</script>
```

Processing Instructions

XML allows the use of special instructions in order to pass information to programs that may read the document. A processing instruction begins with "<?" and ends with "?>". Immediately after the "<?" is a target name that is used to let a program know who the content of the processing instruction is intended for. For example, the following is a processing instruction intended for a program that is looking for the name agent.

```
<?agent process="yes" priority="high">
```

XML Declaration

Most XML documents begin an XML declaration of the form:

```
<?xml version="1.0">
```

Although the XML declaration looks like a processing instruction, it is technically not. If present, it must be the first thing in a document.

XML and DTDs

A DTD defines the structure of an XML document with a list of legal elements. It can be declared either within your XML document or as an external reference. If an XML document conforms to the rules set out by a DTD, the XML is said to be valid with respect to that DTD.

For example, consider the following XML document that contains an internal DTD that begins with "<!DOCTYPE" and ends with "]>".

```
<?xml version="1.0"?>
<!DOCTYPE note [
  <!ELEMENT note (to,from,heading,body)>
  <!ELEMENT to      (#PCDATA)>
  <!ELEMENT from    (#PCDATA)>
  <!ELEMENT heading (#PCDATA)>
  <!ELEMENT body    (#PCDATA)>
]>
<note>
  <to>Bob    </to>
  <from>Marilyn</from>
  <heading>Reminder</heading>
  <body>Don't forget to bring the cheese</body>
</note>
```

The !DOCTYPE syntax in the second line defines this as a document of type note. The third line defines the note element as having four elements: to, from, heading, and body. The fourth line defines the to element as type #PCDATA, which means it may contain text. All the other elements are similarly defined.

A DTD may also be external to an XML source document. If so, the following syntax is used.

```
<!DOCTYPE root-element SYSTEM "filename">
```

Defining Attributes in DTDs

DTDs may also be used to specify attributes using the following form.

```
<!ATTLIST element-name attribute-name   attribute-type
default-value>
```

For example, the DTD

```
<!ATTLIST payment type CDATA "check">
```

establishes the validity of the XML

```
<payment type="check"/>
```

The attribute-type can have the values given in Table A-1.

As an example, consider the following attribute declaration as part of a DTD:

```
<!ELEMENT square EMPTY>
    <!ATTLIST square width CDATA "0">
```

Table A-1 Possible Values of the Attribute-Type in an XML DTD

Value	Explanation
CDATA	The value is character data
(en1|en2|..)	The value must be one from an enumerated list
ID	The value is a unique id
IDREF	The value is the id of another element
IDREFS	The value is a list of other ids
NMTOKEN	The value is a valid XML name
NMTOKENS	The value is a list of valid XML names
ENTITY	The value is an entity
ENTITIES	The value is a list of entities
NOTATION	The value is the name of a notation
xml:	The value is a predefined XML value

This maps to the following XML:

```
<square width="100"></square>
```

The element square is defined as an empty element with a width attribute of type CDATA. If no width attribute is given, the attribute has a default value of 0.

Default Attribute Value

The syntax for default attribute values is as follows:

```
<!ATTLIST element-name attribute-name attribute-type
"default-value">
```

The following DTD example uses default values:

```
<!ATTLIST payment type CDATA "check">
```

Here is an example of XML that is conformant with this DTD:

```
<payment type="check"/>
```

Specifying a default value for an attribute means that the attribute will be assigned a value even if the author of the XML document does not supply one. Table A-2 shows possible default attribute values.

Table A-2 Default Attribute Values in an XML DTD

Value	Explanation
value	The attribute's default value
#DEFAULT	The attribute's default value
#REQUIRED	The attribute value must be included in the element
#IMPLIED	The attribute does not have to be included
#FIXED	The attribute value is fixed

Implied Attribute

The syntax for implied attribute values is as follows:

```
<!ATTLIST element-name attribute-name attribute-type #IMPLIED>
```

This is a DTD example using implied values:

```
<!ATTLIST contact fax CDATA #IMPLIED>
```

And the following XML conforms to this DTD:

```
<contact fax="214-555-6677"/>
```

Use an implied attribute in a DTD when you don't want to force the author to include an attribute and you don't have a default value.

References

Books

Elliotte Rusty Harold, *XML Bible* (Foster City, CA: IDG Books, 1999).

Elliotte Rusty Harold and W. Scott Means, *XML in a Nutshell: A Desktop Quick Reference* (Sebastopol, CA: O'Reilly, 2001).

Web

http://www.w3schools.com/xml/
Online XML tutorial.

http://www.ucc.ie/xml/
Frequently asked questions about XML with many good links.

Appendix B

SOAP Version 1.2 Part 1: Messaging Framework

W3C Working Draft 17 December 2001

This version:

> http://www.w3.org/TR/2001/WD-soap12-part1-20011217/

Latest version:

> http://www.w3.org/TR/soap12-part1/

Previous version:

> http://www.w3.org/TR/2001/WD-soap12-part1-20011002/

Editors:

> Martin Gudgin, DevelopMentor
>
> Marc Hadley, Sun Microsystems
>
> Jean-Jacques Moreau, Canon
>
> Henrik Frystyk Nielsen, Microsoft

Abstract

SOAP version 1.2 is a lightweight protocol for exchange of information in a decentralized, distributed environment. It is an XML based protocol at the core of which is an envelope that defines a framework for describing what is in a message and how to process it and a transport binding framework for exchanging messages using an underlying protocol. Adjuncts to the envelope and binding framework include a set of encoding rules for expressing instances of application-defined data types and a convention for representing remote procedure calls and responses. Part 1 (this document) describes the SOAP envelope and SOAP transport binding framework; Part 2[1] describes adjuncts to the envelope and binding framework.

Status of This Document

This section describes the status of this document at the time of its publication. Other documents may supersede this document. The latest status of this document series is maintained at the W3C.

This is the third W3C Working Draft of the SOAP Version 1.2 specification for review by W3C members and other interested parties. It has been produced by the XML Protocol Working Group (WG), which is part of the XML Protocol Activity.

For a detailed list of changes since the last publication of this document, refer to appendix **C Part 1 Change Log**. A list of open issues against this document can be found at http://www.w3.org/2000/xp/ Group/xmlp-issues.

Comments on this document should be sent to xmlp-comments @w3.org (public archive[13]). It is inappropriate to send discussion emails to this address.

Discussion of this document takes place on the public xml-dist-app @w3.org mailing list[14] per the email communication rules in the XML Protocol Working Group Charter[15].

This is a public W3C Working Draft. It is a draft document and may be updated, replaced, or obsoleted by other documents at any time.

It is inappropriate to use W3C Working Drafts as reference material or to cite them as other than "work in progress". A list of all W3C technical reports can be found at http://www.w3.org/TR/.

Table of Contents

1 Introduction

SOAP version 1.2 provides a simple and lightweight mechanism for exchanging structured and typed information between peers in a decentralized, distributed environment using XML. SOAP does not itself define any application semantics such as a programming model or implementation specific semantics; rather it defines a simple mechanism for expressing application semantics by providing a modular packaging model and mechanisms for encoding application defined data. This allows SOAP to be used for a large variety of purposes ranging from messaging systems to remote procedure call (RPC) invocations. In previous versions of this specification the SOAP name was an acronym. This is no longer the case.

Part 1 of the SOAP specification (this document) describes:

1. The SOAP envelope (**4 SOAP Envelope**). This construct defines an overall framework for expressing what is in a message, who should deal with it, and whether it is optional or mandatory.
2. The SOAP binding framework (**5 SOAP Protocol Binding Framework**). This defines an abstract framework for exchanging SOAP envelopes between peers using an underlying protocol for transport. The SOAP HTTP binding [1](SOAP in HTTP) defines a concrete instance of a binding to the HTTP protocol[2].

Part 2[1] describes adjuncts to the envelope and binding framework including the SOAP encoding rules [1](SOAP Encoding) that define a serialization mechanism that can be used to exchange instances of application-defined datatypes and the SOAP RPC representation [1](SOAP for RPC) that defines a convention that can be used to represent remote procedure calls and responses.

1.1 Design Goals

Two major design goals for SOAP are simplicity and extensibility. SOAP attempts to meet these goals by omitting features often found in messaging systems and distributed object systems such as:

❏ Distributed garbage collection;
❏ Boxcarring or batching of messages;
❏ Objects-by-reference (which requires distributed garbage collection);
❏ Activation (which requires objects-by-reference).

Note that it is possible to implement such features using SOAP but they are out of scope for this specification.

1.2 Notational Conventions

The keywords "MUST", "MUST NOT", "REQUIRED", "SHALL", "SHALL NOT", "SHOULD", "SHOULD NOT", "RECOMMENDED", "MAY", and "OPTIONAL" in this document are to be interpreted as described in [3].

The namespace prefixes "env" and "enc" used in the prose sections of this document are associated with the SOAP namespace names "http://www.w3.org/2001/12/soap-envelope" and "http://www.w3. org/2001/12/soap-encoding" respectively.

The namespace prefixes "xs" and "xsi" used in the prose sections of this document are associated with the namespace names "http:// www.w3.org/2001/XMLSchema" and "http://www.w3.org/2001/ XMLSchema-instance" respectively, both of which are defined in the XML Schemas specification[4],[5].

Note that the choice of any namespace prefix is arbitrary and not semantically significant.

Namespace URIs of the general form "http://example.org/ . . ." and "http://example.com/ . . ." represent an application-dependent or context-dependent URI[6].

1.3 Example of SOAP Message

The following example shows a simple notification message expressed in SOAP. The message contains a header block `alertcontrol` and the body `alert` both of which are application defined and not defined by SOAP. The header contains information which may be of use to intermediaries as well as the ultimate destination of the message. The body contains the actual notification message to be delivered.

1.4 SOAP Terminology

1.4.1 Protocol Concepts

SOAP

The formal set of conventions governing the format and processing rules of a SOAP message and basic control of interaction between SOAP nodes generating and accepting SOAP messages for the purpose of exchanging information along a SOAP message path.

SOAP binding

The formal set of rules for carrying a SOAP message within or on top of another protocol (underlying protocol) for the purpose of transmission. Example SOAP bindings include carrying a SOAP message within an HTTP entity-body, or over a TCP stream.

Example: SOAP message containing a header block and a body

```
<?xml version="1.0" ?>
<env:Envelope xmlns:env="http://www.w3.org/2001/12/soap-envelope">
 <env:Header>
  <n:alertcontrol xmlns:n="http://example.org/alertcontrol">
   <n:priority>1</n:priority>
   <n:expires>2001-06-22T14:00:00-05:00</n:expires>
  </n:alertcontrol>
 </env:Header>
 <env:Body>
  <m:alert xmlns:m="http://example.org/alert">
   <m:msg>Pick up Mary at school at 2pm</m:msg>
  </m:alert>
 </env:Body>
</env:Envelope>
```

SOAP node

A SOAP node processes a SOAP message according to the formal set of conventions defined by SOAP. The SOAP node is responsible for enforcing the rules that govern the exchange of SOAP messages and accesses the services provided by the underlying protocols through SOAP bindings. Non-compliance with SOAP conventions can cause a SOAP node to generate a SOAP fault (see also SOAP receiver and SOAP sender).

1.4.2 Data Encapsulation Concepts

SOAP message

A SOAP message is the basic unit of communication between peer SOAP nodes.

SOAP envelope

The outermost syntactic construct or structure of a SOAP message defined by SOAP within which all other syntactic elements of the message are enclosed.

SOAP header block

A syntactic construct or structure used to delimit data that logically constitutes a single computational unit within the SOAP header. SOAP header blocks are direct children of the SOAP `Header` (**4.2 SOAP Header**) *element information item*. The type of a SOAP header block is identified by the fully qualified name of the outer *element information item* of the block, which consists of its namespace URI and local name.

SOAP header

A collection of zero or more SOAP header blocks each of which may be targeted at any SOAP receiver within the SOAP message path.

SOAP body

A collection of zero or more *element information items* targeted at the ultimate SOAP receiver in the SOAP message path.

SOAP fault

A special SOAP *element information item* which contains fault information generated by a SOAP node.

The following diagram illustrates how a SOAP message is composed.

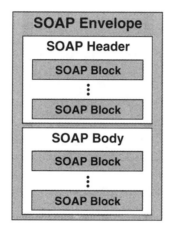

1.4.3 Message Sender and Receiver Concepts

SOAP sender

A SOAP sender is a SOAP node that transmits a SOAP message.

SOAP receiver

A SOAP receiver is a SOAP node that accepts a SOAP message.

SOAP message path

The set of SOAP senders and SOAP receivers through which a single SOAP message passes. This includes the initial SOAP sender, zero or more SOAP intermediaries, and the ultimate SOAP receiver.

Initial SOAP sender

The SOAP sender that originates a SOAP message as the starting point of a SOAP message path.

SOAP intermediary

A SOAP intermediary is both a SOAP receiver and a SOAP sender and is target-able from within a SOAP message. It processes a defined set of blocks in a SOAP message along a SOAP message path. It acts in order to forward the SOAP message towards the ultimate SOAP receiver.

Ultimate SOAP receiver

The SOAP receiver that the initial sender specifies as the final destination of the SOAP message within a SOAP message path. A SOAP message may not reach the ultimate recipient because of a SOAP fault generated by a SOAP node along the SOAP message path.

SOAP Application

A software entity that produces, consumes or otherwise acts upon SOAP messages in a manner conforming to the SOAP processing model.

2 SOAP Message Exchange Model

SOAP messages are fundamentally one-way transmissions from a SOAP sender to a SOAP receiver; however, SOAP messages are often combined to implement patterns such as request/response.

SOAP implementations can be optimized to exploit the unique characteristics of particular network systems. For example, the HTTP binding described in [1](SOAP in HTTP) provides for SOAP response messages to be delivered as HTTP responses, using the same connection as the inbound request.

2.1 SOAP Nodes

A SOAP node can be the initial SOAP sender, the ultimate SOAP receiver, or a SOAP intermediary, in which case it is both a SOAP sender and a SOAP receiver. SOAP does not provide a routing mechanism, however SOAP does recognise that a SOAP sender originates a SOAP message which is sent to an ultimate SOAP receiver, via zero or more SOAP intermediaries.

A SOAP node receiving a SOAP message MUST perform processing according to the SOAP processing model as described in this section and, if appropriate, generate SOAP faults, SOAP responses and send additional SOAP messages, as provided by the remainder of this specification.

2.2 SOAP Actors and SOAP Nodes

In processing a SOAP message, a SOAP node is said to act in the role of one or more SOAP actors, each of which is identified by a URI known as the SOAP actor name. Each SOAP node MUST act in the role of the special SOAP actor named "http://www.w3.org/2001/12/soap-envelope/actor/next", and can additionally assume the roles of zero or more other SOAP actors. A SOAP node can establish itself as the ultimate SOAP receiver by acting in the (additional) role of the anonymous SOAP actor. The roles assumed MUST be invariant during the processing of an individual SOAP message; because this specification deals only with the processing of individual SOAP messages, no statement is made regarding the possibility that a given piece of software might or might not act in varying roles when processing more than one SOAP message.

SOAP nodes MUST NOT act in the role of the special SOAP actor named "http://www.w3.org/2001/12/soap-envelope/actor/none". Header blocks targeted to this special actor are carried with the message to the ultimate receiver, but are never formally "processed".

Such blocks MAY carry data that is required for processing of other blocks.

While the purpose of a SOAP actor name is to identify a SOAP node, there are no routing or message exchange semantics associated with the SOAP actor name. For example, SOAP actors MAY be named with a URI useable to route SOAP messages to an appropriate SOAP node. Conversely, it is also appropriate to use SOAP actor roles with names that are related more indirectly to message routing (e.g. "http://example.org/banking/anyAccountMgr") or which are unrelated to routing (e.g. a URI meant to identify "all cache management software"; such a header might be used, for example, to carry an indication to any concerned software that the containing SOAP message is idempotent, and can safely be cached and replayed.)

Except for "http://www.w3.org/2001/12/soap-envelope/actor/next", "http://www.w3.org/2001/12/soap-envelope/actor/none" and the anonymous actor this specification does not prescribe the criteria by which a given node determines the (possible empty) set of roles in which it acts on a given message. For example, implementations can base this determination on factors including, but not limited to: hardcoded choices in the implementation, information provided by the transport binding (e.g. the URI to which the message was physically delivered), configuration information made by users during system installation, etc.

2.3 Targeting SOAP Header Blocks

SOAP header blocks carry optional actor *attribute information items* (see **4.2.2 SOAP actor Attribute**) that are used to target them to the appropriate SOAP node(s). SOAP header blocks with no such *attribute information item* are implicitly targeted at the anonymous SOAP actor, implying that they are to be processed by the ultimate

SOAP receiver. This specification refers to the (implicit or explicit) value of the SOAP actor attribute as the SOAP actor for the corresponding SOAP header block.

A SOAP header block is said to be targeted to a SOAP node if the SOAP actor (if present) on the block matches (see [7]) a role played by the SOAP node, or in the case of a SOAP header block with no actor *attribute information item,* if the SOAP node is acting in the role of the ultimate SOAP receiver.

A SOAP Node that acts in the role of the anonymous actor with respect to a particular SOAP message becomes the ultimate recipient of that SOAP message. Such a SOAP node is responsible for processing all parts of the message intended for the anonymous actor, including the body, according to the rules described in this section. The SOAP message path for that message ends at the ultimate recipient. However, the ultimate recipient may delegate all or part of its responsibility to other entities. The ultimate recipient may happen to use distinct SOAP message exchanges to interact with such entities. Nevertheless, responsibility for the processing of parts of a SOAP message targetted at the anonymous actor rests with the ultimate recipient of that message

2.4 Understanding SOAP Headers

It is likely that specifications for a wide variety of header functions will be developed over time, and that some SOAP nodes MAY include the software necessary to implement one or more such extensions. A SOAP header block is said to be understood by a SOAP node if the software at that SOAP node has been written to fully conform to and implement the semantics conveyed by the combination of local name and namespace name of the outer-most *element information item* of that block.

SOAP header blocks carry optional mustUnderstand *attribute information items* (see **4.2.3 SOAP mustUnderstand Attribute**). When the value of such an *attribute information item* is "true" or "1", the SOAP block is said to be mandatory.

For every mandatory SOAP header block targeted to a node, that node MUST either process the block according to the semantics conveyed by the combination of local name and namespace name of the outer-most element information item of that block; or not process the SOAP message at all, and instead generate a fault (see **2.6 Processing SOAP Messages** and **4.4 SOAP Fault**).

Mandatory blocks MUST be presumed to somehow modify the semantics of other headers or body elements. Tagging SOAP blocks as mandatory thus assures that such changes in semantics will not be silently (and, presumably, erroneously) ignored.

The mustUnderstand *attribute information item* is not intended as a mechanism for detecting errors in routing, misidentification of nodes, failure of a node to serve in its intended role(s), etc., any of which may result in a failure to even attempt processing, and the subsequent removal, of a given SOAP header block from a SOAP envelope. This specification therefore does not require any fault to be generated based on the presence or value of this attribute on a SOAP header block not targeted at the current processing node, for example when it is suspected that such a block has survived erronously due to a routing or targeting error at a preceeding intermediairy. In particular, it is not an error for a mandatory header block targeted to a role other than the ones assumed by the ultimate SOAP receiver to reach that node without having been processed.

2.5 Structure and Interpretation of SOAP Bodies

A SOAP body consists of zero or more namespace qualified *element information items,* which are the immediate children of the Body *element information item.* The ultimate SOAP receiver MUST correctly process such body elements. However, Part 1 of this specification (this document) mandates no particular structure or interpretation of such elements, and provides no standard means for specifying the processing to be done.

When multiple body elements are present, such elements MAY represent a single unit of work to be performed, MAY represent multiple separate processing steps, possibly but not necessarily in order, MAY represent data or metadata, MAY convey a mixture of work units and data, etc. The ultimate SOAP recipient MAY use the local name(s) and namespace name(s), on any or all body elements, to determine the processing to be performed. Indeed, the SOAP RPC convention (see [1]Using SOAP for RPC) uses just such a method. Conversely, other information in the body and/or headers MAY be used to make such a determination.

2.6 Processing SOAP Messages

This section sets out the rules by which SOAP messages are processed. Unless otherwise stated, processing must be semantically equivalent to performing the following steps separately, and in the order given. Note however that nothing in this specification should be taken to prevent the use of optimistic concurrency, roll back, or other techniques that might provide increased flexibility in processing order as long as all SOAP messages, SOAP faults and application-level side effects are equivalent to those that would be obtained by direct implementation of the following rules in the order shown below.

1. Determine the set of roles in which the node is to act. The contents of the SOAP envelope, including header blocks and the body, MAY be inspected in making such determination.
2. Identify all header blocks targeted at the node that are mandatory.
3. If one or more of the header blocks identified in the preceding step are not understood by the node then generate a single SOAP MustUnderstand fault (see **4.4.6 MustUnderstand Faults**). If such a fault is generated, any further processing MUST NOT be done. Faults relating to the existence or contents of the body MUST NOT be generated in this step.
4. Process all header blocks targeted at the node and, in the case of the ultimate SOAP recipient, the SOAP body. A SOAP node MUST process all SOAP header blocks targeted at it. A SOAP node MAY choose to ignore the processing implied by non-mandatory SOAP header blocks targeted at it.
5. In the case of a SOAP intermediary, and where the message is to be forwarded further along the message path, remove all SOAP header blocks targeted at the node, and possibly insert new SOAP header blocks.

In all cases where a SOAP header block is processed, the SOAP node must understand the SOAP block and must do such processing in a manner fully conformant with the specification for that block. The ultimate recipient MUST process the SOAP body, in a manner consistent with **2.5 Structure and Interpretation of SOAP Bodies**.

If processing is unsuccessful, exactly one fault MUST be generated by the node. Header-related faults other than mustUnderstand faults (see **4.4 SOAP Fault**) MUST be SOAP Sender or DataEncoding Unknown faults (see **4.4.5 SOAP Fault Codes**) and MUST conform to the specification for the corresponding SOAP header block.

Faults relating to the body MUST be SOAP Sender or DataEncoding Unknown faults (see **4.4.5 SOAP Fault Codes**).

SOAP nodes can make reference to any information in the SOAP envelope when processing a SOAP block. For example, a caching function can cache the entire SOAP message, if desired.

The processing of particular SOAP header block MAY control or determine the order of processing for other SOAP header blocks and/or the SOAP body. For example, one could create a SOAP header block to force processing of other SOAP header blocks in lexical order. In the absence of such a controlling block, the order of header and body processing is at the discretion of the SOAP node; header blocks MAY be processed in arbitrary order, and such processing MAY precede, be interleaved with, or MAY follow processing of the body. For example, a "begin transaction" header block would typically precede, a "commit transaction" would likely follow, and a "logging" function might run concurrently with body processing.

If the SOAP node is a SOAP intermediary, the SOAP message pattern and results of processing (e.g. no fault generated) MAY require that the SOAP message be sent further along the SOAP message path. Such relayed SOAP messages MUST contain all SOAP header blocks and the SOAP body from the original SOAP message, in the original order, except that SOAP header blocks targeted at the SOAP intermediary MUST be removed (such SOAP blocks are removed regardless of whether they were processed or ignored). Additional SOAP header blocks MAY be inserted at any point in the SOAP message, and such inserted SOAP header blocks MAY be indistinguishable from one or more just removed (effectively leaving them in place, but emphasizing the need to reinterpret at each SOAP node along the SOAP message path.)

Note:

The above rules apply to processing at a single node. SOAP extensions MAY be designed to ensure that mandatory (and other) headers are processed in an appropriate order, as the message moves along the message path towards the ultimate recipient. Specifically, such extensions might specify that a (Sender) fault is generated if some SOAP header blocks have inadvertently survied past some intended point in the message path. Such extensions MAY depend on the presence or value of the `mustUnderstand` *attribute information item* in the surviving headers when determining whether an error has occurred.

3 Relation to XML

All SOAP messages have an XML Information Set[10].

A SOAP node MUST ensure that all *element information items* and *attribute information items* in messages that it generates are correctly namespace qualified. A SOAP node MUST be able to process SOAP namespace information in messages that it receives. It MUST treat messages with incorrect namespace information as described in **4.1.2 Envelope Versioning Model**.

This document defines the following namespaces[7]:

❑ The SOAP envelope has the namespace identifier "http://www.w3.org/2001/12/soap-envelope"

❑ The SOAP MustUnderstand Fault has the namespace identifier "http://www.w3.org/2001/12/soap-faults"

❏ The SOAP `Upgrade` element has the namespace identifier "http://www.w3.org/2001/12/soap-upgrade"

Schema documents for these namespaces can be found by dereferencing the namespace identifiers. These schemas are normative.

A SOAP message MUST NOT contain a Document Type Declaration. On receipt of a SOAP message containing a Document Type Declaration, a SOAP receiver MUST generate a fault (see **4.4 SOAP Fault**) with a faultcode of "DTDNotSupported". A SOAP message SHOULD NOT contain processing instruction information items. A SOAP receiver MUST ignore *processing instruction information items* in SOAP messages it receives.

A SOAP message MUST NOT impose any XML schema processing (assessment and validation) requirement on the part of any receiving SOAP node. Therefore, SOAP REQUIRES that all *attribute information items,* whether specified in this specification or whether they belong to a foreign namespace be caried in the serialized SOAP envelope.

4 SOAP Envelope

A SOAP message has an XML Infoset that consists of a *document information item* with exactly one child, which is an *element information item* as described below.

The document *element information item* has:

❏ A local name of `Envelope`;

❏ A namespace name of *http://www.w3.org/2001/12/soap-envelope*;

❏ Zero or more namespace qualified *attribute information items;*

❏ One or two *element information item* children in order as follows:
1. An optional Header *element information item,* see **4.2 SOAP Header**;
2. A mandatory Body *element information item,* see **4.3 SOAP Body**;

4.1 Envelope Encoding and Versioning

4.1.1 SOAP encodingStyle Attribute

SOAP defines an encodingStyle *attribute information item* which can be used to indicate the encoding rules used to serialize a SOAP message.

The encodingStyle *attribute information item* has:

❏ A local name of encodingStyle

❏ A namespace name of *http://www.w3.org/2001/12/soap-envelope*

Editorial note: MJG   20010802

The following sentence conflicts with the definition of the Body

---

It may appear on any *element information item* in the SOAP message. Its scope is that of its owner *element information item* and that *element information item's* descendants, unless a descendant itself owns such an *attribute information item.*

The encodingStyle *attribute information item* is of type *anyURI* in the namespace *http://www.w3.org/2001/XMLSchema.* Its value identifies a set of serialization rules that can be used to deserialize the SOAP message.

Example: Example values for the encodingStyle attribute

```
encodingStyle="http://www.w3.org/2001/12/soap-encoding"
encodingStyle="http://example.org/encoding/"
encodingStyle=""
```

The serialization rules defined by SOAP (see [1]SOAP Encoding) are identified by the URI "http://www.w3.org/2001/12/soap-encoding". SOAP messages using this particular serialization SHOULD indicate this using the SOAP `encodingStyle` *attribute information item*. In addition, all URIs syntactically beginning with "http://www.w3.org/ 2001/12/soap-encoding" indicate conformance with the SOAP encoding rules defined in [1](SOAP Encoding), though with potentially tighter rules added.

A value of the zero-length URI (`""`) explicitly indicates that no claims are made for the encoding style of contained elements. This can be used to turn off any claims from containing elements.

4.1.2 Envelope Versioning Model

SOAP does not define a traditional versioning model based on major and minor version numbers. If a SOAP message is received by a SOAP 1.2 node in which the document *element information item* does NOT have a namespace name of *http://www.w3.org/2001/12/ soap-envelope* the SOAP node MUST treat this as a version error and generate a VersionMismatch SOAP fault (see **4.4 SOAP Fault**). See **A Version Transition From SOAP/1.1 to SOAP Version 1.2** for further details.

Any other malformation of the message structure MUST be treated as a Sender SOAP fault.

4.2 SOAP Header

SOAP provides a flexible mechanism for extending a SOAP message in a decentralized and modular way without prior knowledge between the communicating parties. Typical examples of extensions that can be implemented as SOAP header blocks are authentication, transaction management, payment, etc.

The Header *element information item* has:

- ❑ A local name of Header
- ❑ A namespace name of *http://www.w3.org/2001/12/soap-envelope*
- ❑ Zero or more namespace qualified *attribute information item* children.
- ❑ Zero or more namespace qualified *element information item* children.

All child *element information items* of the SOAP Header are called SOAP header blocks.

Each SOAP header block *element information item:*

- ❑ MUST be namespace qualified;
- ❑ MAY have an encodingStyle *attribute information item*
- ❑ MAY have an actor *attribute information item*
- ❑ MAY have a mustUnderstand *attribute information item*

4.2.1 Use of Header Attributes

The SOAP header block *attribute information items* defined in this section determine how a SOAP receiver should process an incoming SOAP message, as described in **2 SOAP Message Exchange Model**.

A SOAP sender generating a SOAP message SHOULD only use the SOAP header block *attribute information items* on child *element information items* of the SOAP Header *element information item.*

A SOAP receiver MUST ignore all SOAP header block *attribute information items* that are applied to other descendant *element information items* of the SOAP Header *element information item.*

Example: Example header with a single header block

```
<env:Header xmlns:env="http://www.w3.org/2001/12/soap-envelope" >
  <t:Transaction xmlns:t="http://example.org/2001/06/tx"
env:mustUnderstand="1" >
    5
  </t:Transaction>
</env:Header>
```

SOAP header block *attribute information items* MUST appear in the SOAP message itself in order to be effective; default values which may be specified in an XML Schema or other description language do not affect SOAP processing (see **3 Relation to XML**).

4.2.2 SOAP actor Attribute

As described in **2 SOAP Message Exchange Model**, not all parts of a SOAP message may be intended for the ultimate SOAP receiver. The actor *attribute information item* is to be used to indicate the SOAP node at which a particular SOAP header block is targeted.

The actor *attribute information item* has the following Infoset properties:

- ❑ A local name of actor;
- ❑ A namespace name of http://www.w3.org/2001/12/soap-envelope;
- ❑ A specified property with a value of true.

The type of the actor *attribute information item* is *anyURI* in the namespace http://www.w3.org/2001/XMLSchema. The value of the actor *attribute information item* is a URI that names a role that a SOAP node may assume.

Omitting the SOAP actor *attribute information item* implicitly targets the SOAP header block at the ultimate SOAP receiver. An empty value for this attribute is equivalent to omitting the attribute completely, i.e. targeting the block at the ultimate SOAP recipient.

4.2.3 SOAP mustUnderstand Attribute

As described in **2.4 Understanding SOAP Headers**, the SOAP mustUnderstand *attribute information item* is used to indicate whether the processing of a SOAP header block is mandatory or optional at the target SOAP node.

The mustUnderstand *attribute information item* has the following Infoset properties:

- ❏ A local name of mustUnderstand;
- ❏ A namespace name of http://www.w3.org/2001/12/soap-envelope;
- ❏ A specified property with a value of true.

The type of the mustUnderstand *attribute information item* is boolean in the namespace http://www.w3.org/2001/XMLSchema. Omitting this attribute information item is defined as being semantically equivalent to including it with a value of "false".

4.3 SOAP Body

The SOAP Body *element information item* provides a simple mechanism for exchanging mandatory information intended for the ultimate SOAP receiver of a SOAP message. Example uses of SOAP Body include marshalling RPC calls and error reporting.

The Body *element information item* has:

- ❏ A local name of Body
- ❏ A namespace name of *http://www.w3.org/2001/12/soap-envelope*
- ❏ Zero or more *element information item* children.

Editorial note: MJG   20010802

The description of Body does not allow additional attributes.

All child *element information items* of the SOAP Body *element information item:*

Editorial note: MJG   20011025

The requirement that direct children of the SOAP body be namespace qualified is a change from previous drafts. The XML Protocol Working Group solicits feedback from implementors on this change.

- ❏ MUST be namespace qualified.
- ❏ MAY have an `encodingStyle` *attribute information item*

SOAP defines one particular direct child of the SOAP body, the SOAP fault, which is used for reporting errors (see **4.4 SOAP Fault**).

4.4 SOAP Fault

The SOAP `Fault` *element information item* is used to carry error and/or status information within a SOAP message. If present, the SOAP Fault MUST appear as a direct child of the SOAP body and MUST NOT appear more than once within a SOAP Body.

The `Fault` *element information item* has:

- ❏ A local name of `Fault`;
- ❏ A namespace name of *http://www.w3.org/2001/12/soap-envelope;*
- ❏ Two or more child *element information items* in order as follows:
  1. A mandatory `faultcode` *element information item,* see **4.4.1 SOAP faultcode Element**;
  2. A mandatory `faultstring` *element information item,* see **4.4.2 SOAP faultstring Element**;

3. An optional `faultactor` *element information item,* see **4.4.3 SOAP faultactor Element**;

4. An optional `detail` *element information item,* see **4.4.4 SOAP detail Element**.

4.4.1 SOAP faultcode Element

The `faultcode` *element information item* has:

- ❑ A local name of `faultcode`;
- ❑ A namespace name which is empty

The type of the `faultcode` *element information item* is *QName* in the *http://www.w3.org/2001/XMLSchema* namespace. It is intended for use by software to provide an algorithmic mechanism for identifying the fault. SOAP defines a small set of SOAP fault codes covering basic SOAP faults (see **4.4.5 SOAP Fault Codes**)

4.4.2 SOAP faultstring Element

The `faultstring` *element information item* has:

- ❑ A local name of `faultstring`;
- ❑ A namespace name which is empty.

The type of the `faultstring` *element information item* is *string* in the *http://www.w3.org/2001/XMLSchema* namespace. It is intended to provide a human readable explanation of the fault and is not intended for algorithmic processing. This *element information item* is similar to the 'Reason-Phrase' defined by HTTP[2] and SHOULD provide at least some information explaining the nature of the fault.

4.4.3 SOAP faultactor Element

The `faultactor` *element information item* has:

- ❑ A local name of `faultactor`;
- ❑ A namespace name which is empty

The type of the `faultactor` *element information item* is *anyURI* in the *http://www.w3.org/2001/XMLSchema* namespace. It is intended to provide information about which SOAP node on the SOAP message path caused the fault to happen (see **2 SOAP Message Exchange Model**). It is similar to the SOAP `actor` *attribute information item* (see **4.2.2 SOAP actor Attribute**) but instead of indicating the target of a SOAP header block, it indicates the source of the fault. The value of the `faultactor` *element information item* identifies the source of the fault. SOAP nodes that do not act as the ultimate SOAP receiver MUST include this *element information item* The ultimate SOAP receiver MAY include this *element information item* to indicate explicitly that it generated the fault.

4.4.4 SOAP detail Element

The `detail` *element information item* has:

- ❑ A local name of `detail`;
- ❑ A namespace name which is empty;
- ❑ Zero or more *attribute information items;*
- ❑ Zero or more child *element information items.*

The `detail` *element information item* is intended for carrying application specific error information related to the SOAP Body. It MUST be present when the contents of the SOAP Body could not be processed successfully. It MUST NOT be used to carry error information about any SOAP header blocks. Detailed error information for SOAP header blocks MUST be carried within the SOAP header blocks themselves.

The absence of the `detail` *element information item* indicates that a SOAP Fault is not related to the processing of the SOAP Body. This can be used to find out whether the SOAP Body was at least partially processed by the ultimate SOAP receiver before the fault occurred, or not.

All child *element information items* of the detail *element Information Item* are called detail entries.

Each such *element information item:*

❏ MAY be namespace qualified;

❏ MAY have an encodingStyle *attribute information item.*

The SOAP encodingStyle *attribute information item* is used to indicate the encoding style used for the detail entries (see **4.1.1 SOAP encodingStyle Attribute**).

4.4.5 SOAP Fault Codes

Editorial note: MJG   20011130

Previous versions of this specification supported a hierarchical notation for fault codes using a 'dot' notation. This support has been removed in this draft and will also be omitted from the next version of this specification unless significant evidence for the contrary is provided.

SOAP faultcode values are XML qualified names [7]. The faultcodes defined in this section MUST be used as values for the SOAP faultcode *element information item* when describing faults defined by SOAP 1.2 Part 1 (this document). The namespace identifier for these SOAP faultcode values is "http://www.w3.org/2001/12/soap-envelope". Other specifications may define their own fault codes. Use of this namespace is recommended (but not required) in the specification of such faultcodes.

The faultcode values defined by this specification are listed in the following table.

Name	Meaning
VersionMismatch	The processing party found an invalid namespace for the SOAP Envelope *element information item* (see **4.1.2 Envelope Versioning Model**)
MustUnderstand	An immediate child *element information item* of the SOAP Header *element information item* that was either not understood or not obeyed by the processing party contained a SOAP mustUnderstand *attribute information item* with a value of "true" (see **4.2.3 SOAP mustUnderstand Attribute**)
DTDNotSupported	The SOAP message contained a Document Type Definition (see **3 Relation to XML**).
DataEncodingUnknown	A header or body targetted at the current SOAP node is scoped (See **4.1.1 SOAP encodingStyle Attribute**) with a data encoding that the current node does not support.
Sender	A Sender faultcode indicates that the message was incorrectly formed or did not contain the appropriate information in order to succeed. For example, the message could lack the proper authentication or payment information. It is generally an indication that the message should not be resent without change. See also **4.4 SOAP Fault** for a description of the SOAP fault detail sub-element.

Name	Meaning
Receiver	The Receiver faultcode indicates that the message could not be processed for reasons not directly attributable to the contents of the message itself but rather to the processing of the message. For example, processing could include communicating with an upstream SOAP node, which did not respond. The message may succeed at a later point in time. See also **4.4 SOAP Fault** for a description of the SOAP fault `detail` sub-element.

4.4.6 MustUnderstand Faults

When a SOAP node generates a MustUnderstand fault, it SHOULD provide, in the generated fault message, header blocks as described below which detail the qualified names (QNames, per the XML Schema Datatypes specification[5]) of the particular header block(s) which were not understood.

Each such header block *element information item* has:

❑ A local name of `Misunderstood`;

❑ A namespace name of *http://www.w3.org/2001/12/soap-faults;*

❑ A `qname` *attribute information item* as desribed below.

The `qname` *attribute information item* has the following Infoset properties:

❑ A local name of `qname`;

❑ A namespace name which is empty;

❑ A specified property with a value of true.

The type of the `qname` *attribute information item* is *QName* in the *http://www.w3.org/2001/XMLSchema* namespace. Its value is the QName of a header block which the faulting node failed to understand.

Consider the following message:

Example: SOAP envelope that will cause a SOAP MustUnderstand fault if Extension1 or Extension2 are not understood

```
<?xml version="1.0" ?>
<env:Envelope xmlns:env='http://www.w3.org/2001/12/soap-envelope'>
  <env:Header>
    <abc:Extension1 xmlns:abc='http://example.org/2001/06/ext'
                    env:mustUnderstand='1' />
    <def:Extension2 xmlns:def='http://example.com/stuff'
                    env:mustUnderstand='1' />
  </env:Header>
  <env:Body>
    . . .
  </env:Body>
</env:Envelope>
```

The above message would result in the fault message shown below if the recipient of the initial message does not understand the two header elements `abc:Extension1` and `def:Extension2` .

Note that when serializing the `qname` *attribute information item* there must be an in-scope namespace declaration for the namespace name of the misunderstood header and the value of the *attribute information item* must use the prefix of such a namespace declaration.

Note also that there is no guarantee that each MustUnderstand error contains ALL misunderstood header QNames. SOAP nodes MAY generate a fault after the first header block that causes an error

Example: SOAP fault generated as a result of not understanding Extension1 and Extension2

```xml
<?xml version="1.0" ?>
<env:Envelope xmlns:env='http://www.w3.org/2001/12/soap-envelope'
                    xmlns:f='http://www.w3.org/2001/12/soap-faults' >
  <env:Header>
    <f:Misunderstood qname='abc:Extension1'
                      xmlns:abc='http://example.org/2001/06/ext' />
    <f:Misunderstood qname='def:Extension2'
                      xmlns:def='http://example.com/stuff' />
  </env:Header>
  <env:Body>
    <env:Fault>
      <faultcode>env:MustUnderstand</faultcode>
      <faultstring>One or more mandatory headers not understood</faultstring>
    </env:Fault>
  </env:Body>
</env:Envelope>
```

containing details about that single header block only, alternatively SOAP nodes MAY generate a combined fault detailing all of the MustUnderstand problems at once.

5 SOAP Protocol Binding Framework

5.1 Introduction

SOAP provides a simple messaging framework with a core set of functionality which is primarily concerned with providing extensibility. The SOAP processing model (**2 SOAP Message Exchange Model**) describes the behavior of a single SOAP node with respect to the processing of an individual message.

The sending and receiving of SOAP messages by a SOAP node is mediated by a binding to an underlying protocol. A SOAP underlying protocol binding operates between adjacent SOAP nodes along a SOAP message path. A binding does not provide a separate processing model and does not constitute a SOAP node by itself. Rather a SOAP binding is an integral part of a SOAP node. There is no requirement that the same underlying protocol is used for all hops along a SOAP message path.

As part of communicating between SOAP nodes it may be necessary to introduce a variety of abstract features generally associated with the exchange of messages in a protocol environment. Although SOAP poses no constraints on the potential scope of such features, typical examples include "reliability", "security", "correlation", and "routing". In addition, the communication may require message exchange patterns (MEPs) beyond the one-way MEP that SOAP provides. MEPs are considered to be a type of feature; unless otherwise stated, references to the term "feature" apply also to MEPs.

In some cases, underlying protocols are equipped, either directly or through extension, with mechanisms for providing certain features, in whole or in part. Features are the modular components from which the contract between SOAP nodes and the bindings they support are formed. The SOAP binding framework provides a framework for describing these features and how they relate to SOAP nodes. A SOAP binding specification declares the features provided by a binding and describes how the services of the underlying protocol are used to honor the contract formed by the declaration of features supported by that binding. In addition, a binding specification defines the requirements for building a conformant implementation of the binding being specified.

The combination of the SOAP extensibility model and the SOAP binding framework provides some flexibility in the way that particular features can be expressed: they can be expressed entirely within the

SOAP envelope (as blocks), outside the envelope (typically in a manner that is specific to the underlying protocol), or as a combination of such expressions. It is up to the communicating nodes to decide how best to express particular features; often when a binding-level implementation for a particular feature is available, utilizing it when appropriate will provide for optimized processing.

Editorial note: HFN   20011201

Some discussion continues on how best to represent the balance of responsibility between binding specifications in particular, vs. other software at the SOAP node, when dealing with features that are represented entirely within the SOAP envelope. The paragraph above may need some additional work to clarify.

5.2 Goals of the Binding Framework

As described above, SOAP messages can be transported using a variety of underlying protocols. SOAP Part 2: Adjuncts[1] includes the specification for a binding to HTTP. Additional bindings can be created by specifications that conform to the binding framework introduced in this chapter. The goals of the binding framework are:

1. To set out the requirements and concepts that are common to all binding specifications.
2. To facilitate homogenous description of bindings that support common features.
3. To facilitate homogenous description of bindings that support common features.

Note, that the second and third goals above are related: two or more bindings may offer a given optional feature, such as reliable delivery, with one operating using an underlying protocol that directly facilitates the feature (the protocol is reliable), and the other providing the logic (logging and retransmission) in the binding. The feature can be made available to applications in a consistent manner, regardless of which binding is used.

5.3 Binding Framework

The creation, transmission, and processing of a SOAP message, possibly through one or more intermediaries, is specified in terms of a distributed state machine. The state consists of information known to a SOAP node at a given point in time, including but not limited to the contents of messages being assembled for transmission or received for processing. The state at each node can be updated either by local processing, or by information received from an adjacent node.

Section **2 SOAP Message Exchange Model** of this specification describes the processing that is common to all SOAP nodes when receiving a message. The purpose of a binding specification is to augment those core SOAP rules with any additional processing that may be particular to the binding, and to specify the manner in which the underlying protocol is used to transmit information between adjacent nodes in the message path.

Thus, the distributed state machine that manages the transmission of a given SOAP message through its message path is the combination of the core SOAP processing (see **2 SOAP Message Exchange Model**) operating at each node, in conjunction with the binding specifications connecting each pair of nodes.

As described above, SOAP can be augmented with optional features, (such as reliable message delivery, request/response MEPs, multicast MEPs, etc.). The specification of each such feature MUST include the following:

1. The information (state) required at each node to implement the feature.

2. The processing required at each node in order to fulfill the obligations of the feature.
3. The information transmitted from node to node, and in the case of MEPs, any requirements to generate additional messages (such as responses to requests in a request/response MEP).

Every binding specification MUST support the transmission and processing of one-way messages as described in this specification. A binding specification MAY state that it supports additional features, in which case the binding specification MUST provide for maintaining state, performing processing, and transmitting information in a manner consistent with the specification for those features.

In cases where multiple features are supported by a binding specification the specifications for those features must provide any information necessary for their successful use in combination; this binding framework does not provide any explicit mechanism for ensuring such compatibility of multiple features.

The binding framework provides no fixed means of naming or typing the information comprising the state at a given node. Individual feature and binding specifications are free to adopt their own conventions for specifying state. Note, however, that consistency across bindings and features is likely to be enhanced in situations where multiple feature specifications adopt consistent conventions for representing state. For example, multiple features may benefit from a consistent specification for an authentication credential, the transaction ID, etc. The HTTP binding in SOAP Part 2[1] illustrates one such convention.

As described in **4 SOAP Envelope**, each SOAP message is modeled as an XML Infoset that consists of a *document information item* with exactly one child: the envelope *element information item.* Therefore, the minimum responsibility of a binding in transmitting a message is to specify the means by which the SOAP XML Infoset is transferred to and reconstituted by the binding at the receiving SOAP node and to specify the manner in which the transmission of the envelope is effected using the facilities of the underlying protocol. The binding framework does NOT require that every binding use the XML 1.0[8] serialization as the "on the wire" representation of the Infoset; compressed, encrypted, fragmented representations and so on can be used if appropriate.

Bindings MAY depend on state that is modeled as being outside of the SOAP XML Infoset (e.g. retry counts), and MAY transmit such information to adjacent nodes. For example, some bindings take a message delivery address (typically URI) that is not within the envelope; the HTTP binding in Part 2[1] (see Using SOAP in HTTP) transmits an HTTP field named SOAPAction that is not contained within the SOAP XML Infoset.

5.4 Binding to Application-Specific Protocols

Some underlying protocols may be designed for a particular purpose or application profile. SOAP bindings to such protocols MAY use the same endpoint identification (e.g., TCP port number) as the underlying protocol, in order to reuse the existing infrastructure associated that protocol.

However, the use of well-known ports by SOAP may incur additional, unintended handling by intermediaries and underlying implementations. For example, HTTP is commonly thought of as a "Web browsing" protocol, and network administrators may place certain restrictions upon its use, or may interpose services such as filtering, content modification, routing, etc. Often, these services are interposed using port number as a heuristic.

As a result, binding definitions for underlying protocols with well-known default ports or application profiles SHOULD document potential (harmful?) interactions with commonly deployed infrastructure at those default ports or in-conformance with default application profiles. Binding definitions SHOULD also illustrate the use of the binding on a non-default port as a means of avoiding unintended interaction with such services.

5.5 Security Considerations

Editorial note: MJG   20010926

This section will in a future revision provide some guidelines for the security considerations that should be taken into account when using the binding framework defined in this document.

6 Use of URIs in SOAP

SOAP uses URIs for some identifiers including, but not limited to, values of the encodingStyle (see **4.1.1 SOAP encodingStyle Attribute**) and actor (see **4.2.2 SOAP actor Attribute**) *attribute information items*. To SOAP, a URI is simply a formatted string that identifies a web resource via its name, location, or via any other characteristics.

Although this section only applies to URIs directly used by information items defined by this specification, it is RECOMMENDED but NOT REQUIRED that application-defined data carried within a SOAP envelope use the same mechanisms and guidelines defined here for handling URIs.

URIs used as values in information items identified by the "http://www.w3.org/2001/12/soap-envelope"   and   "http://www.w3.org/

2001/12/soap-encoding" XML namespaces can be either relative or absolute. In addition, URIs used as values of the local, unqualified href attribute information item can be relative or absolute.

SOAP does not define a base URI but relies on the mechanisms defined in XML Base[11] and RFC 2396[6] for establishing a base URI against which relative URIs can be made absolute.

The underlying protocol binding MAY define a base URI which can act as the base URI for the SOAP envelope (see **5 SOAP Protocol Binding Framework** and the HTTP binding[1]).

SOAP does not define any equivalence rules for URIs in general as these are defined by the individual URI schemes and by RFC 2396[6]. However, because of inconsistencies with respect to URI equivalence rules in many current URI parsers, it is RECOMMENDED that SOAP senders do NOT rely on any special equivalence rules in SOAP receivers in order to determine equivalence between URI values used in a SOAP message.

The use of IP addresses in URIs SHOULD be avoided whenever possible (see RFC 1900[16]). However, when used, the literal format for IPv6 addresses in URI's as described by RFC 2732[12] SHOULD be supported.

SOAP does not place any a priori limit on the length of a URI. Any SOAP node MUST be able to handle the length of any URI that it publishes and both SOAP senders and SOAP receivers SHOULD be able to deal with URIs of at least 8k in length.

7 References

7.1 Normative References

1

W3C Working Draft "SOAP Version 1.2 Part 2: Adjuncts", Martin Gudgin, Marc Hadley, Jean-Jacques Moreau, Henrik Frystyk Nielsen, 2 10 2001. (See http://www.w3.org/TR/2001/WD-soap12-part2-20011217/.)

2

IETF "RFC 2616: Hypertext Transfer Protocol—HTTP/1.1", R. Fielding, J. Gettys, J. C. Mogul, H. Frystyk, T. Berners-Lee, January 1997. (See http://www.ietf.org/rfc/rfc2616.txt.)

3

IETF "RFC 2119: Key words for use in RFCs to Indicate Requirement Levels", S. Bradner, March 1997. (See http://www.ietf.org/rfc/rfc2119.txt.)

4

W3C Recommendation "XML Schema Part 1: Structures", Henry S. Thompson, David Beech, Murray Maloney, Noah Mendelsohn, 2 May 2001. (See http://www.w3.org/TR/2001/REC-xmlschema-1-20010502/.)

5

W3C Recommendation "XML Schema Part 2: Datatypes", Paul V. Biron, Ashok Malhotra, 2 May 2001. (See http://www.w3.org/TR/2001/REC-xmlschema-2-20010502/.)

6

IETF "RFC 2396: Uniform Resource Identifiers (URI): Generic Syntax", T. Berners-Lee, R. Fielding, L. Masinter, August 1998. (See http://www.ietf.org/rfc/rfc2396.txt.)

7

W3C Recommendation "Namespaces in XML", Tim Bray, Dave Hollander, Andrew Layman, 14 January 1999. (See http://www.w3.org/TR/1999/REC-xml-names-19990114/.)

8

W3C Recommendation "Extensible Markup Language (XML) 1.0 (Second Edition)", Tim Bray, Jean Paoli, C. M. Sperberg-McQueen, Eve Maler, 6 October 2000. (See http://www.w3.org/TR/2000/REC-xml-20001006.)

9

W3C Recommendation "XML Linking Language (XLink) Version 1.0", Steve DeRose, Eve Maler, David Orchard, 27 June 2001. (See http://www.w3.org/TR/2001/REC-xlink-20010627/.)

10

W3C Recommendation "XML Information Set", John Cowan, Richard Tobin, 24 October 2001. (See http://www.w3.org/TR/2001/REC-xml-infoset-20011024/.)

11

W3C Recommendation "XML Base", Johnathan Marsh, 27 June 2001. (See http://www.w3.org/TR/2001/REC-xmlbase-20010627/.)

12

IETF "RFC 2732: Format for Literal IPv6 Addresses in URL's", R. Hinden, B. Carpenter, L. Masinter, December 1999. (See http://www.ietf.org/rfc/rfc2732.txt.)

7.2 Informative References

13

XML Protocol Comments Archive (See http://lists.w3.org/ Archives/Public/xmlp-comments/.)

14

XML Protocol Discussion Archive (See http://lists.w3.org/ Archives/Public/xml-dist-app/.)

15

XML Protocol Charter (See http://www.w3.org/2000/09/XML-Protocol-Charter.)

15

W3C Note "Simple Object Access Protocol (SOAP) 1.1", Don Box, David Ehnebuske, Gopal Kakivaya, Andrew Layman, Noah Mendelsohn, Henrik Nielsen, Satish Thatte, Dave Winer, 8 May 2000. (See http://www.w3.org/TR/SOAP/.)

16

IETF "RFC 1900: Renumbering Needs Work", B. Carpenter, Y. Rekhter, February 1996. (See http://www.ietf.org/rfc/ rfc1900.txt.)

A Version Transition from SOAP/1.1 to SOAP Version 1.2

The SOAP/1.1 specification[15] says the following on versioning in section 4.1.2:

"SOAP does not define a traditional versioning model based on major and minor version numbers. A SOAP message MUST have an Envelope element associated with the "http://schemas.xmlsoap.org/

soap/envelope/" namespace. If a message is received by a SOAP application in which the SOAP `Envelope` element is associated with a different namespace, the application MUST treat this as a version error and discard the message. If the message is received through a request/response protocol such as HTTP, the application MUST respond with a SOAP VersionMismatch faultcode message (see section 4.4) using the SOAP "http://schemas.xmlsoap.org/soap/envelope/" namespace."

That is, rather than a versioning model based on shortnames (typically version numbers), SOAP uses a declarative extension model which allows a sender to include the desired features within the SOAP envelope construct. SOAP says nothing about the granularity of extensions nor how extensions may or may not affect the basic SOAP processing model. It is entirely up to extension designers be it either in a central or a decentralized manner to determine which features become SOAP extensions.

The SOAP extensibility model is based on the following three basic assumptions:

1. SOAP versioning is directed only at the SOAP envelope. It explicitly does not address versioning of blocks, encodings, protocol bindings, or otherwise.
2. A SOAP node must determine whether it supports the version of a SOAP message on a per message basis. In the following, "support" means understanding the semantics of the envelope version identified by the QName of the `Envelope` element information item:
   ❑ A SOAP node receiving an envelope that it doesn't support must not attempt to process the message according to any other processing rules regardless of other up- or downstream SOAP nodes.

❑ A SOAP node may provide support for multiple envelope versions. However, when processing a message a SOAP node must use the semantics defined by the version of that message.

3. It is essential that the envelope remains stable over time and that new features are added using the SOAP extensibility mechanism. Changing the envelope inherently affects interoperability, adds complexity, and requires central control of extensions—all of which directly conflicts with the SOAP requirements.

The rules for dealing with the possible SOAP/1.1 and SOAP Version 1.2 interactions are as follows:

1. Because of the SOAP/1.1 rules, a compliant SOAP/1.1 node receiving a SOAP Version 1.2 message will generate a Version-Mismatch SOAP fault using an envelope qualified by the "http://schemas.xmlsoap.org/soap/envelope/" namespace identifier.

2. A SOAP Version 1.2 node receiving a SOAP/1.1 message may either process the message as SOAP/1.1 or generate a SOAP VersionMismatch fault using the "http://schemas.xmlsoap.org/soap/envelope/" namespace identifier. As part of the SOAP VersionMismatch fault, a SOAP Version 1.2 node should include the list of envelope versions that it supports using the SOAP upgrade extension identified by the "http://www.w3.org/2001/12/soap-upgrade" identifier.

The upgrade extension consists of an Upgrade *element information item.*

The Upgrade *element information item* contains an ordered list of namespace identifiers of SOAP envelopes that the SOAP node supports in the order most to least preferred.

The Upgrade *element information item* has:

❑ A local name of Upgrade;

❑ A namespace name of *http://www.w3.org/2001/12/soap-upgrade;*

❑ One or more envelope child *element information items* as described below.

The envelope *element information item* has:

❑ A local name of envelope;

❑ A namespace name which is empty;

❑ An unqualified *attribute information item* with a local name of qname and a type of QName in the "http://www.w3.org/2001/XMLSchema" namespace.

The value of the qname *attribute information item* specifies the qualified name of an element that the SOAP node accepts as the top-level element of a SOAP message

Following is an example of a VersionMismatch fault generated by a SOAP Version 1.2 node including the SOAP upgrade extension:

Example: VersionMismatch fault generated by a SOAP Version 1.2 node, and including a SOAP upgrade extension

```
<?xml version="1.0" ?>
<env:Envelope
xmlns:env="http://schemas.xmlsoap.org/soap/envelope/">
  <env:Header>
    <V:Upgrade xmlns:V="http://www.w3.org/2001/12/soap-upgrade">
      <envelope qname="ns1:Envelope"
      xmlns:ns1="http://www.w3.org/2001/12/soap-envelope"/>
    </V:Upgrade>
  </env:Header>
  <env:Body>
    <env:Fault>
      <faultcode>env:VersionMismatch</faultcode>
      <faultstring>Version Mismatch</faultstring>
    </env:Fault>
  </env:Body>
</env:Envelope>
```

The following is an example of some future SOAP node which returns multiple envelope elements in the Upgrade element. This SOAP node prefers the Envelope element in the "http://www.example.org/2002/10/soap-envelope" namespace but will also accept the Envelope element in the "http://www.w3.org/2001/12/soap-envelope" namespace.

Example: VersionMismatch fault generated by some future SOAP node, and including a SOAP upgrade extension with multiple envelope elements

```
<?xml version="1.0" ?>
<env:Envelope
xmlns:env="http://schemas.xmlsoap.org/soap/envelope/">
  <env:Header>
    <V:Upgrade xmlns:V="http://www.w3.org/2001/12/soap-upgrade">
      <envelope qname="ns1:Envelope"
xmlns:ns1="http://www.example.org/2002/10/soap-envelope"/>
      <envelope qname="ns2:Envelope"
xmlns:ns2="http://www.w3.org/2001/12/soap-envelope"/>
    </V:Upgrade>
  </env:Header>
  <env:Body>
    <env:Fault>
      <faultcode>env:VersionMismatch</faultcode>
      <faultstring>Version Mismatch</faultstring>
    </env:Fault>
  </env:Body>
</env:Envelope>
```

Note that existing SOAP/1.1 nodes are not likely to indicate which envelope versions they support. If nothing is indicated then this means that SOAP/1.1 is the only supported envelope.

B Acknowledgements (Non-Normative)

This document is the work of the W3C XML Protocol Working Group.

Members of the Working Group are (at the time of writing, and by alphabetical order): Yasser al Safadi (Philips Research), Vidur Apparao (Netscape), Don Box (DevelopMentor), Charles Campbell (Informix Software), Michael Champion (Software AG), Dave Cleary (web-Methods), Ugo Corda (Xerox), Paul Cotton (Microsoft Corporation), Ron Daniel (Interwoven), Glen Daniels (Allaire), Doug Davis (IBM), Ray Denenberg (Library of Congress), Paul Denning (MITRE Corporation), Frank DeRose (TIBCO Software, Inc.), James Falek (TIBCO Software, Inc.), David Fallside (IBM), Chris Ferris (Sun Microsystems), Daniela Florescu (Propel), Dietmar Gaertner (Software AG), Rich Greenfield (Library of Congress), Martin Gudgin (Develop-Mentor), Hugo Haas (W3C), Marc Hadley (Sun Microsystems), Mark Hale (Interwoven), Randy Hall (Intel), Gerd Hoelzing (SAP AG), Oisin Hurley (IONA Technologies), Yin-Leng Husband (Compaq), John Ibbotson (IBM), Ryuji Inoue (Matsushita Electric Industrial Co., Ltd.), Scott Isaacson (Novell, Inc.), Kazunori Iwasa (Fujitsu Software Corporation), Murali Janakiraman (Rogue Wave), Mario Jeckle (Daimler-Chrysler Research and Technology), Eric Jenkins (Engenia Software), Mark Jones (AT&T), Anish Karmarkar (Oracle), Jeffrey Kay (Engenia Software), Richard Koo (Vitria Technology Inc.), Jacek Kopecky (IDOOX s.r.o.), Yves Lafon (W3C), Tony Lee (Vitria Technology Inc.), Michah Lerner (AT&T), Henry Lowe (OMG), Richard Martin (Active Data Exchange), Noah Mendelsohn (Lotus Development), Jeff Mischkinsky (Oracle), Nilo Mitra (Ericsson Research Canada), Jean-Jacques Moreau (Canon), Highland Mary Mountain (Intel), Masahiko Narita (Fujitsu Software Corporation), Mark Needleman (Data Research Associates), Eric Newcomer (IONA Technologies), Henrik Frystyk Nielsen (Microsoft Corporation), Mark Nottingham (Akamai Technologies), David Orchard (BEA Systems),

Kevin Perkins (Compaq), Jags Ramnaryan (BEA Systems), Andreas Riegg (Daimler-Chrysler Research and Technology), Herve Ruellan (Canon), Marwan Sabbouh (MITRE Corporation), Shane Sesta (Active Data Exchange), Miroslav Simek (IDOOX s.r.o.), Simeon Simeonov (Allaire), Nick Smilonich (Unisys), Soumitro Tagore (Informix Software), Lynne Thompson (Unisys), Patrick Thompson (Rogue Wave), Asir Vedamuthu (webMethods) Ray Whitmer (Netscape), Volker Wiechers (SAP AG), Stuart Williams (Hewlett-Packard), Amr Yassin (Philips Research) and Jin Yu (Martsoft Corp.).

Previous members were: Eric Fedok (Active Data Exchange), Susan Yee (Active Data Exchange), Dan Frantz (BEA Systems), Alex Ceponkus (Bowstreet), James Tauber (Bowstreet), Rekha Nagarajan (Calico Commerce), Mary Holstege (Calico Commerce), Krishna Sankar (Cisco Systems), David Burdett (Commerce One), Murray Maloney (Commerce One), Jay Kasi (Commerce One), Yan Xu (DataChannel), Brian Eisenberg (DataChannel), Mike Dierken (DataChannel), Michael Freeman (Engenia Software), Bjoern Heckel (Epicentric), Dean Moses (Epicentric), Julian Kumar (Epicentric), Miles Chaston (Epicentric), Alan Kropp (Epicentric), Scott Golubock (Epicentric), Michael Freeman (Engenia Software), Jim Hughes (Fujitsu Limited), Dick Brooks (Group 8760), David Ezell (Hewlett Packard), Fransisco Cubera (IBM), David Orchard (Jamcracker), Alex Milowski (Lexica), Steve Hole (MessagingDirect Ltd.), John-Paul Sicotte (MessagingDirect Ltd.), Vilhelm Rosenqvist (NCR), Lew Shannon (NCR), Art Nevarez (Novell, Inc.), David Clay (Oracle), Jim Trezzo (Oracle), David Cleary (Progress Software), Andrew Eisenberg (Progress Software), Peter Lecuyer (Progress Software), Ed Mooney (Sun Microsystems), Mark Baker (Sun Microsystems), Anne Thomas Manes (Sun Microsystems), George Scott (Tradia Inc.), Erin Hoffmann (Tradia Inc.), Conleth O'Connell (Vignette), Waqar Sadiq (Vitria Technology Inc.), Randy Waldrop (webMethods), Bill Anderson (Xerox), Tom Breuel (Xerox), Matthew MacKenzie (XMLGlobal

Technologies), David Webber (XMLGlobal Technologies), John Evde-
mon (XMLSolutions) and Kevin Mitchell (XMLSolutions).

The people who have contributed to discussions on xml-dist-app@w3.
org are also gratefully acknowledged.

C Part 1 Change Log (Non-Normative)

C.1 SOAP Specification Changes

Date	Author	Description
20011213	MJH	Updated namespace URIs, fixed spelling error.
20011211	MJH	Added section headings for faultcode, faultstring, faultactor and detail elements.
20011211	MJH	Fixed a number of spelling errors and grammatical problems throughout the document. Applied some limited rewording to improve readability.
20011211	MJH	Removed duplicate description of "must happen" extension from section 2.
20011206	MJH	Removed more mentions of body blocks.
20011206	MJH	Limited rewording and removal of duplication from section 2. In particular, removed namespace definition for mU and actor (this is in section 4) and massaged text in processing model to remove duplication and improve readability.
20011206	MJH	Incorporated Chris Ferris suggested changes to glossary and section 2.
20011206	MJH	General editorial work on new sections. Added references and other tagging as required.
20011206	MJH	Incorporated agreed changes to URIs in SOAP section (remove duplication with XML base and cite XML base more strongly).

Date	Author	Description
20011206	MJH	Incorporated issue 155 resolution.
20011205	JJM	Elevated the header removal step to a processing model step.
20011204	MJH	Added bibref to Use of URIs section and tidied up the language in that section.
20011204	MJH	Modified soapEncoding descriptive text—Issues 159 and 166.
20011204	JJM	Added text to section 2.2, second paragraph, to indicate none blocks may carry data for processing of other blocks.
20011204	JJM	Section 2.2, four paragraph, added "anonymous actor" to the list.
20011204	JJM	Section 2.3, remove text for SOAP body blocks.
20011204	JJM	Section 2.3, replace "has assumed the role of the anonymous actor" by "is the ultimate receiver".
20011204	JJM	Section 2.4, incorporated 2 paragraph previously in section 2.
20011204	JJM	Added section 2.5 (text from Noah).
20011204	JJM	Added an extra step to the processing model (now section 2.6).
20011204	JJM	Simplified step 3, and moved the previous text further below in the same section (2.6).
20011204	JJM	Section 2.6, incorporated text from section 4.
20011204	JJM	Section 4.2.2, removed explanation of next and none roles.
20011204	JJM	Section 4.2.2, added text to indicate the meaning of an empty actor attribute.
20011204	JJM	Trimmed section 4.2.3, as the text is now in section 2.
20011204	JJM	Removed section 4.3.1, since body processing is now in section 2.6.
20011204	JJM	Added ednote to flag the definition for SOAP block is out of date.

Date	Author	Description
20011204	JJM	Reformated section 5 (Binding Framework).
20011204	JJM	Reformated section 6 (Use of URIs in SOAP). Removed non ASCII characters.
20011204	JJM	Added missing "att" and "attval" around elements and attributes in section 6.
20011204	JJM	Fixed a number of lax references in section 6.
20011201	HFN	Added SOAP Protocol Binding Framework.
20011201	HFN	Added section on URIs and XML Base.
2001129	MJG	Incorporated resolution text for Issue 146 into Section 2.3.
2001129	MJG	Changed "Client" and "Server" fault codes to be "Sender" and "Receiver" respectively as resolution of Issue 143.
2001129	MJG	Removed dot notation from spec. Added "DTDNotSupported" fault code to fault code table.
20011122	MJH	Incorporated resolution to issue 172 (criteria for generating version mismatch fault into **4.1.2 Envelope Versioning Model**. Removed duplication of versioning error text and associated ednote from **3 Relation to XML**.
20011029	MJH	Changed "default actor" to "anonymous actor".
20011029	MJH	Amended relation to XML section (Issue 135).
20011029	MJH	Amended section 2.5 (Issue 157).
20011029	MJH	Removed citation of ABNF—not used in part 1.
20011029	MJH	Amended section 1.3 (Issue 150).
20011029	MJH	Amended section 1.1 (Issue 149).
20011029	MJH	Amended introductory text (Issue 148).
20011029	MJH	Amended introductory text (Issue 147).
20011029	MJH	Amended abstract (Issue 147).

Date	Author	Description
20011026	MJG	Amended text in Section 2.5 bullet 2 (Issue 158).
20011026	MJG	Amended text in Section 2.4 para 2 (Issue 156).
20011026	MJG	Amended text in Section 2.1 para 2 (Issue 152).
20011026	MJG	Amended prose related to DTDs and PIs (Issue 4).
20011026	MJG	Added text to state that SOAP is no longer an acronym (Issue 125).
20011026	MJG	Amended description of Upgrade extension in Appendix A to be Infoset based.
20011026	MJG	Added an example of returning multiple versions in the VersionMismatch header to Appendix A (Issue 119).
20011026	MJG	Added definition of SOAP Application to glossary (Issue 139).
20011026	MJG	Added xml declaration to all XML examples with a root of env:Envelope or xs:schema (Issue 10).
20011025	MJG	Changed MAY to MUST regarding namespace qualification of SOAP body blocks (Issue 141).
20011011	MJG	Added para to section 2.2 on criteria (or lack thereof) for determining whether a SOAP node acts as a particular actor.
20010926	MJG	Updated member list.
20010926	MJG	Removed extra double quotes around certain URLs.
20010921	MJG	Changed targetNamespace attribute of faults schema to http://www.w3.org/2001/09/soap-faults.
20010921	MJG	Changed targetNamespace attribute of upgrade schema to http://www.w3.org/2001/09/soap-upgrade.
20010921	MJG	Changed targetNamespace attribute of envelope schema to http://www.w3.org/2001/09/soap-envelope.

Date	Author	Description
20010921	MJG	Modified content model of Envelope complex type in envelope schema to disallow content after the Body element.
20010920	JJM	Included MarkN's text regarding issue 11 and 13 as amended by Stuart in the specification and expand the ednote appropriately.
20010920	JJM	Change the namespace of the envelope to http://www.w3.org/2001/09/ . . .
20010918	JJM	Incorporated several editorial comments from Stuart Williams.
20010918	JJM	Removed reference to trailer from the "SOAP Envelope" section.
20010914	JJM	Fixed issues 124, 126, 127, 128 and 132.
20010914	JJM	Used the rewrite from Mark Nottingham for section "SOAPAction attribute".
20010914	JJM	Incoporated text from Mark Nottingham clarifying the role of none blocks.
20010914	JJM	Reference the XML InfoSet Proposed Recommandation instead of the Candidate Recommandation.
20010911	JJM	Changed XML Information Set into a normative reference. Changed XML Protocol Comments Archive, Discussion Archive and Charter into non-normative references. Removed "as illustrated above" from section 2. Added missing parantheses in sections 2.5 and 4.1.1.
20010905	MJH	Wordsmithed abstract and introduction to better reflect split into parts 1 and 2. Rationalised list of references so only cited works appear. Removed encoding schema changes. Added bibref entries for cross references to Part 2, fixed links so they target the HTML instead of XML version of the doc.
20010831	JJM	Added a close paragraph tag before starting a new olist or ulist.

Date	Author	Description
20010831	JJM	Properly declared the language for the spec, so that we can generate valid HTML.
20010830	MJG	Added an element declaration for a Fault element of type Fault to the envelope schema.
20010830	JJM	Removed terminology not relevant for part1.
20010830	JJM	Moved some introductory examples to part2.
20010830	JJM	Moved SOAP example appendix to part2.
20010830	JJM	Added a paragraph to section 1 pointing to part2 for encoding, rpc and http binding.
20010829	JJM	Added a placeholder for the forthcoming Transport Binding Framework section.
20010829	JJM	Updated the spec's title.
20010829	JJM	Replaced specref with xspecref for references to Part2 items.
20010829	JJM	Added bibliography entry for SOAP 1.2 Part 2.
20010829	JJM	Removed former sections 5, 6, 7 and 8.
20010829	JJM	Did split the spec into two parts.
20010829	JJM	Refered to the proper DTD and stylesheet.
20010829	JJM	Updated the list of WG members: one person per line in the XML file, for easier updating.
20010816	MJH	Replaced a mustUnderstand="1" with mustUnderstand="true". Slight rewording in mu description.
20010810	MJH	Merged in RPC fault rules text from Jacek. Added new DataEncodingUnknown fault code to SOAP Fault Codes section. Added editorial notes about introduction of new fault code namespace for RPC.
20010809	MJH	Merged in "mustHappen" descriptive text from Glen and Noah.

Date	Author	Description
20010809	MJH	Fixed language around "default" values of attributes.
20010809	MJH	Removed HTTP extension framework, added editorial note to describe why.
20010808	MJH	Added Infoset "specified" property text from Chris.
20010808	MJH	Removed assumption 4 from version transition appendix.
20010808	MJH	Added reference to SOAP 1.1 specification to references section, removed SOAP 1.1 author list from acknowledgments section.
20010807	MJH	Converted specification from HTML to XML conforming to W3C XMLSpec DTD. Numerous resulting formatting changes.
20010720	MJG	Applied Infoset terminology to sections 1, 2, 3 and 4.
20010629	MJG	Amended description of routing and intermediaries in Section 2.1.
20010629	JJM	Changed "latest version" URI to end with soap12.
20010629	JJM	Remove "previous version" URI.
20010629	JJM	Removed "Editor copy" in <title>.
20010629	JJM	Removed "Editor copy" in the title.
20010629	JJM	Added "Previous version" to either point to SOAP/1.1, or explicitly mention there was no prior draft.
20010629	JJM	Pre-filed publication URIs.
20010629	JJM	Incorporated David's suggested changes for the examples in section 4.1.1 to 4.4.2.
20010629	JJM	Fixed some remaining typos.
20010629	MJH	Fixed a couple of typos.
20010628	MJG	Made various formatting, spelling and grammatical fixes.
20010628	MJG	Moved soap:encodingStyle from soap:Envelope to children of soap:Header/soap:Body in examples 1, 2, 47, 48, 49 and 50.

Date	Author	Description
20010628	MJG	Changed text in Section 2.1 from 'it is both a SOAP sender or a SOAP receiver' to 'it is both a SOAP sender and a SOAP receiver'.
20010628	MJG	Fixed caption on Example 24.
20010628	MJH	Fixed a couple of capitalisation errors where the letter A appeared as a capital in the middle of a sentence.
20010628	MJH	Updated figure 1, removed ednote to do so.
20010622	HFN	Removed the introductory text in terminology section 1.4.3 as it talks about model stuff that is covered in section 2. It was left over from original glossary which also explained the SOAP model.
20010622	HFN	Moved the definition of block to encapsulation section in terminology.
20010622	HFN	Removed introductory section in 1.4.1 as this overlaps with the model description in section 2 and doesn't belong in a terminology section.
20010622	HFN	Removed reference to "Web Characterization Terminology & Definitions Sheet" in terminology section as this is not an active WD.
20010622	HFN	Added revised glossary.
20010622	HFN	Added example 0 to section 1.3 and slightly modified text for example 1 and 2 to make it clear that HTTP is used as a protocol binding.
20010622	MJG	Added http://example.com/ . . . to list of application/context specific URIs in section 1.2.
20010622	MJG	Updated examples in section 4.1.1 to be encodingStyle attributes rather than just the values of attributes.
20010622	MJG	Added table.norm, td.normitem and td.normtext styles to stylesheet. Used said styles for table of fault code values in section 4.4.1.

Date	Author	Description
20010622	MJG	In Appendix C, changed upgrade element to Upgrade and env to envelope. Made envelope unqualified. Updated schema document to match.
20010622	MJG	Moved MisunderstoodHeader from envelope schema into seperate faults schema. Removed entry in envelope schema change table in Appendix D.2 that refered to additon of said element. Modified example in section 4.4.2 to match. Added reference to schema document to section 4.4.2.
20010622	MJH	Added binding as a component of SOAP in introduction. Fixed a couple of typos and updated a couple of example captions.
20010622	MJG	Made BNF in section 6.1.1 into a table.
20010622	MJG	Made BNFs in section 5.1 clause 8 into tables. Added associated 'bnf' style for table and td elements to stylesheet.
20010622	MJG	Amended text regarding namespace prefix mappings in section 1.2.
20010622	MJG	Added link to schema for the http://www.w3.org/2001/06/soap-upgrade namespace to Appendix C. Updated associated ednote.
20010622	MJG	Added reference numbers for XML Schema Recommendation to text prior to schema change tables in Appendix D.2 and linked said numbers to local rcferences in this document.
20010622	MJG	Reordered entries in schema change classification table in Appendix D.2.
20010622	MJG	Changed type of mustUnderstand and root attributes to standard boolean and updated schema change tables in Appendix D.2 accordingly.
20010622	JJM	Manually numbered all the examples (53 in total!).
20010622	JJM	Added caption text to all the examples.
20010622	JJM	Replaced remaining occurrences of SOAP/1.2 with SOAP Version 1.2 (including <title>).

Date	Author	Description
20010621	HFN	Added ednote to section 4.2.2 and 4.2.3 that we know they have to be incorporated with section 2.
20010621	HFN	Added version transition appendix C.
20010621	HFN	Applied new styles to examples.
20010621	HFN	Changed term "transport" to "underlying protocol.
20010621	HFN	Changed example URNs to URLs of the style http://example.org/ . . .
20010621	MJH	Updated the Acknowledgements section.
20010621	JJM	Added new style sheet definitions (from XML Schema) for examples, and used them for example 1 and 2.
20010621	JJM	Incorporated David Fallside's comments on section Status and Intro sections.
20010620	HFN	Changed the status section.
20010620	HFN	Changed title to SOAP Version 1.2 and used that first time in abstract and in body.
20010620	HFN	Removed question from section 2.4 as this is an issue and is to be listed in the issues list.
20010620	HFN	Moved change log to appendix.
20010615	JJM	Renamed default actor to anonymous actor for now (to be consistent).
20010615	JJM	Fixed typos in section 2.
20010614	JJM	Updated section 2 to adopt the terminology used elsewhere in the spec.
20010613	MJH	Updated mustUnderstand fault text with additions from Martin Gudgin.
20010613	MJH	Added schema changes appendix from Martin Gudgin.

Date	Author	Description
20010613	MJH	Added mustUnderstand fault text from Glen Daniels.
20010612	MJH	Fixed document <title>.
20010612	MJH	Moved terminology subsection from message exchange model section to introduction section.
20010612	MJH	Fixed capitalisation errors by replacing ". . . A SOAP . . ." with ". . . a SOAP . . ." where appropriate.
20010612	MJH	Removed trailing "/" from encoding namespace URI.
20010612	MJH	Fixed links under namespace URIs to point to W3C space instead of schemas.xmlsoap.org.
20010612	MJH	Removed some odd additional links with text of "/" pointing to the encoding schema following the text of the encoding namespace URI in several places.
20010611	MJH	Incorporated new text for section 2.
20010611	JJM	Changed remaining namespaces, in particular next.
20010609	JJM	Changed the spec name from XMLP/SOAP to SOAP.
20010609	JJM	Changed the version number from 1.1 to 1.2.
20010609	JJM	Changed the namespaces from http://schemas.xmlsoap.org/soap/ to http://www.w3.org/2001/06/soap-.
20010609	JJM	Replaced the remaining XS and XE prefixes to env and enc, respectively.
20010601	MJH	Updated the examples in section 1, 6 and appendix A with text suggested by Martin Gudgin to comply with XML Schema Recommendation.
20010601	JJM	Updated the examples in section 4 and 5 with text suggested by Martin Gudgin, to comply with XML Schema Recommendation.

Date	Author	Description
20010531	HFN	Removed appendices C and D and added links to live issues list and separate schema files.
20010531	MJH	Added this change log and updated schemas in appendix C to comply with XML Schema Recommendation.

C.2 XML Schema Changes

The envelope schema has been updated to be compliant with the XML Schema Recomendation[4][5]. The table below shows the categories of change.

Class	Meaning
Addition	New constructs have been added to the schema
Clarification	The meaning of the schema has been changed to more accurately match the specification
Deletion	Constructs have been removed from the schema
Name	The schema has been changed due to a datatype name change in the XML Schema specification
Namespace	A namespace name has been changed
Semantic	The meaning of the schema has been changed
Style	Style changes have been made to the schema
Syntax	The syntax of the schema has been updated due to changes in the XML Schema specification

The table below lists the changes to the envelope schema.

Class	Description
Namespace	Updated to use the http://www.w3.org/2001/XMLSchema namespace
Namespace	Value of targetNamespace attribute changed to http://www.w3.org/2001/06/soap-envelope
Clarification	Changed element and attribute wildcards in Envelope complex type to namespace="##other"
Clarification	Changed element and attribute wildcards in Header complex type to namespace="##other"

Class	Description
Clarification	Added explicit namespace="##any" to element and attribute wildcards in Body complex type
Clarification	Added explicit namespace="##any" to element and attribute wildcards in detail complex type
Clarification	Added an element wildcard with namespace="##other" to the Fault complex type
Name	Changed item type of encodingStyle from uri-reference to anyURI
Name	Changed type of actor attribute from uri-reference to anyURI
Name	Changed type of faultactor attribute from uri-reference to anyURI
Semantic	Added processContents="lax" to all element and attribute wildcards

Class	Description
Semantic	Changed type of the mustUnderstand attribute from restriction of boolean that only allowed 0 or 1 as lexical values to the standard boolean in the http://www.w3.org/2001/XMLSchema namespace. The lexical forms 0, 1, false, true are now allowed.
Style	Where possible comments have been changed into annotations
Syntax	Changed all occurences of maxOccurs="*" to maxOccurs="unbounded"
Syntax	Added <xs:sequence> to all complex type definitions derived implicitly from the ur-type
Syntax	Added <xs:sequence> to all named model group definitions

In addition several changes occured in the names of datatypes in the XML Schema specification and some datatypes were removed. The following table lists those changes.

Datatype	Class	Description
timeDuration	Renamed	New name is duration
timeInstant	Renamed	New name is dateTime
recurringDuration	Removed	The recurringDuration datatype no longer exists.
recurringInstant	Removed	The recurringInstant datatype no longer exists.
binary	Removed	The binary datatype has been replaced by the hexBinary and base64Binary datatypes.
month	Renamed	New name is gYearMonth

Datatype	Class	Description
timePeriod	Removed	The timePeriod datatype no longer exists
year	Renamed	New name is gYear
century	Removed	The century datatype no longer exists
recurringDate	Renamed	New name is gMonthDay
recurringDay	Renamed	New name is gDay

Glossary

.NET

A Microsoft development framework that integrates earlier Microsoft technologies with newer technologies built around XML. Microsoft's .NET packages earlier COM+ component services and the ASP Web Development framework with XML and support for XML protocols such as SOAP, WSDL, and UDDI.

ANSI (American National Standards Institute)

The United States government body responsible for approving U.S. standards in many different areas, including computers and communications.

API (application program interface)

The calling conventions by which an application accesses the services of a software library. An API provides a level of abstraction between the application and the library to ensure code portability.

ASC X12 (Accredited Standards Committee X12)

The U.S. standards organization responsible for defining national and industry EDI messaging protocols.

B2B (business-to-business)

Electronic commerce between businesses, replacing the exchange of paper documents.

B2C (business-to-consumer)

Electronic commerce between businesses and their consumers, usually through a Web browser.

B2E (business-to-employee)

Communication between an organization and its workers using the Internet and related technologies.

BizTalk

Both a Microsoft framework for XML-based B2B e-commerce and the name of the Windows-based server that supports the BizTalk Framework. Related to BizTalk is the Web site www.biztalk.org that acts as a repository for XML schemas that describe the structure of BizTalk documents for various businesses and business processes.

C# (pronounced "C sharp")

An object-oriented language that allows programmers to build applications for the new Microsoft .NET platform. C# is similar to Java in that programs are compiled to an intermediate language and then interpreted at runtime.

C++

An object-oriented programming language developed by Bjorne Stroustrop at Bell Labs. C++ adds object-oriented features to the C programming language. In both C and C++, the term C++ has the technical meaning "add 1 to C," so that the name of the language is also a play on words.

CA (certificate authority)

A trusted third-party organization or company that issues digital certifications used to create digital signatures and public and private key pairs. A CA guarantees that the individual or company granting a certificate is in fact that entity. CAs usually maintain relationships with banks or credit card companies that confirm a claimed identity.

Canonicalization

An XML technique that reduces an XML document to its essential (or canonical) form. Canonicalization addresses the fact that when XML is read and processed using standard XML parsing and processing techniques, some surface representation information may be lost or modified. Some of the actions taken in creating a canonical form include replacing character and parsed entity references, replacing CDATA sections with their character content, removing the XML declaration and DTD, converting empty elements to start-end tag pairs, replacing special characters in attribute values and character content by character references, and adding default attributes to each element.

CICS (Customer Information Control System)

IBM's general-purpose online transaction processing software. First released in 1968 and continuing to evolve, CICS is an application server that runs on a range of operating systems from the desktop to the largest mainframe. When many computing and data-access tasks must be executed as a single atomic operation, the operations are grouped together as a unit of work or a transaction.

CLR (Common Language Runtime)

A Microsoft Windows-based execution environment for over 15 languages that sits behind the .NET framework. Languages including Visual Basic, C++, Perl, C#, and COBOL compile to an Intermediate Language that executes in the CLR.

COM (Component Object Model)

The Microsoft Component Object Model that for the past decade has been the standard for components that run on Windows machines. Tools such as Visual C++ and Visual Basic facilitate the creation of COM components. Many features of the Windows operating system are implemented using COM and many companies have significant investment in COM-based systems.

COM+ (extension to Component Object Model)

Services that include transactions, security, synchronization, and events-handling for both COM and .NET component-based applications.

CORBA (Common Object Request Broker Architecture)

A vendor-independent tightly coupled architecture and infrastructure from the Object Management Group that applications use to communicate over networks. Based on the IIOP protocol, CORBA programs can interoperate with other CORBA programs independent of vendor, operating system, programming language, and network. CORBA requires purchasing a CORBA implementation from a vendor and compiling code with CORBA libraries.

CSS (cascading style sheets)

A simple mechanism for adding style (such as fonts, colors, or spacing) to Web documents. Multiple levels of CSS can be used to allow selective overriding of styles.

DCOM (Distributed Component Object Model)

Often called "COM on the wire," DCOM supports distributed object communication across platforms by running a protocol called Object Remote Procedure Call.

DHTML (Dynamic HTML)

An extension of HTML that provides greater control over the layout of a Web page and allows Web pages to change based on user interaction without requiring additional communication with the server.

digital certificate

Digital documents issued by a trusted certificate authority.

digital signature

The use of public-key encryption to authenticate the identity of the sender and validate the content of the message. Analogous to signing one's name across the face of a document.

DLL (dynamic link library)

A library of software-support modules that is linked to application programs when they run rather than during compilation. This means that the same library code can be shared between several programs rather than each program containing its own copy of the library module it uses. DLLs, however, suffer from problems when one application requires a version of a DLL that is incompatible with what another application requires.

DOM (Document Object Model)

A platform- and language-neutral interface defined by the W3C that allows programs and scripts to access and update the content, structure, and style of documents.

DTD (document type definition)

A description of the structure and the elements and attributes that define a class of XML documents. A DTD can be declared within an XML document or as an external reference. An XML document that conforms to a DTD is said to be valid with respect to the DTD.

EAI (enterprise application integration)

The use of middleware to integrate application programs, databases, and legacy systems involved in an organization's critical business processes.

ebXML (Electronic Business XML)

A global initiative to define processes around which businesses can interact over the Web. It is a technology aimed at bringing the benefits of B2B data exchange to a global audience of small, medium, and large businesses. It has been developed under the auspices of the United Nations' technical and e-business group (UN/CEFACT) and OASIS, the international, nonprofit consortium of technology companies formed to promote open, collaborative development of interoperability specifications based on standards such as XML and SGML.

EDI (Electronic Data Interchange)

A collection of standard message formats that businesses may use to exchange data across any underlying network. EDI message formats are undergoing a transition to XML formats, creating a new XML/EDI framework.

EJB (Enterprise JavaBeans)

A component architecture for building distributed object-oriented business applications in Java. EJB is the basis for J2EE, a framework that provides services such as transactions, security, and persistence to programs executing in EJB containers.

FTP (File Transfer Protocol)

A client-server protocol allowing a user on one computer to transfer files to and from another computer over a TCP/IP network. The protocol may also be used to transport SOAP and XML.

GovTalk

The British government initiative to use XML as the basis for exchanging information between government systems, and between the government and its citizens.

GUI (graphical user interface)

The use of graphics and images rather than just words to represent interaction with a program.

HR-XML

A nonprofit consortium dedicated to enabling an XML-based e-commerce and human resources data interchange format for human resources.

HTML (Hypertext Markup Language)

A tag-based language widely used across the Web to render documents in browsers. The intent of HTML is to leave the formatting details up to a browser. The tags defined in HTML are intended as hints on how to display content.

HTTP (HyperText Transfer Protocol)

A protocol for distributed, collaborative, hypermedia information systems, in use since 1990, for initiating requests and moving data across the Web. It has found use beyond its original function for hypertext transfer and is currently used to communicate with servers and to distribute XML and SOAP messages.

HTTPS (HyperText Transfer Protocol over Secure Sockets Layer)

A protocol for the transfer of encrypted information between computers over the Web. HTTPS is essentially HTTP using a Secure Socket Layer, an encryption protocol for moving data securely across the Web. HTTPS is widely used for online purchasing and the exchange of private information.

IDE (Integrated Development Environment)

A system that supports the process of writing software. An IDE may include a programming-language-specific syntax-directed editor, graphical tools for program entry, and integrated support for compiling, running, and debugging programs.

IDL (Interface Definition Language)

A language that provides a standard interface between objects and is used as the base mechanism for object interaction. CORBA uses an IDL so that objects written in different programming languages can communicate.

IE (Microsoft Internet Explorer)

Microsoft's World Wide Web browser, which is the main rival to Netscape Navigator. Both support the same core features and offer incompatible extensions. Microsoft's bundling of IE with Windows 95 became the subject of a U.S. Department of Justice antitrust trial in late 1998.

IETF (Internet Engineering Task Force)

An open international community of network designers, vendors, and researchers whose goal is to coordinate the operation, management, and evolution of the Internet and to resolve protocol and architectural issues.

IIOP (Internet Inter-ORB Protocol)

A protocol that allows different implementations of a CORBA ORB to communicate with each other.

IL (Intermediate Language)

A term used to describe the result of the compilation of programs designed for execution by a runtime engine that interprets the IL for execution on a specific platform. Both Java and programming languages that are supported by .NET are compiled into ILs.

InfoSet (XML Information)

A W3C initiative to provide a consistent set of definitions for use in other specifications that need to refer to the information in a well-formed XML document.

J2EE (Java 2 Enterprise Edition)

A specification for the development and deployment of Java-based enterprise server applications. J2EE applications are hosted within a container that provides transaction, security, and persistence services, simplifying the work of the developer. J2EE has recently been extended to include support for XML and Web services.

Java

An object-oriented programming language developed by Sun Microsystems in 1995. Java has aspects of both C++ and Smalltalk. It is supports single inheritance and automatic garbage collection for reclaiming used memory. It is the underlying language for J2EE.

JAXB (Java Architecture for XML Binding)

A Java API with an accompanying toolset that automates the mapping between XML documents and Java objects. Based on an XML Schema, JAXB automatically generates Java classes that provide access to XML data.

JAXM (Java API for XML Messaging)

A Java API that enables applications to send and receive XML messages using SOAP.

JAXP (Java API for XML Processing)

A Java API that supports the processing of XML documents using DOM, SAX, and XSLT. JAXP enables applications to parse and transform XML documents independent of a particular XML processing implementation.

JAXR (Java API for XML Registries)

A Java API for a set of distributed registry services that enable B2B integration based on protocols under development by ebXML.org and OASIS. The JAXR specification assumes that all communication between a registry and clients will be based on JAXM.

JAX-RPC (Java API for XML Remote Procedure Calls)

A Java API that supports building Web applications that incorporate XML-based RPC as defined in the SOAP specification.

JCP (Java Community Process)

An open organization of Java developers and licensees chartered to develop and revise Java technology specifications. JCP reflects the trend toward open, collaborative development in order to identify design problems early in the development lifecycle.

JDBC (Java Database Connectivity)

A Java API that lets developers tabulate data sources from a Java program. JDBC provides connectivity to a wide range of SQL databases as well as data sources such as spreadsheets or flat files.

JINI (pronounced "Genie")

A network-centric computing architecture which enables plug-and-play on the network. JINI clients request services through Java interfaces, and JINI services deliver code to clients based on the service request.

JMS (Java Message Service)

A standard Java-based interface to the message services of a MOM. JMS handles publish-subscribe, point-to-point, and request-reply messaging.

JRMP (Java Remote Method Protocol)

The transport protocol for Java RMI, which is the basis for communication using Enterprise JavaBeans.

JSP (Java Server Pages)

A Java technology that uses XML-like tags and scriptlets written in Java to provide the logic for generating Web page content.

JSR (Java Specification Request)

A document submitted to the Java Community Process by one or more members to propose the development of a new specification or major revision to an existing specification.

loose coupling

A term that describes distributed systems where senders and receivers aren't required to know each other or be active at the same time. Communication in loosely coupled systems occurs through an intermediary that brokers communication between participants. The intermediary may be message-oriented middleware or a tuple space as found in JavaSpaces and TSpaces.

MathML

An XML language for describing mathematics. It may be used as a basis for machine-to-machine communication and is used to standardize the display of mathematical expressions in Web pages.

metadata

Literally data about data. XML element and attribute names are considered metadata in that they may be used to describe the data contained in a document.

metainformation

Literally information about information.

metalanguage

Literally a language about languages. XML is a metalanguage because it can be used to define other tag-based languages.

MIME (Multi-Purpose Internet Mail Extensions)

A standard for multi-part, multimedia electronic mail and hypertext documents on the Internet. MIME provides the ability to transfer nontextual data, such as graphics, audio, and fax.

MISMO (Mortgage Industry Standards Maintenance Organization)

An organization that is working to define XML vocabularies for electronic commerce issues in the mortgage industry.

MOM (Message–Oriented Middleware)

A reliable way for programs to create, send, receive, and read messages in a distributed, loosely coupled network. MOM ensures reliable asynchronous electronic communication, with options for guaranteed message delivery, receipt notification, and transaction control.

MQSeries

An IBM middleware product used to integrate software applications on dissimilar systems. It supports a messaging scheme requiring the application that receives a message to confirm receipt. If no confirmation materializes, the message is resent by the MQSeries.

MTS (Microsoft Transaction Server)

Microsoft middleware that offers both a transaction monitor and distributed object communication.

namespaces

XML namespaces provide a simple method for qualifying element and attribute names used in XML documents by associating them with namespaces identified by URI references.

OASIS (Organization for the Advancement of Structured Information Standards)

A nonprofit international consortium that creates interoperable industry specifications based on public XML and SGML standards. OASIS supports vertical industry applications, conformance tests, and interoperability specifications that make vertical standards usable.

OFX (Open Financial Exchange)

An XML-based language enabling brokerage clients to download account information directly into their accounting and tax-preparation software, such as Quicken or TurboTax. OFX also supports the exchange of financial information between financial services companies, their technology outsourcers, and consumers using Web- and PC-based software.

OMG (Object Management Group)
The consortium responsible for defining a cross-compatible distributed object standard known as CORBA. The first CORBA standard appeared in 1991.

ORB (Object Request Broker)
A central object bus over which objects interact transparently with other local or remote objects. CORBA uses an ORB through which a client can acquire an object reference to a CORBA server object and make method calls on the object reference as if the CORBA server object were local in the client's address space. The ORB is responsible for locating the requested object's implementation, preparing it to receive requests, communicating requests to the object, and returning the reply to the client.

ORPC (Object Remote Procedure Call)
The transport protocol built on the earlier DCE model of RPC and used as the basis for DCOM communication.

PKI (public-key infrastructure)
A system of digital certificates and certificate authorities that verifies and authenticates the validity of parties involved in electronic commerce.

public-key cryptography
A technology based on a complex mathematical formula to generate two separate but related keys, one open to public view and the other private, known only to one individual. Documents encrypted with

the private key can only be decrypted with the public key and assure the reader that the document was generated by the owner of the public key (that is, that the document is authentic). Documents encrypted with the public key can only be decrypted by the owner of the public key.

RDF (Resource Description Framework)

A foundation for processing metadata. It provides interoperability between applications that exchange machine-understandable information on the Web. RDF emphasizes facilities to enable automated processing of Web resources.

registry

A server that is part of the Web services framework and that provides information describing the services of a Web entity or business. The registry describes a company and its services across three directories: white pages that store the addresses and contact information of companies in the registry, yellow pages that organize entries by industry classification, and green pages that provide detailed descriptions of services offered.

RMI (Remote Method Invocation)

Java's technology for doing distributed object communication across networks based on the Java Remote Method Protocol. RMI is based on Java's capability to serialize objects where objects can be transmitted as a byte stream across networks. Because object serialization is specific to Java, both the RMI server and client objects must be written in Java.

RPC (Remote Procedure Call)

A protocol that allows a program running on one host to cause code to be executed on another host without the programmer explicitly writing networking code. A RPC is initiated by the caller (client) sending a request message to a remote system (the server) to execute a specific procedure or function using arguments supplied by the client.

SAX (Simple API for XML)

A standard interface for event-based XML parsing, developed collaboratively by the members of the XML-DEV mailing list.

schema

A general term that refers to the structure and content of a document. In the XML world schemas take the form of either DTDs or XML Schemas.

Semantic Web

An extension of the current Web in which information is given well-defined meaning, better enabling computers and people to work in cooperation. Tim Berners-Lee is a driving force behind the W3C's Semantic Web initiative.

SGML (Standard Generalized Markup Language)

An international standard for the description of marked-up electronic text. More precisely, SGML is a metalanguage, that is, a means of formally describing a language. SGML is the precursor to XML, a simpler metalanguage for describing languages.

Smalltalk

The pioneering object-oriented programming system developed at Xerox PARC in the 1970s. Smalltalk took the concepts of class and message from an earlier language, Simula-67, and made them part of the programming vocabulary. The Java programming language has been influenced by many of the concepts found in Smalltalk.

SMIL (Synchronized Multimedia Integration Language)

A broad-based effort to use XML to define instructions for the creation of Web-based interactive multimedia presentations. SMIL provides an XML alternative to technologies such as Flash or JavaScript that are widely used to control animation in browsers.

SMTP (Simple Mail Transfer Protocol)

A protocol for the reliable and efficient delivery of mail over the Internet.

SOAP (Simple Object Access Protocol)

An XML-based protocol for exchanging information in a decentralized, distributed environment. SOAP defines an XML envelope for delivering XML content across HTTP as well as other protocols and specifies a set of rules for servers to follow when receiving a SOAP message. SOAP supports the notion of message paths whereby servers can perform intermediate processing along a path from a SOAP source to final destination.

SOAP with Attachments

A binding for a SOAP message that allows additional information to be transported with the message using HTTP's multipart (MIME) messaging. This allows information such as DTDs, style sheets, and digital digests to be sent as auxiliary information with a single SOAP message.

SSL (Secure Sockets Layer)

A protocol developed by Netscape for delivering documents securely over the Web, using public and private keys.

Sun ONE (Sun Open Net Environment)

Sun's standards-based platform for building and deploying Web-based applications and Web services.

SVG (Scalable Vector Graphics)

A W3C Recommendation that defines an XML grammar for creating vector-based 2D graphics for the Web and other applications. SVG is an alternative to delivering GIF or JPEG images to browsers. Because SVG is defined as an XML grammar, SVG graphics can easily be generated dynamically on Web servers using standard XML tools and delivered with a style sheet to a browser for rendering.

TELNET

The Internet protocol for creating a connection with a remote machine.

tight coupling

A term used by Glenford Myers to describe the dependence between two modules that complicates their design and limits their ability for reuse. In the context of the Web, "tightly coupled systems" refers to networks whose ability to transmit data is coupled with the technology used to transport the data from one place to another. Tight coupling stands in opposition to loose coupling.

TP Monitor (Transaction-Processing Monitor)

A program that monitors a transaction to insure that it completes in an all-or-none manner.

TSpaces

IBM's implementation of the loosely-coupled P2P distributed computing model introduced as part of the Linda system at Yale in the 1980s. Similar to Sun's JavaSpaces architecture.

TupleSpace

The part of the Linda distributed computing model that acts as a central repository for communication primitives known as tuples.

Linda supports asynchronous interprocess communication through synchronous communication with a central tuple space.

UDDI (Universal Description, Discovery, and Integration)

A protocol for describing Web services components. UDDI allows businesses to register with an Internet directory so they can advertise their services and companies can find each other and carry out transactions over the Web.

UML (Unified Modeling Language)

An industry-standard language for specifying, constructing, and documenting the artifacts of software systems. It supports the software development process through the provision of numerous standard diagrams that describe the structure and interactions of object-based systems.

UN/CEFACT (United Nations Centre for Trade Facilitation and Electronic Business)

A United Nations organization whose objective is to develop recommendations and standards to help foster cooperative relationships between private business and public organizations.

UN/EDIFACT (United Nations Directories for Electronic Data Interchange for Administration, Commerce and Transport)

A United Nations organization set up to improve the ability of business, trade, and administrative organizations from developed, developing, and transitional economies to exchange products and relevant services effectively, thereby contributing to the growth of global commerce.

URI (Uniform Resource Identifier)

A short string used to identify a Web resource such as a document, image, downloadable file, or electronic mailbox.

URL (Uniform Resource Locator)

An informal term (no longer used in technical specifications) associated with popular URI schemes such as HTTP, FTP, and mailto.

VB (Visual Basic)

A programming language widely used to develop Microsoft applications.

VB.NET

Visual Basic, updated to support .NET features.

VisualStudio.NET

A development environment for building applications that are tightly integrated with the Microsoft Windows platform and the Microsoft .NET Enterprise Server environment.

VoiceXML (Voice Extensible Markup Language)

An XML language for programming dialogs for voice-enabled devices over the Web. VoiceXML has built-in features for collecting data from forms and presenting choices as menus.

W3C (World Wide Web Consortium)

An organization that develops interoperable technologies in the form of specifications, guidelines, software, and tools, with the objective of leading the Web to its full potential as an infrastructure for information, commerce, and communication.

Web services

An umbrella term that describes a process and protocols for discovering software as services across the Web. Key protocols in Web services include UDDI and WSDL.

WebLogic

BEA's software platform built around J2EE that provides application program interfaces for XML enterprise Java and Web services.

WebSphere

IBM's software platform, built around J2EE, that provides application program interfaces for XML enterprise Java and Web services.

World Wide Web

An Internet-based, client-server, hypertext, distributed, information retrieval system, originating at the CERN laboratories in Geneva, Switzerland. On the Web all content is presented to the user as a hypertext link in HTML format. A client program called a browser runs on a user's computer and provides the capability to follow links or to send a query to a server.

WSDL (Web Services Description Language)

An XML description of both the service interface and the implementation details of how to connect to and use a particular Web service.

XForms

A specification of Web forms that can be used with a wide variety of platforms including desktop computers, handheld computers, cell phones, and information appliances.

XHTML (Extensible Hypertext Markup Language)

A family of current and future document types and modules that extend HTML. XHTML is XML based and designed to work as part of the XML family of technologies.

X-KISS (XML Key Information Service Specification)

Part of the XML Key Management Specification. X-KISS defines a protocol for a trust service that resolves public-key information contained in XML Signature elements.

XKMS (XML Key Management Specification)
A W3C initiative that targets the delegation of trust processing decisions to one or more specialized trust processors, to give businesses an easier way to manage digital signatures and data encryption.

X-KRSS (XML Key Registration Service Specification)
Part of the XML Key Management Specification. X-KRSS defines a protocol for the registration of public keys.

XLink
A technology that allows elements to be inserted into XML documents in order to create and describe links between resources. It uses XML syntax to create structures that can describe links similar to the simple unidirectional hyperlinks of today's HTML, as well as more sophisticated links.

XML (Extensible Markup Language)
The universal format for structured documents and data on the Web.

XML Encryption
A W3C specification for the encryption of a all or part of an XML document.

XML Query
A W3C initiative to provide query facilities for extracting data from XML documents.

XML Schema
A W3C Recommendation (May 2001) that expresses shared vocabularies providing a means for defining the structure, content, and semantics of XML documents.

XML Signature

A W3C specification that defines processing rules and syntax for specifying the integrity, message authentication, and/or signer authentication for data located within an XML document.

XML-RPC (XML Remote Procedure Call)

A protocol for doing remote procedure calls over the Web where the information about what procedure to call and what parameters to pass are encoded as XML in the body of an HTTP POST request to a server.

XPath

An expression language used to access or refer to parts of an XML document.

XPointer

An expression language that supports addressing the internal structures of XML documents so that links may be composed that connect directly to specific parts of a document rather than the entire document.

XQuery

A query language that uses the structure of XML to express queries across all kinds of data, whether structured as XML or viewed as XML via middleware.

XSL (Extensible Stylesheet Language)

A language for expressing style sheets. It consists of three parts: XSL Transformations, a language for transforming XML documents; XPath, an expression language used by XSLT to access or refer to parts of an XML document (XPath is also used by the XML Linking specification); and XSL Formatting Objects, an XML vocabulary for specifying formatting semantics.

XSL-FO (XSL Formatting Objects)

An XML vocabulary for specifying formatting semantics.

XSLT (XSL Transformations)

A language for transforming XML documents into other XML documents.

Index

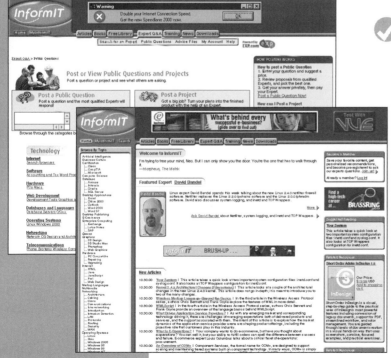

Register
Your Book